WORKING IT OUT AT WORK

Julie Hay has been active within the transactional analysis community for many years. She is a past president of both the European and the International Transactional Analysis Associations. She served as Vice Chair of the UK-based Institute of Transactional Analysis and was one of the three founders and then inaugural chairperson of the UK-based Institute of Developmental Transactional Analysis.

In 2009 she founded the International Centre for Developmental Transactional Analysis - see www.icdta.net.

She has also set up the International Centre for Developmental Super-Vision - see www.icdsv.net.

Julie has designed several TA qualifications that she provides in cooperation with an international group of TA colleagues, all of whom have accreditation from the International and/or European Associations. See www.icdta.net and www.icdsv.net for details or contact Julie on julie@adinternational.com.

Julie continues to provide ongoing TA training within the UK and currently leads a programme in the Ukraine - see www.adinternational.com. She regularly works in other countries and is available as a pro bono 'travelling trainer' under the auspices of ITAA and EATA for groups in economically-disadvantaged areas of the world.

Julie provides consultancy services, coaching and supervision by arrangement. In addition to transactional analysis, Julie has many years experience of designing and running assessment and development centres, and of setting up in-house mentoring and coaching schemes. She is also a Licensed NLP (neuro linguistic programming) Trainer.

She was a founder and then President 2006-2008 of the European Mentoring and Coaching Council.

The questionnaires contained in this book can be purchased from www.sherwoodpublishing.com

WORKING IT OUT AT WORK
UNDERSTANDING ATTITUDES AND BUILDING RELATIONSHIPS

Julie Hay

SHERWOOD PUBLISHING
• • • developing people

HERTFORD UK

Published by

Sherwood Publishing

Wildhill, Broadoak End, Hertford SG14 2JA, UK

www.sherwoodpublishing.com

email: sherwood@adinternational.com

This edition first published 2009

A catalogue record of this book is available from the British Library.

ISBN 978-1-907037-01-6

Design by Diane Richardson, info@drdm.eu

Reprinted 2012 by Atlas Print Group

TO TERRY AND STEVE

who bring me such joy and are proof that 'scripty' behaviour

can lead to wonderful consequences

CONTENTS

LIST OF FIGURES

ACKNOWLEDGEMENTS

My main thanks for making this book possible go to the many groups of participants who have attended my training workshops and enabled me to test out my ideas and develop them into the workable formats that are included in the following pages.

Special thanks are also due to Andrew Dellors, a manager in the Probation Service, for the brainstorming session which led to the title of this book.

I thank the following for permission to reproduce their diagrams, or variations of them, as referenced below: Taibi Kahler, Steve Karpman, Richard Erskine, Pam Levin, Marilyn Zalcman.

I also thank Graham Barnes, who gave permission even though he does not believe his model is as useful as I think it is.

And last but by no means least, I acknowledge my debt to Eric Berne for originating the field of knowledge known as transactional analysis from which many of the ideas in this book are drawn, and those writers since him who have added to his original work and generously shared their own ideas.

REFERENCES
Barnes, Graham – *"On Saying Hello; The Script Drama Diamond and Character Role Analysis"* Transactional Analysis Journal, 1981 11(1) pp 22-32

Erskine, Richard G and Zalcman, Marilyn J. – *"The Racket System: A Model for Racket Analysis"* Transactional Analysis Journal, Jan 1979 9(1) pp 51-59

Kahler, Taibi with Capers, Hedges – *"The Miniscript"* Transactional Analysis Journal, 1974 4(1) pp 26-42

Karpman, Stephen – *"Fairy Tales and Script Drama Analysis"* Transactional Analysis Bulletin, 1986 7(26) pp 39-43

Levin, Pamela – *"The Cycle of Development"* Transactional Analysis Journal, 1982 12(2) pp 129-139

ABOUT THIS BOOK

The basis for this book is transactional analysis, a wide-ranging set of theories and techniques with an underlying philosophy of mutual self-respect and caring. After a period in the 1970's when it became almost too popular (with best-sellers Games People Play, I'm OK You're OK and Born to Win – and a number of untrained people claiming far more knowledge of the approach than was warranted), transactional analysis has continued to develop and there are now many new concepts. There are now TA associations in many countries, as well as a worldwide association with members in over 65 countries, plus thriving associations for Europe and South America. With its own special blend of academically respectable theory and user-friendly jargon, transactional analysis continues to be an excellent framework for helping people understand human nature.

Julie Hay is internationally accredited as an expert on organisational and educational applications of transactional analysis. She is a Past President of both the European and the International Transactional Analysis Associations, founder of the International Centre for Developmental Transactional Analysis, and author of the highly successful Transactional Analysis for Trainers, 2nd edition Sherwood Publishing 2009. She has taught transactional analysis for over 30 years in industry, the public sector, local and central government, and in Europe, Australasia, India, Asia, North, Central and South America.

With more than 40 years experience as an employee, supervisor, manager, trade unionist, trainer and consultant, Julie is now Managing Director of Psychological Intelligence Ltd. She operates as a consultant, facilitator and mentor to individuals, teams and organisations, designs assessment and development centres, and provides training in interpersonal skills and teamwork.

Names used in examples in this book have been changed to preserve confidentiality

CHAPTER 1:   **INTRODUCTION**

Do you think you'd get along better with people if you understood more about human nature?

Are you puzzled when you see people behaving in ways that don't seem to be in their own best interests?

Would you like to improve your communication and team skills so you can build better relationships with people at work?

If you've answered yes to any of these questions, keep on reading. This book contains a wide range of ideas and practical suggestions for developing yourself to be as effective as possible at dealing with people in the working environment.

The content of the book is based on models and methods that I have been teaching on training courses for many years. I have presented the ideas to many different people:

- in a wide range of occupations, such as clerical staff and administrators, warehouse operators and storekeepers, airline cabin crew and pilots, nurses, pharmacists and doctors, computer operators and programmers, maintenance and design engineers, accounts clerks and accountants, machine operators and team leaders, probation officers and social workers, training officers and consultants, salespeople and buyers...
- in many different organisations and industry sectors, such as manufacturing, information technology, retail, engineering, oil, government departments and agencies, local authorities, healthcare and medicine, travel, financial markets, banking and insurance...
- with different perspectives and responsibilities, such as shop floor employees, shop stewards, supervisors, middle and senior managers, board members, personnel professionals, volunteers, freelance consultants...
- and in different parts of the world, including the UK, France, Finland, the Netherlands, Italy, Germany, Russia, the Ukraine, Romania, Lithuania, Armenia, Macedonia, Serbia, Mexico, USA, Canada, India, Australia, Singapore...

Along the way, the ideas have been tested and refined, so that this book now contains the results of all that trial and error. The concepts have been 'worked over' and developed, so I'm confident that you'll find plenty here that will be directly relevant to you.

I have included several questionnaires as appendices. These are for your personal use so please don't copy them - if you want more copies for friends or colleagues, you can buy them in packs at www.sherwoodpublishing.com at a very low cost. I will mention each questionnaire at an appropriate point in the text so you can fill them in and score them as you go along. I will suggest that you complete the questionnaires before you read the theory, so you are not trying to second-guess your results. Keep in mind that these are intended to be fun! They are not psychometric instruments that have been tested on thousands of people - they are simple little questionnaires that match the models in this book and provide you with an option for increasing your self awareness. Don't take the results too seriously!!

HOW TO USE THIS BOOK

The sequence in this book goes from the broader aspects of attitudes into descriptions of more specific elements of our styles, and then into a framework that pulls together several of the concepts, followed by even more focused ideas on particular approaches to problems. I then show how these different elements form part of an overall pattern, and finish with information about the process of change.

Before you read on, however, I suggest that you do something that I always ask participants on courses to do. Stop and think about the areas in your working life in which you would like to be more effective. All of us are good at some things and not so good at others. In order to develop our abilities, we need to identify the aspects where we want to change. We also need to focus on a clear outcome – what do we actually want to achieve? It may be that you struggle with particular types of people, or that you lack the skills you need in specific circumstances. Whatever it is, identify some precise instances when you feel you are not as competent as you would like to be. Keep these in mind as you read on, so that you can apply the ideas to real problems and check that you are acquiring some additional insights and options.

There are a lot of ideas and concepts in this book. You will almost certainly find that some appeal to you more than others. I invite you to choose – to pick out those aspects that are most helpful and meaningful to you. There is no need to work hard at understanding everything. We are all different, so we have different preferences and priorities. Use what makes most sense for you now and feel free to skip the bits that seem superfluous. Or read those parts again in a few months time – you will almost certainly find that you can then see the relevance of a few more elements.

JARGON

There is a fair amount of jargon in this book. I have deliberately retained the 'technical' terminology, in the same way that anyone who studies a subject needs to learn the customary words that are used. Most jobs have their own vocabularies, which provide specific labels so that people know precisely what is being talked about – or don't know at all if they haven't learnt the jargon. Even hobbies have their own languages; television ensures most non-golfers are familiar with birdies and eagles but fewer of us would understand the terms used by CB radio hams.

Jargon is important for two reasons: so we understand each other and so we can be specific. If we want to look closely at our attitudes and our behaviour, we need some fairly precise words so we know what we are talking about. If I am to explain concepts to you, we need to share a common set of labels. These labels will also allow us to be economical with words, as we can then refer to ideas without having to give a detailed description every time we mention them. Using the customary labels will also allow you to compare what I write with other books on the same subject – although if you do, you will see that I have updated some labels and introduced some new ones. Having retained the jargon, I will of course explain each term as I use it. I have also included a glossary so you can look up any terms. The glossary is right at the end of the book so it will be easy to turn to.

One other point about terminology – as a trainer, I have observed the usefulness of memory aids. I am therefore a fan of 'donkey bridges', which are the gimmicky ways that we can label things to aid recall, such as making a list of items all start with the same letter, or spell a word. You will find instances of this technique throughout this book. If you hate gimmicks like this, feel free to change my words. Misery is optional!

HOW AND WHY?

Writing a book to tell you how to do things sounds a lot more reasonable than a book to help you understand why. However, as a trainer I know that teaching someone skills and techniques is often not enough. Knowing what to do is no help if you feel unable to change your behaviour. Many times we know at a logical level that what we are doing is unhelpful but we go ahead and do it anyway. It is an endearing aspect of human nature that we keep on doing things that don't work – indeed we often do it even harder! That's why we raise our voices when talking to foreigners. If they don't understand our language, it really doesn't help to say it louder – but we still shout and feel frustrated when they look blankly at us.

So, this book is about why as well as how. The more we understand what leads people – including ourselves – to think, feel and act as they do, the better we can get along with each other. Having some frameworks for analysing what happens, and why it happens, allows us to develop our skills at interacting, influencing, building relationships and working in teams.

People are like icebergs – as I show in Figure 1.1, the relatively small amount that shows above the surface is controlled by the great mass that is hidden beneath the waves. As we go further below the surface, we have less and less conscious awareness of what is contained there. We can be confident that there will be a number of useful aspects that keep us balanced. We can also be sure that there will be unhelpful aspects too, including some that we have no conscious awareness of. These become our hang-ups and sometimes interfere with our ability to interact with the world in genuine and skilful ways.

This book is therefore about –
- knowing what might be below the surface,
- knowing how this affects what shows above the surface,

Figure 1.1: The Iceberg

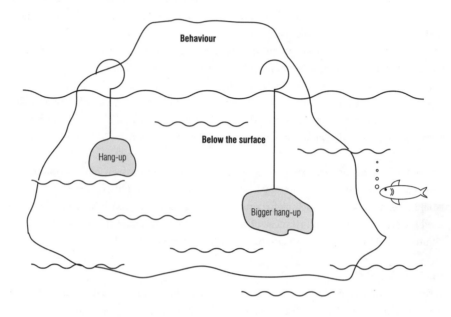

- knowing how to use the useful parts below the surface,
- knowing how to change the parts that act like sabotage mechanisms,
- and knowing how to translate all of this into more effective behaviour above the water line.

TRANSACTIONAL ANALYSIS

Having told you I've retained the jargon, I'm now starting to use it! The main source of ideas for this book is *transactional analysis* (TA for short). TA consists of a range of interlocking yet self-contained theories and techniques. Underlying these is a philosophy about the value and potential of human beings.

I had been at work for over 15 years before I learned about TA. Prior to that, I had been an 'ordinary' employee, a supervisor, a trade union representative and a manager. I had worked in a variety of organisations, and in a range of occupations. I had sometimes been sent on training courses to learn how to do my job, to learn how to operate in a team, to learn how to be a better supervisor or manager – even at one point to learn how to be a better shop steward. Along the way, I'd become a trainer myself and begun to teach other people how to behave. When I did, I often had the same nagging doubts that I'd experienced as a participant – did it really work? It was one thing to know what to do to be skilful but quite another to put it into practice. Even the trainers didn't always follow their own advice. When I was introduced to TA, I realised that I had at last found a way of understanding and explaining the effect of the iceberg.

Unfortunately, TA acquired a bad reputation during the 1960's. It became regarded as the latest fad from California. Eric Berne, the originator, had written a best-selling book called Games People Play but this led to a 'bandwagon' effect. People who knew little about the subject started to teach it to others. Techniques that had been developed for therapy were applied inappropriately in work settings. Because the ideas seemed so simple, people didn't recognise that you still had to make an effort to put them into effect. TA's success nearly became its downfall.

However, even though many more cults have since emerged from California, TA has continued to develop. A worldwide network of transactional analysts now exists. New theories have been added and techniques have been devised that relate specifically to organisations. There are internationally agreed accreditation processes for anyone who wants to teach TA to others, or to use it to help people learn and grow. At the same time, the ideas are still straightforward enough for most people to understand and use them for their own development.

I hope you will find the ideas as useful as I did. I hope too that you will work through the suggested activities and questionnaires. We can't change other people – but we can change our own attitudes and behaviour – and when we do we usually trigger different responses. The way to increase our interpersonal effectiveness, therefore, is to concentrate on what we are doing and what kind of 'invitation' our own behaviour is sending to other people. So use the book to understand and open up your attitudes, and you will find that other people will 'become' easier to deal with.

THEORIES VERSUS COMMONSENSE

"A theory is commonsense that someone else has spent their life devising."

I say this because I find that the response to well thought out theories is often "But this is just commonsense!" Good theories are commonsense; the test of a useful theory is that it fits the world as you know it.

What we often overlook, however, is that sometimes commonsense is anything but a reliable theory – it may be no more than a generalisation based on a few instances only. There are plenty of examples of this – old wives tales, opinions of only one person, distortions of the facts, half-remembered (and therefore half-forgotten) references to things that happened in the past, genuine misunderstandings, and so on.

If we are going to rely on commonsense, we need to ensure that it really checks out against reality. The ideas I present in this book have been developed over several years, so they represent the combined theorising of several specialists and the combined commonsense of lots of people who have applied them in lots of situations. They have been checked out many times, so I have no hesitation in recommending them to you. I anticipate that they will add quite a lot to your own commonsense models.

CHAPTER 2:   WINDOWS ON THE WORLD

WHAT IS AN ATTITUDE?

A long time ago I was a newly-appointed supervisor in a local authority building maintenance department. The authority was a typical, traditional style hierarchy, in which staff were expected to follow the rules. One member of staff refused, in front of my manager, to operate the new systems I was being paid to introduce. To my surprise, the manager transferred him almost immediately. The reason he gave was that "his *attitude* was wrong – you can't have people refusing to obey someone on a higher grade."

A few years after that I was asked to introduce a Youth Training Scheme within an international airline, just after a major redundancy programme under which 20,000 people had left. I had to describe the scheme to the same trade union officials who had recently been told there would be no guaranteed jobs for apprentices as they reached the end of their training. Fortunately, they said they were "taking the *attitude* that they might as well agree, albeit reluctantly, as otherwise there would be even more young people out of work."

Some time ago, I bought fax rolls from the shop where I had just purchased a new fax machine. When the fax paper in the machine ran out – in the middle of someone sending me a long fax – I discovered that the new rolls did not fit. When I returned them to the supplier and asked for a refund I was given one. However, that was all I was given. I got no apology for the inconvenience, just a comment that I must sign a form because "Head Office have the attitude that we might be stealing the money from the till if we can't prove the customer exists."

So what is an *attitude*? The word itself must be one of the most over-used and ill-defined in our language. Ask people what they mean by it and they use other words, such as: belief, point of view, position, stance, stand, mood, disposition, feeling, humour, mind, spirit, temper, demeanour, air, bearing… and you may think of more. Someone who read an advance copy of this book sent me two full pages of their definition!

When most of us refer to someone's attitude, we are simply using a shorthand label for their individual blend of beliefs, behaviours and emotions. We can observe the behaviours, and sometimes the emotions, and they may tell us about the beliefs. However, we cannot truly see inside them so we make assumptions. The way this works is shown in figure 2.1.

Figure 2.1: Attitude Labelling

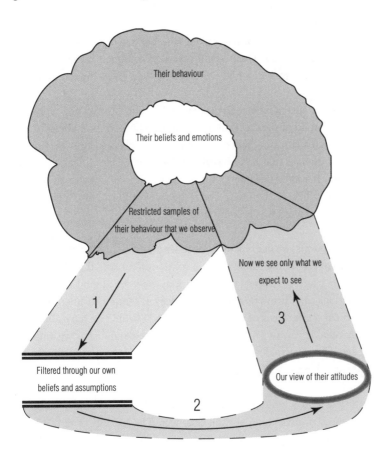

Somewhere in the core is their personality (another over-used word that has lost its meaning in everyday speech). Their attitude, therefore, is the way that personality comes across to the outside world. However, we generally only see a restricted sample of another person's behaviour. We go on to extrapolate from that and make assumptions that it is representative of much more.

Tom spoke little during section meetings, preferring to develop his ideas on paper. Mary, who saw him only in these meetings, assumed this meant he had nothing to offer, and that he lacked confidence. Brian, on the other hand, saw the reports Tom wrote, so knew that he had plenty of useful ideas. Brian also noticed that Tom was good at one-to-one presentations to the customers. These different conclusions came to light at annual appraisal time, when Brian, the supervisor, discussed Tom's performance with Brian's own manager, Mary.

Similar examples occur when recruitment decisions are being made. Some managers believe they can 'read' personalities instantly. As candidates enter the room, these managers are subtly influenced by apparently irrelevant aspects such as the old school tie, a resemblance to someone from the past, or even whether the candidate takes a seat without first being invited to do so. These small pieces of evidence are noticed almost subconsciously but have a big impact on how the manager then views the candidate.

George was a manager in an engineering company who took on two new apprentice instructors. George was proud of the fact that he recognised his own prejudices, and had therefore appointed an instructor who held different political beliefs to his own. However, George was unaware of the fact that he had still decided that such political views could only be held by an idiot. It was noticeable to both instructors that one was always given the benefit of the doubt, whereas the other was frequently criticised by George – even though their performance at work was broadly similar.

Having made our assumptions, we use our 'attitude assessment' to predict how the person will behave in the future. We "know" their attitude so we can 'foretell' their behaviour. If they deviate too much from our expectations, we may have to amend our labelling. However, a few variations can always be rationalised away as temporary aberrations. We are now relating to them on the basis of the personality and attitude we have allocated to them – a reasonably reliable way of getting most people to respond just as we anticipate. Persist in treating someone as arrogant and they will eventually behave accordingly; treat someone as friendly and that too will generally turn out to be correct.

Susan was a secretary in a busy building contractor's office. She claimed to be able to tell whether suppliers' representatives (and anyone else) would be friendly or not. What she used as her primary evidence was eye colour! Brown-eyed people were trustworthy and therefore friendly: blue-eyed people could not be trusted and were correspondingly unfriendly. This theory was based on many years of empirical evidence – i.e. lots of people had smiled at her but only the brown-eyed ones had really meant it! What she overlooked was her own response to them. She smiled at brown-eyed people when she first met them, treated them with respect, and was responded to in the same way. She did not smile at blue-eyed people when she met them, their smile would freeze on their lips, and she would conclude that it was artificial. You can guess the longer term result.

So, in our assessments of others, an additional twist occurs – our own behaviour is being used as fodder for their interpretation of our attitude. They too will respond on the basis of such conclusions. Perhaps they alter their behaviour in line with their perceptions about our personality and attitudes. It can become very difficult to unravel the 'real' people underneath the layers of interactions.

Clearly, our attitudes and those of others are key elements in our relationships. The more we understand the process by which attitudes are formed, the more accurately we will be able to assess the best approach to use with other people. We will also be more alert to the ways our own beliefs can lead us into unhelpful assumptions and misperceptions. This in turn will mean we are more open-minded about others, so that we will be seen to have an understanding attitude ourselves.

WINDOWS ON THE WORLD

We can identify some common patterns when we are 'attitude labelling'. There are four core themes that operate like windows on the world. The frames of our windows on the world are our frames of reference – the beliefs and core attitudes that we have about ourselves and others. Depending on our choice of frame, we may well look out on the world through the equivalent of distorting glass. The distortions will not be random; it will be as if over the years we will have carefully ground them into the window glass so that we see only those things that we expect to see and that will reinforce our existing attitudes. Like rose-coloured spectacles, we notice only what we are already determined to notice.

Figure 2.2 summarises four ways in which we may view the world. Known also as life positions because they reflect a position we take towards life itself, these windows on the world consist of four options based on our underlying beliefs about ourselves and other people. The four are permutations of whether we think we are OK or not OK, and whether we think other people are OK or not OK. A similar concept is implied when we talk about win/win, win/lose, and so on in our interactions.

Before you read on, have a look at the Windows on the Worlds Questionnaire on page 178. Check out your scores and then see how the following descriptions fit you.

Figure 2.2: Windows on the World

Are you an IOK-YOK or a SHNOK?

These strange sounding labels are a way of emphasising that we may take a positive or a negative view of the world. An IOK–YOK is someone operating on the basis of I'm OK, You're OK. SHNOK, on the other hand, stands for Somebody Here is Not OK - so includes all three variations that have a not OK position within them.

Most of us recognise, most of the time, that the position of mutual respect is summarised by IOK–YOK. This view of the world gives us the greatest chance of getting on with other people. We will accept that compromises may be needed so that each of us can satisfy most of our own needs without impinging too much on the needs of others. We set out to problem solve and to look for ways of working and living alongside each other. In other words, we operate to a win/win philosophy.

Jalal became group leader of a team handing customer queries in a well-known computer manufacturers. One of the team, Howard, was the company expert on a particular model but wanted to move into a different department and undertake developmental work on a new system. There was a recruitment embargo in effect, so Jalal would not be allowed a replacement member of staff. Company policy permitted Jalal to refuse a transfer if the person was a key worker. Jalal's predecessor had in fact already vetoed a transfer. Jalal, on the other hand, invited Howard to investigate options. After a three-way discussion between Jalal, Howard and the other manager, it was agreed Howard would work one day a week on systems development.

Jalal judged that a motivated employee for part of the week was better than a full-time demotivated one. Howard responded by introducing several time-saving ideas and producing a training manual for his colleagues so they could share his expertise. The other manager got some much needed development work underway.

Unfortunately, we do not always operate as Jalal did. Indeed, Jalal didn't always manage to be so well-balanced and understanding. Like all of us, he occasionally had bad days, when he would wonder why on earth he hadn't just insisted Howard stay put.

When we have an off day, we slide into one of the other life positions and see the world through a distorted frame of reference. It seems strange to conclude that we would settle for a distorted view when a more reasonable one is available. To understand, recall what it was like to be a young child, wanting to be able to forecast the consequences of our actions and to know how things fit together. Small children find it hard to cope with ambiguity (as do many of us still as adults). We want to know how to behave so that our parents will love us and approve of us. So we think about what happens to us and then invent our own theory to explain events. Unfortunately for us, being children, we also believe that we cause things to happen. Our theory, therefore, is deficient because it puts all the onus on us and makes no allowances for external influences. When something goes wrong, we assume it is our fault; when something goes right we take the full credit.

INOK–YOK

Within that context, we note that we are smaller than just about everybody else around us. Only babies are smaller than us and they don't do much as far as we can see. We are not able to do many of the things others can, such as eat with utensils instead of fingers, fasten buttons and zips, carry things without dropping them. We do not understand that we will be able to do these things when we are older so we begin to believe that there must be something wrong with us. We come to the conclusion that we are at fault and others are capable – we start to look out through the I'm not OK, You're OK, or INOK–YOK, window.

Having devised our theory, we test it out. We observe what happens: do we continue to be incapable while others succeed; perhaps people tell us that we are clumsy or a nuisance. If there is enough of this type of evidence to support our hypothesis, we conclude that we were right. We then begin to filter information, rejecting any that contradicts our theory and thereby reinforcing our selected life position.

We begin to have an air of helplessness. Because we have got used to being helped, we start to pause before attempting things, expecting that someone else will step in and do it for us. People respond to our non-verbal message and do indeed take over the task. When we are children this will be appropriate when the task is too difficult, such as using a dangerously sharp knife. However, if we establish this pattern strongly we will exhibit it also as grown-ups. Faced with a new project, we hang back so that our manager starts to organise the work on our behalf. We may well be passed over for promotion because we fail to show our true abilities – it is likely we then get described as 'lacking confidence'.

Megan often opted for this window. She was a Nursing Sister in a large metropolitan hospital, in charge of a small ward. She had taken several years to reach this position, mainly because she exhibited a recurring pattern of temporary inability to make decisions. She did not do this in connection with patient care – otherwise she would soon have lost her job. Where Megan had problems was in supervising and organising the nurses. She would dither and worry about how to allocate duties. Often Sarah, one of the more experienced nurses, would become impatient and sort out the rosters herself. Megan would always be grateful but Sarah felt resentful that she was having to do Megan's job for her.

In this way, Megan reinforced her unfortunate window on the world in two ways. First, by seeing Sarah behave competently, Megan was reminded of her own apparent incompetence. Second, when she sensed that Sarah was resentful, Megan was able to blame herself for alienating such a good member of her team.

INOK–YNOK

A different view of the world will have arisen for some of us when we were small. Perhaps there was insufficient evidence to support an INOK–YOK view. We will then have experimented with an alternative scenario, in which we decide that everyone is at fault.

One traumatic event in an otherwise satisfactory childhood may make such an impact that we jump to this conclusion. Maybe our parents are going through a difficult time and are unable to care for us properly. Perhaps we spent time with people who were depressed or cynical, and who taught us not to trust, or not to expect to be successful. Whatever the reason, we test out the view from the I'm not OK, You're not OK, or INOK–YNOK, window. Again, if it seems to fit we become selective about the data we then take notice of.

When we slide back to this window as adults, we see only the worst in everyone and everything. We expect to fail, we expect other people to fail, we even expect the fates to conspire against us. We adopt a rather hopeless air, signalling to others that we have very pessimistic expectations. The self-fulfilling nature of our manner is such that people avoid our company (unless they are feeling miserable too). We then conclude that this proves our point and that we are right to be wary when people seem to withdraw their friendship before we can really get to know them.

Frank was employed several years ago as an administrative officer in the UK offices of an American oil company. Senior managers from the USA made regular visits. Sometimes they would dismiss someone during one of these visits, usually on the recommendation of local management. Frank always regarded their visits with foreboding. He was convinced that the dismissals were unfair, but also blamed the victims for being stupid enough not to see it coming. Eventually, Frank talked himself out of a job – he became so obviously cynical about the company and so openly critical that local management added him to the dismissal list for the next visit.

IOK–YNOK

Our third option as children is the I'm OK, You're not OK, or IOK–YNOK, combination. This arises when we decide that our problems are purely temporary. As soon as we are older, we will be able to do all the things the bigger people can do. In fact, we will do them better. Now we look for evidence of other people's failings in order to check that our theory is correct. We pay attention only to the times when we do something well, and blame others for any shortcomings on our part.

As adults, we will then appear to be conceited. We may make it our business to tell other people how they ought to behave, whilst at the same time letting them see that we really do not believe they are capable of taking our excellent advice. Our relationships may last only a short time, as we push people away with our criticisms and one-up attitude.

Bill was a technical director in a frozen-foods processing plant. He was highly autocratic, expecting instant obedience even from the senior managers reporting to him. When several of them decided to attend a short presentation on stress organised by the company medical department, he sent his secretary along with a message that they must report to his office immediately to deal with a problem. When they arrived, he harangued one of them in front of the others over a mistake that had been discovered. Bill sometimes wondered why so few senior managers stayed working for him for long. He usually concluded it was because they couldn't cope with his high standards.

The examples I've given are chosen to illustrate some fairly extreme cases. However, you probably recognise bits of each position in yourself and others. This is because each of us is likely to have considered the view through each of the unhelpful windows during childhood. We may now show elements of each on different occasions. Sometimes we may even cycle through all three very quickly. However, there is likely to be one that we visit more often. We will have become accustomed to this more when we were young, and will now revert to this at times of stress.

IOK–YOK

The picture is not all gloomy. Fortunately, we will also have experienced occupying the IOK-YOK slot for plenty of the time. Provided we don't apply IOK–YOK like Pollyanna, and expect that everyone will always behave in an okay manner, there is a good case for arguing that this win/win position is actually different in kind and substance from the other three. When looking through this particular window, it may well be that the view is clear and undistorted. We may see things as they really are. We are even able to recognise that other people may be viewing through their unhelpful windows.

This means we understand that they will sometimes behave illogically because their perceptions are being filtered by an out-of-date pattern. We can separate a person's behaviour from their innate worth as a human being. All of us have bad days sometimes, when we do things we regret afterwards. By keeping in mind that a skewed perception is occurring, we can be more tolerant of apparent shortcomings. In true assertive fashion, we can object to the behaviour whilst continuing to respect the individual.

With a little thought, you can if you want chart the relative proportions of time that you occupy each of the four positions:

Think of a typical day or week and review what happened specifically in terms of your life positions. Make a note of occasions when you now realise you were looking through each of the four windows. Estimate how much time you think each window is in effect. You can then draw your personal 'blob' onto the diagram as shown in Figure 2.3 to represent how much of each window you recognise, or plot a simple bar chart to show the relative proportions. Think about how you might spend more time in IOK-YOK in future.

Your Attitude to this Book

Hopefully, you are reading this book through the clear, IOK–YOK window. If so, you will be ready to consider the ideas I put forward and will also trust your own judgment in determining whether they are useful for you. You will be operating on the basis that I will probably be competent and will therefore have written a helpful and relevant book. You too are competent, so you will be able to understand the theories and models I describe and you

Figure 2.3: An Example of a Life Positions Blob

| I'm not OK | I'm OK |
| You're OK | You're OK |

| I'm not OK | I'm OK |
| You're not OK | You're not OK |

will see how they might be applied to your circumstances. When you have read the book, you will make selections of what you want to use from it – this may include approaches that are new for you; it may equally give you fresh insights into areas you already know about; and you might instead come to the conclusion that you prefer different frameworks altogether.

On the other hand, you might have slipped into IOK–YNOK. If so, you are likely to find a lot wrong with what I've written. You may already suspect that this kind of approach is a waste of time – you are reading the book only to confirm that you know better. If you stay at the same window, you will probably employ some interesting mental manoeuvres to maintain your frame of reference. For example, the book may be too simplistic (if I've focused on practical application rather than theory), or too heavy (if I've put more emphasis on theory). Or perhaps you already know some of the concepts and can find places where I seem to have misunderstood them.

Perhaps you're at a different window, marked INOK–YOK. In that case, you may expect that I'm an expert and that you will not be clever enough to understand the complex things I've written. Maybe you have a history of not understanding books! Or perhaps you find it difficult to put the ideas into practice. You may even wish I were with you so I could help you by telling you exactly what to do. Even if I did, you still might not succeed at applying the models to your own situation. In that case, this will be yet another admirable book that you somehow fail to apply.

Or let's suppose that you're looking through the INOK–YNOK window. If so, you may well be pretty cynical about books that purport to explain people and their attitudes. You are already convinced that people are tricky, they can't be trusted, and they only read books like this so they can learn to manipulate more skilfully. You also suspect that no-one really changes anyway – we're all stuck with our unhelpful habits and nothing can be done about it! This book will be like so many others: full of unworkable ideas and really written just to make money for the author.

Do you recognise any grains of truth in these three exaggerated descriptions? If so, check out your scores on the Windows on the World Questionnaire that I mentioned earlier.

Often, being aware of the nature of life positions is enough to break the spell that we appear to be under. If this is not so for you right now, I suggest you stop reading and do something that will leave you feeling less stressed. Perhaps something energetic would help, or something relaxing and peaceful. Maybe you need more time with your family, your friends, or on your own. Work out how you could spend some time in a way that you enjoy and then do so before you read on.

THE DISPOSITION DIAMOND

I have said already that our attitude is an amalgam of our beliefs, behaviour and emotions. When I described the windows on the world I focused mainly on our beliefs. Often, our behaviour and feelings will seem to be in line with our beliefs, so that what others observe is in fact the same as we are thinking and feeling. However, we also experience situations where our beliefs, behaviour and emotions do not coincide – we may behave in a one-up manner to disguise the fact that we feel one-down, or we may believe we know better than others but still act outwardly as if we accept their control. The disposition diamond in Figure 2.4 is a diagram that allows us to represent beliefs, behaviour and emotions as if they exist separately. This gives us a better understanding of what is happening when these facets operate as if they are three different levels.

Figure 2.4: Disposition Diamond

Please note that the Disposition Diamond is my adaptation of ideas I first heard several years ago from another presenter. He now asks that I preface any reference to his work with the statement that he "does not consider this, or similar such models, as sufficiently valid for use in a general manner to describe human communication." I disagree with him because I have found that the model gives people a helpful insight into what is going on inside them. I leave you to draw your own conclusions once you've read the next few pages.

At the top of the diamond is our core **belief**. This contains our basic view of the world – our opinion of how OK or not OK we have judged ourselves and others to be. This will be the window through which we observe events. It will be what we think about ourselves and other people.

Our **behaviour**, on the other hand, consists of what we actually demonstrate to others. We may appear to act as if we are superior, inferior or pessimistic. IOK–YNOK behaviour consists of telling other people what to do and generally pushing them around. The old autocratic style of management worked like this. INOK–YOK mode indicates a willingness to be controlled by others, and to let them push us around. INOK–YNOK behaviour is probably the most frustrating to others; it encompasses actions that demonstrate a lack of faith in our own and anyone else's abilities. In this stance, we pour a lot of cold water onto any attempts to improve the situation.

The **emotional** level is hidden from others whenever our behaviour does not reflect how we are really feeling. This may be because we are deliberately hiding our feelings. However, it may also occur when we are out of touch with our true emotions; something that may well apply if we have learned that particular feelings have led to unpleasant consequences. Whether deliberately hidden or not, our emotions may reflect the life positions. IOK–YNOK feelings include righteousness, triumph, and smugness. INOK–YOK emotions are to do with embarrassment, shame, guilt. INOK–YNOK feelings relate to despair, hopelessness and a sensation of being unloved. Genuine feelings of being glad, sad, mad (angry) and scared have somehow been repressed and temporarily lost to us when we are locked into one of the unhelpful emotional conditions.

It is this combination of beliefs, behaviour and emotions that is picked up by other people and forms the basis for their opinion of our attitude. They are unlikely to separate out the different levels within us – indeed, they cannot do this unless they are unusually intuitive. It is worth considering, therefore, some of the common combinations that occur.

If you understand statistics, you will already have calculated that there are 27 possible permutations. Don't worry – it appears very probable that there are in fact only six combinations, as shown in figures 2.5 – 2.10. This is because we seem to use one of each of the three unhelpful positions in each section of the diamond - so we have the set of IOK-YNOK, INOK-YOK and INOK-YNOK spread across the diamond. We can therefore concentrate just on what each of those combinations would be like.

The Martyr: Belief IOK–YNOK Behaviour INOK–YOK Emotion INOK–YNOK

Shown in Figure 2.5, this is the pattern that applies when we martyr ourselves in order to listen patiently to other people and give them advice, which they usually ignore, on how to sort out their lives. We believe that we know best when it comes to understanding people and relationships. We then behave in a way that implies that we are here to help them, regardless of any plans we might have had of our own. Neglecting our own work in order to listen patiently to a colleague is an example of this. Under the surface, however, we are likely to feel despair when we sense that, yet again, we lack the skill and they lack the willpower to change.

The Moaner: Belief IOK–YNOK Behaviour INOK–YNOK Emotion INOK–YOK

Again we believe we know best. However, as shown in Figure 2.6. we feel that we are inadequate in some way. We are likely to behave, therefore, as if we do not expect to be listened to. We probably grumble about how stupid people are to ignore what we think is the obvious solution to a problem. "No-one takes any notice of me, even though I've seen it all before. I've told them what to do but they're incapable of acting on my advice!" Deep down, we feel as if we are useless while others seem more emotionally balanced.

The Bully: Belief INOK–YOK Behaviour IOK–YNOK Emotion INOK–YNOK

Shown in Figure 2.7, this pattern matches the archetypal bully. We believe we are less able in some way than others. We feel despair. So we camouflage these underlying doubts by behaving as if we know it all. We tell others how to behave; if challenged we become even more autocratic and unreasonable. Outside our awareness, we are digging in for fear that our weaknesses will be exposed.

Figure 2.5: The Martyr

Figure 2.6: The Moaner

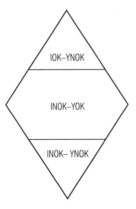

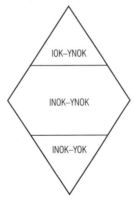

Figure 2.7: The Bully

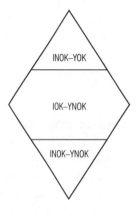

Figure 2.8: The Sufferer

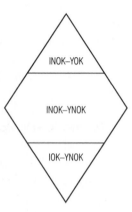

The Sufferer: Belief INOK–YOK Behaviour INOK–YNOK Emotion IOK–YNOK

As in Figure 2.8, now we behave as if we are hurt but cannot be helped. We develop an aura of suffering but signal to others that they are so unfeeling that they could not possibly offer us comfort. We believe that we are less capable or intelligent than others but feel that we experience more genuine emotions. We feel, therefore, that our own emotional needs should take precedence over the feelings of others. Indeed, we may be so 'emotional' that we fail to recognise that other people have any feelings.

The Do-Gooder: Belief INOK–YNOK Behaviour IOK–YNOK Emotion INOK–YOK

Figure 2.9 illustrates how we secretly believe that no-one knows what they are doing. The world is probably doomed. However, other people's feelings are more important than ours, so we set out to save them from themselves. We are the typical do-gooder, out to tell everyone how to live their lives better. We may campaign for censorship because we believe that all of us must be protected from evil influences. At work, we put our energies into setting up procedures so that no-one will make mistakes. We are poor at delegation because we want to save people from their own incompetence.

The No-Hoper: Belief INOK–YNOK Behaviour INOK–YOK Emotion IOK–YNOK

Finally, in Figure 2.10, it shows that we believe that no-one is really capable. In spite of this, we need to deal with our emotions, which are so much more valid to us than the feelings of others. We therefore display our emotions and excuse ourselves by claiming we just can't help feeling as we do. We seek out others to lean on, expecting them to take care of us in some way. We are likely to confide in others and then act as if they are responsible for resolving the situation for us. Under the surface, though, we have no real expectation that they will achieve any more than we would.

Figure 2.9: The Do-Gooder

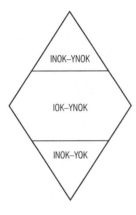

Figure 2.10: The No-Hoper

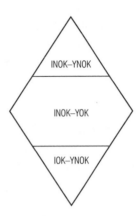

AUTONOMY

There is no diagram for Belief IOK–YOK Behaviour IOK–YOK Emotion IOK–YOK! This grouping is not something you would find on the Disposition Diamond. Once we are into an IOK–YOK perception of the world, we are outside the unhelpful confines of the Diamond. We are believing, behaving and feeling in ways that reflect the reality of the situation we are in. We may believe that someone's behaviour is unacceptable without believing also that they are unacceptable as a person. We will behave in ways that imply trust and respect of others, without taking stupid risks or assuming that everyone will respond in the way we hope. And we will experience genuine emotions, of sadness, fear, anger or happiness, in line with whatever is happening in our lives at the current moment.

When this happens, we have achieved a condition of autonomy. Autonomy has three elements:
- *awareness* – being in the here and now, knowing who we are, being conscious of our feelings and reactions, recognising our own belief systems and being able to consider their relevance to our current situation;
- *alternatives* – having a range of alternative ways of being, in terms of our behaviour and our emotions, and being able to choose consciously how we will respond;
- *attachment* – open to real connection with other human beings, prepared to be honest and candid, inviting mutual trust, respect and caring.

Humans are social animals; we need connection with other humans in order to function well. Our frames of reference are devices we create when we are small, to protect us from our fear when we cannot make the world behave as we would like. It is truly unfortunate that we so often seem to finish up with a Jekyll and Hyde arrangement, where the distortions take over and prevent us seeing that everyone else wants that connection too. With a better understanding of the frameworks we have selected, and an awareness of what we really want to achieve, we can set about unravelling the knots we unwittingly tied around ourselves.

UNDERSTANDING YOURSELF

We all have an innate drive towards being as psychologically healthy as we can be. We therefore strive to attain as much autonomy as possible, so that we can fulfil our potential and have good relationships with other people. Regrettably, sometimes we do not understand what is holding us back. The more we can understand about ourselves and others, the more we can increase our range of options and become open to real connection and community.

If you explored your life position as I suggested earlier, you have probably already identified some actions that will help you look through the clear IOK–YOK window more often. You can now add further to your awareness by completing your personal disposition diamond:

Sketch yourself a diamond shape with the three divisions. Make it large enough for you to insert appropriate details relating to the attitude you typically adopt. The questions below will help you select some areas to focus on if you are dissatisfied with the result.

You may find it helpful to answer the questions with a particular colleague or work situation in mind. It can also be enlightening to complete another diamond showing how you believe the other person would complete it for themselves. This encourages you to put yourself in their shoes – a great way to increase your awareness of them and of ways of interacting more effectively with them.

Finally, I invite you to think again about how you approach the rest of this book. I look forward to your company on an IOK–YOK journey towards self-awareness leading to personal and professional development.

- *What significant problems arise at work because of my beliefs about myself and others?*
- *What am I afraid might happen if I spent more time believing that I and others are equally OK?*
- *What opportunities do I now recognise for moving to the IOK-YOK window?*

- *What unsatisfactory interactions occur because of my behaviour?*
- *What negative consequences do I fear if I change my behaviour to an IOK-YOK style?*
- *What options do I have for adopting IOK-YOK behaviour in specific situations?*
- *With whom do I stand the best chance of a successful outcome?*

- *What emotions am I hiding or ignoring?*
- *What am I scared would happen if I were to show my genuine feelings?*
- *In which situations can I appropriately show how I really feel?*
- *Who is most likely to respond in a constructive way?*

CHAPTER 3: **STRESS STRATEGIES**

The ways in which we view the world have a major impact on how we deal with stress. Indeed, our life positions may be the cause of stress as well as the result. If we are looking for things to go wrong, they probably will! We also have other ways of dealing with the world that tend to distort reality and stimulate unhealthy levels of stress in ourselves and others.

Freda was a coach driver for a company that operated both local and long-haul trips. She preferred the longer trips because she got time at the other end to enjoy herself, the passengers would collect money for her, and the longer shifts meant she got bonus payments. Frances was the route allocator. Frances dreaded Freda coming into the office. Frances knew she was meant to share the longer routes but she couldn't bring herself to do that when Freda was about. Frances wasn't sure how this happened because Freda never said anything directly. It was just that she somehow gave the impression that she would be deeply wounded if her 'friend' Frances didn't give her special treatment.

RACKETS

What Freda was doing was operating a *racket*. I use the term racket here in the sense of a protection racket – a form of manipulative behaviour that is designed to force others to do what we want. Gangsters had protection rackets in order to extract money from their victims. We may operate rackets that threaten severe discomfort to others if they fail to modify their behaviour to suit us. For example, we may be seen as the sort of person who will sulk if we are not given first choice about when to take our lunch break, or we may establish a reputation for angry scenes if the work is not completed exactly as we require. Rather than risk these consequences, people may reluctantly comply with our demands.

The major difference between our rackets and those operated by gangsters of old is the level of awareness. Gangsters knew exactly what they were doing, and their victims were left in no doubt about the threat. Our rackets, on the other hand, are another aspect of our reality which we have created and then pushed into our subconscious. When we engage in our rackets, we do not know we are doing so. Our 'victims', too, are not consciously aware of being manipulated; they recognise their mounting discomfort but do not realise that they are responding to a message being sent to them at a hidden, psychological level. On the other hand, when we deliberately choose to manipulate someone, we are not racketeering (although we are still unlikely to be in the psychologically healthy win/win mode).

Some people display high levels of racketeering at work. There are the managers who 'shoot the messenger' – get so angry at bad news that no-one dares to tell them that their pet project is not working. There is the member of staff who gets upset and agitated whenever a new task is allocated – so the supervisor gives the work to someone else rather than cope with the emotional outburst. There is the employee who throws tantrums at appraisal time if told that performance is in any way inadequate – so the boss backs down and gives a higher rating than is warranted. These are just some examples of how a racket seems to make people do what we want, or stop doing what we don't want.

Remember that our rackets are outside our awareness. Freda did not deliberately play on Frances' sensitive nature to get preferential treatment. The person who gets agitated about a new task really does feel agitated, and genuinely feels relieved if the work is allocated elsewhere. Even the tantrums seem to the person concerned to be the only way they can behave in the circumstances.

All of this racketeering generates high levels of negative stress in ourselves and others. We may not be aware of our own stress but it is there, in the energy we are unconsciously using to push down our real feelings and control our behaviour. We may exhaust ourselves through creating a sense of agitation, or anxiety, or by tensing our bodies so that particular body language signals are sent out.

Other people feel stressed because they are uncomfortable around us. They may use up a lot of energy feeling angry, or they too may be busy damping down their responses in order to avoid a conflict, or so that other people won't see how upset or anxious they are in response to our behaviour.

Racket Variations

Our rackets may actually appear in several forms. We may have a feeling racket where we generate an 'artificial' emotion such as guilt or anxiety, or we may have racket feelings which are substitutes for the appropriate feelings in the particular circumstances. There are thinking rackets such as confusion; we may engage in racket fantasising about how we might feel in the future; and our rackets may also be seen as short sequences of behaviours. What these varied formulations have in common is the notion that a racket is essentially an internal psychological process. We can infer the existence of a racket through our observations of behaviour although we cannot actually see the process itself.

Rackets as artificial feelings are 'created' in response to the norms of society. For example, we may feel guilty when we forget to send a birthday card on time, instead of sad because the other person may be hurt by our thoughtlessness. The artificiality here refers only to the manufactured nature of the feeling; the feeling itself is no less real in its impact on us. The range of feelings generated by us in accordance with our beliefs and value systems will be just as vivid as other, genuine emotions; our guilt is just as stressful as our sadness would have been.

So how do we create a feeling? We use three processes, the same as when genuine feelings occur. We 'do something' with;

- our **body**
- our **breathing**
- our **brain**

With our **body**, we adopt a particular posture. With anger, we usually pull ourselves more upright. We also tighten our muscles, particularly in our hands, arms and jaw. With depression, we slump. We may even have a characteristic way of sitting, and leaning to one side or the other.

We unconsciously change our **breathing** to suit. For anger to be expressed, we take deeper, faster breaths so that we can 'explode' angry-sounding words from our mouths. Depression, on the other hand, requires us to sigh a lot – so we take shallow breaths only and breathe it out again as soon as we can. Keeping our body slumped ensures there's not too much room in our lungs for air anyway.

Finally, our **brain** is also an important part of the feeling dynamic. We think about what is happening and compare it to what we believe should be happening. In anger, our thinking is something like "How dare they behave like that!" or "I'll soon sort them out!" In depression, we tell ourselves "How awful things are!", "It never changes!", or "I'll always have problems!"

These three, our body, our breathing and our brain, combine so that we experience a feeling. With a genuine feeling, there will be some purpose achieved. Sadness is necessary so that we can let go and move on. Anger generates energy so that we can take action to deal with something. Fear stimulates us to move away from danger. Happiness creates beneficial effects in our bodies, as when laughter keeps people healthy. Racket feelings do not have the same usefulness as they do not relate to our real needs.

As substitute feelings, rackets are often responses that we learned as children in order to meet parental expectations. Small boys are typically discouraged from showing hurt so they substitute anger until they can no longer recognise the underlying emotion; they then respond aggressively as a habit. Girls are often given the opposite messages, and grow up programmed to burst into tears when a more genuine response would be anger. A common substitution for both sexes is the anger displayed when someone arrives home later than expected; generally this masks the fear we have been experiencing while we worried in case they had been in an accident. Instead of showing our relief and caring that they are home safely at last, we angrily accuse them of not bothering to let us know where they were.

Rackets as fantasies occur when we worry about a forthcoming event in a way that is not related to preparing ourselves to deal with it. Perhaps we are due to make a presentation to a large group. Genuine feelings in response to this might be being scared; to allay our fear we need to prepare well so we can go into the session knowing we have good notes to rely on. Racket fantasising consists of imagining the presentation going badly, scaring ourselves more by visualising all the things that could go wrong, and distracting ourselves in this way from doing the necessary preparation. We sit and worry instead of getting ready!

Helpful, Helpless, Hurtful Rackets

Rackets as interactions can be classified into three broad groups, based on whether they are by nature concerned with being helpful, being helpless, or being hurtful. Helpful rackets occur when we try to do things for other people that they do not need done for them. They then feel obliged to accept our help even though they feel smothered by it. Helpless rackets arise when we act as if we cannot solve problems for ourselves, so that other people feel trapped into dealing with the world on our behalf. Hurtful rackets revolve around passing on our pain to others, as when we blame them for how we feel.

Simon had a helpful racket. He was a social worker in a residential home for the elderly. He liked to feel needed. Without realising it, he subtly influenced the elderly people in his care to act helpless so he could do things for them. Sometimes this was over small things, such as fetching them tea when they might have gone to the kitchen and made it themselves. At other times what Simon did was more serious, as when he insisted on bathing them when they longed for some privacy, or talked for and over them when their relatives came to visit.

Megan, the Nursing Sister in Chapter 2, had a helpless racket. This was why Sarah did her work for her and then felt manipulated.

Bill, the frozen foods director, had a hurtful racket. By taking out his temper on the managers, he was able to avoid recognising his own feelings of inadequacy when mistakes happened. He always blamed someone else, in a way that made it almost impossible for them to challenge him.

It is not essential to have a victim, or partner, to operate a racket; we can do so alone. If someone fails to speak to us, we can feel upset whether they did so intentionally or not. Indeed, we will often overlook the option of checking with them and will instead tell ourselves that "of course it was deliberate, and I'll feel even worse if I speak to them and they still ignore me."

Racket Clues

You can identify your own rackets using a checklist of clues; the more you say yes to, the more likely that you are racketeering:

- *Is the sensation or situation repetitive?*
- *Can I predict how it will end?*
- *Do I sense a hidden agenda?*
- *Do I end up feeling bad in some way?*

- *Does the feeling seem inappropriate to the event?*
- *Does another person back off in some way?*

Identification of our rackets enables us to tackle many of the sources of stress. We can instead deal with situations in a straightforward and aware manner, checking our responses to see that they are relevant and helpful instead of programmed and energy-draining.

If we decide our reaction is not a genuine one, we can change our body, our breathing and/or our brain to move out of the racket. If you suspect your anger is misplaced, try relaxing your forearms or your jaw – and you'll find that the anger dissolves. For depression, sit up straight and breathe evenly and deeply – the extra oxygen will perk you up. For anxiety, check your thinking – is it logical to worry about something that might not happen, especially when the worrying itself is preventing you from taking any action to solve the potential problem.

Better still, shift body, breathing and brain at the same time. Whatever your racket, you'll find you move out of it more quickly if you sit or stand in an upright yet relaxed posture, breathe evenly and normally, and accept that the world will not always behave in ways that match your personal belief systems.

Equally useful is an awareness of other peoples' rackets. We can then act to protect ourselves from the consequences. Once we recognise that we are being stressed through subconscious manipulation, we can begin to choose different and more constructive responses. Remembering that the other person is unaware of the racket is in itself helpful, as it enables us to be more understanding and tolerant of their behaviour.

To obtain maximum benefit from this framework, I recommend that you take time to 'analyse' the situations or people you find difficult. Make notes on what happens, identifying what might be evidence of their racket and of yours (don't assume it will always be them at fault!). Then consider what a more satisfactory outcome would be. Finally, work out how to change your own approach so as to achieve the desired result.

Options to consider include:
- *checking out your thinking and feeling with a trusted colleague to see if it seems a genuine and appropriate response to the situation*
- *being more assertive in telling others what you do or do not want to do*
- *taking time out to explore how you really feel*
- *being more open about your real feelings*
- *asking more questions to establish what the other person does or does not want*
- *gently suggesting to the other person that their true feeling may be different, such as by saying in a questioning way: "If that happened to me, I think I'd feel XYZ." (whatever you think the genuine feeling is) or "Don't you feel XYZ? I think I would in your place."*

THE RACKET SYSTEM

We can extend the idea of rackets into a racket system, as shown in figure 3.1. This is an internal, self-perpetuating system which links our beliefs, our rackety actions and our reinforcements. It consists of a thinking and feeling sequence that occurs internally but which can be related to our behaviour and our interactions with others. This gives us a different way of tackling our limitations; once we identify the closed loop operation of the sequence, we can break into the cycle at any point and substitute a more realistic frame of reference.

Because the elements are beliefs, actions and reinforcements, I think of this system as made up of BARs to our healthy functioning. As I show in Figure 3.2, it is as if we create a whole series of mythical BARs around us, forming a prison of our own making that prevents us making effective contact with the world.

Understanding the racket system gives us insights into why we may avoid decisions that require us to be assertive, and what is happening when our problem solving is adversely affected by stress. And because the system shows how the associated behaviour operates alongside the internal process, we can obtain feedback in an indirect way by noting the responses we appear to generate in other people.

Beliefs

The beliefs in our racket system consist of core beliefs about self, others, and quality of life, together with our emotions and the needs we seek to satisfy. These beliefs influence everything we do. Associated with them are a whole range of more detailed beliefs that form a kind of operating code. I have already explained life positions so I will extend this idea here to show how these affect our ability to think and to handle stress.

In the IOK–YOK life position, we see things clearly. We know we are able to think effectively and will therefore expect to be allowed to use our initiative and make decisions.

Figure 3.1: The Racket System

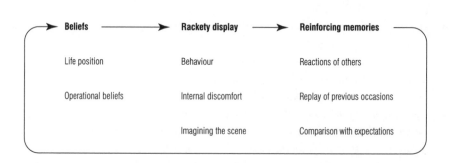

Figure 3.2: BARs to Assertiveness

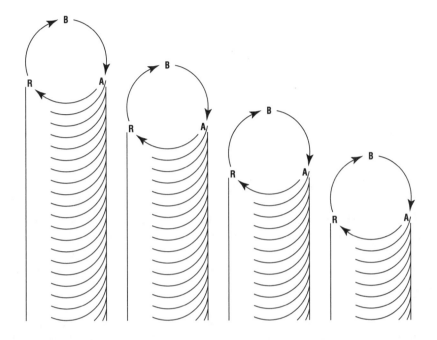

We also respect the thinking ability of others. In stressful situations, we will expect to be able to deal with problems; we will have confidence that other people too can handle stress. At the same time, we are able to balance our expectations of stress capability with the recognition that all of us need support from time to time.

Looking through the INOK–YOK window means we believe we are surrounded by people who are much more capable of handling stress than we are. We will therefore do our best to get them to do our thinking for us. We may attempt to set up a dependency relationship so that they will take care of us and we can abdicate any responsibility for dealing with the stressful situation. Faced with a difficult person, we will prefer to have someone else take over – perhaps we refer them to our supervisor instead of sorting out the problem ourself.

When we spend time in the INOK–YNOK position, we are at our most pessimistic and cynical. Either we seem incapable of thinking, or we believe that our thinking will not make any difference. We do our best to discourage others from thinking too, by letting them know what a waste of time it will be. This adds to the stress for everyone! It's as if we have a multiplier effect – in addition to whatever is happening to cause stress, we generate a second dose of stress about the impossibility of dealing with the stress effectively. This in turn leads other people to feel even more stressed!

Finally, if we are at the IOK–YNOK window, the view prevents us seeing the good in other people. Only we know the right way to think. Our decisions cannot be challenged as no-one else has our ability to analyse a situation. According to us, the quality of our judgment is unmatched. In stressful situations, we become even more dogmatic. We refuse to acknowledge that we might be stressed, insist that we know how to deal with the situation, and make it worse by refusing any help.

Although we will spend a lot of our time at the IOK–YOK window, seeing the world as it really is, we are all likely to slide across to one of the distorting windows when put under stress. Once we do, we then have a whole range of supporting beliefs that we can use to operationalise any of the three less helpful views of the world.

To illustrate this, let's take the example of going to a departmental meeting and couple it with shyness. If we have a belief that we are shy, our most likely life position is INOK–YOK. We probably also believe that many other people are not shy. We believe instead that they are confident and socially skilled. Our belief about our own shyness will have supporting beliefs attached to it, such as that we lack social skills, that no-one wants to talk to us, that we are usually ignored at meetings, that we are not as clever as others, that we have no interesting hobbies to talk about, and so on.

Or perhaps we have a life position of IOK–YNOK, and an operational belief that people cannot be trusted to do as good a job as we would. Associated beliefs might include such things as: only someone with my educational background is clever enough to do this work; people with families will not work hard enough because their priorities are elsewhere; there is only one right way to undertake a task (and I know what it is); people must be criticised to keep them on their toes.

Actions

These clusters of beliefs will form the basis for our rackety actions as we interact with the world. Our rackety actions will include the behaviour we exhibit, the internal experience that accompanies it, and the fantasies that we imagine about it. To continue with our example, what happens when we walk into a room full of people whilst believing that we are shy? Our overt behaviour will probably consist of a 'wallflower act'. We walk in and make for the corner. We keep our eyes downcast. We speak to no-one. In other words, we exhibit the type of behaviour that most people interpret as indicating shyness!

Internally, we are almost certainly experiencing psychosomatic reactions. Our stomach feels knotted or full of butterflies, or we wish we had visited the bathroom before we came in. We may even have been feeling uncomfortable for some time before we actually entered the room – from the point at which we realised we could not avoid the occasion. If someone speaks to us, we will find it hard to concentrate and respond because we are so conscious of the discomfort in our body. Our agitation or our focus on our own sensations will give a signal to others that we are not really paying attention to them.

In our imagination, we are replaying a scene in which no-one speaks to us. We visualise spending the whole time standing alone, trying to look nonchalant. We fantasise that everyone is talking about us and our shyness. Again, we may have started these fantasies beforehand, so that they are well underway by the time we enter the room. The longer we stay in the room, the more vivid and awful are the things we imagine. Each group appears to be deliberately ignoring us, while a glance in our direction is, perversely, interpreted as checking to make sure we are not getting too close.

With the second example, our rackety action is likely to include a lot of checking up on people, asking for reports on them from other people, and insisting on doing important tasks ourselves instead of delegating. We may well feel angry and frustrated in anticipation of the mistakes we are convinced we will soon find. And we will fantasise about how bad the problems will be when they fail to do the job; how we will have to do it again ourselves; how we will have to explain the failures to senior management who may blame us for lack of supervision.

Reinforcements

Our reinforcements are created from three sources: observing the current reactions of other people; checking back in our memory banks to replay old scenes; and evaluating real-life against our fantasies.

By noting the responses of others we are completing the cycle of a self-fulfilling prophecy. We believed we were shy, we therefore behaved as if we had nothing to say to people, and they therefore did not approach us. Hey presto – we were right to believe as we did. We believed people were incompetent, we interfered in the way they were doing the work, they got confused or rebellious – and they did the work badly. Or we believed that we and others were all useless, and we behaved so cynically that they got annoyed and refused to perform at all. In each example, our self-perpetuated disaster movie checked out!

Dredging out our old memories is a technique that allows us to emphasise our expectations of negative current reactions from others; we simply recall previous occasions when our worst fears were confirmed. This can also be done when people fail to respond as we expected. Should someone actually speak to us (in spite of our rackety actions), we will seek to resurrect enough unpleasant memories to override the current experience. We can then decide that this change in response is a fluke as it is so unlike our customary pattern. If necessary, we can even shift to an alternative belief; perhaps they only spoke to us because they are so boring that no-one else will talk to them either.

Comparison of events against our expectations can be another source of confirmation of our beliefs. If our fantasy was good, we can be disappointed when reality fails to match up to it – and we can castigate ourselves for hoping it might be otherwise. If our fantasy was unpleasant, then we can review the evidence we have collected to prove we were right to be so pessimistic.

Breaking out of the closed loop

The closed loop of the racket system means that we believe something, we act in accordance with that belief, we believe that events prove our point, so we have reconfirmed our original belief. As we repeat this loop many times, so it becomes more deeply ingrained. However, the nature of this system means that we have three points at which we can interrupt the cycle. We can change the cycle into a positive one by substituting:

- different beliefs,
- different behaviours,
- or different reactions from others.

Changing our beliefs directly may be difficult because they tend to be set into an interlocking network of values and needs. As I've mentioned already, we may well shift to an alternative belief if the response from others conflicts with our expectations. If someone shows an interest in us although we believe we are shy, we may rationalize by deciding that they only did this because: no-one will talk to them; they had been told to by our/their manager; they were out to steal our ideas; they were practising their assertiveness techniques and we happened to be handy.

However, we can achieve a change through this route. As I wrote in the section on rackets, we can work with a trusted colleague to check out the validity of our beliefs. It is even better if we can do this with more than one person; different people are unlikely to overlook the same things so the more people we talk to, the more we are likely to uncover our personal distortions. We can adopt more positive beliefs.

Behaviour change may be easier than trying to change our beliefs. Governments use this process when they change the law. Making seatbelt wearing compulsory forces people to change their behaviour – and this will be followed later by a change in beliefs as people who initially objected gradually come to accept wearing seatbelts as part of normal behaviour. Eventually, most people will shift to believing that it's a mistake not to fasten a seatbelt, just as many years ago people were 'forced' to change their minds about the acceptability of sending children up chimneys to clean them.

We can also change our behaviour by making a conscious effort to practise new, more resourceful ways of doing things. If we are shy, we can force ourselves to walk up to someone and start a conversation. If we do this by asking them about themselves, they will nearly always respond positively because most people are flattered to find an interested listener. Each time they respond to us we have stimulated a different reinforcement, that will challenge our unhelpful beliefs about no-one wanting to talk to us.

We can get even more of an effect if we become part of a support group or find a friend to work with, so that we can be sure of an okay outcome even if our new behaviour doesn't quite work. Two or three people can get together to practice new ways of behaving. For instance, we can rehearse how we might approach someone, with a colleague playing the part of the other person. In such a role-play we can deliberately put aside our anxieties and ignore the bodily sensations associated with being nervous while we experiment with new ways of behaving. As we do so, the connections back to the old beliefs are being severed. The more we practice, the easier it gets. We begin to recognise that we have indeed acquired the desired skills; this provides us with a new belief to override the old one.

A key to the impact of this type of rehearsal is that our co-role-player can deliberately choose to give us only positive responses. They may do this anyway as the result of our new behaviour. However, they may do it even though we have not quite mastered the requisite skill because they know that we need time and encouragement to become more competent. They can, therefore, change their own reaction into a more positive response. They can also do this in advance of any change by us. This positive-choice reaction is the process by which support groups are so powerful.

We can of course also tackle all three aspects of our racket system at once. In this case, we can check out our beliefs with other people to identify those that need updating, whilst also practising new behaviours, and in a setting where we have already agreed to respond differently to each other. Training courses provide opportunities like this, and there is no reason why we shouldn't get together with colleagues to do the same. All we need is time for those participating to:

- discuss their values and opinions in small groups – and choose more positive beliefs;
- devise and practice new ways of behaving – and build up our repertoire of resourceful actions;
- provide structured responses and feedback to each other – to ensure okay outcomes.

PRO Success

I rename the elements of the BAR to create a simple reminder of what we need instead. PRO, as shown in Figure 3.3, shows how we can create a positive self-fulfilling prophecy.

Figure 3.3: PRO Success

In PRO, we start with positive beliefs, based on IOK–YOK. This means that our operating beliefs are also positive, so we expect to be able to get along with others, we expect they will produce good enough results – and, most importantly, we recognise that someone else may be having a bad day so may not always live up to expectations – and we can deal with that too! For example, if we are going to make a presentation, we can concentrate on thinking about how well prepared we are and how interested the audience will be in the subject.

Our positive beliefs mean that we then exhibit resourceful actions. We can add to this by reminding ourselves of previous occasions when we have felt good in whatever way is appropriate now. For example, if our presentation will be to a challenging audience, we can remind ourselves of previous times when we felt confident about what we were doing. It doesn't even have to be a previous presentation – it is enough to call upon the appropriate resourceful feelings. Perhaps we feel most confident when we are skiing, or cooking, or doing mathematical calculations. Whatever it is, recalling and replaying the confident feelings from that will enable us to go into the presentation feeling the same way. This in turn will mean that we behave confidently, which will stimulate different responses from our audience than if we appeared nervous.

Our positive beliefs and resourceful actions will create a self-fulfilling cycle that leads to okay outcomes. Just as with a BAR, others will respond in ways that reinforce our beliefs – in this case, of course, it will be our IOK–YOK and related positive operating beliefs.

Use PRO to dismantle your BARs. Take each BAR in turn, as you realise what it is, and plan how to convert it into a PRO.

The following prompts may help:
Positive Beliefs
1.   *What belief(s) will be most useful for you in the situation you are preparing for?*
2.   *What belief(s) do other people have that you can 'borrow'?*
3.   *How will you stay in the here-and-now and believe what you wish and not what other people said when you were a child?*

Resourceful Actions
1.   *What behaviours are most likely to get the reactions you want?*
2.   *What behaviours do other people display that you can copy?*
3.   *Who will support you while you practice and rehearse the new behaviours?*

Okay Outcomes
1.   *How will you interpret the reactions of others so that you focus on the positive elements?*
2.   *What will you do to celebrate the okay outcomes and reinforce your positive beliefs?*
3.   *What other BARs will you now dismantle now you know how easy it is?*

MINISCRIPT

Another useful model for understanding our responses to stressful situations is the miniscript. This looks at a much shorter process than the racket system; it is a sequence occurs in a matter of minutes or even seconds. Again, it is a mental and emotional sequence whereby we reinforce our view of the world. We can think of it as a staircase down into deeper and more unpleasant thoughts and feelings. It is called miniscript because it operates as if we are following a short script – as if we have been given the words, actions and feelings just as an actor or actress would be. The sequence is shown in Figure 3.4.

We begin with a myth – an invalid belief that if we can only behave in just the way we should, everything will be alright. As we grew up, we have stored away a message that we will be OK IF... Accompanying this may be a similar belief about other people; they will be OK IF... The IF refers to some magical thinking, similar to superstitions. Rather like avoiding stepping on the cracks in the pavement, or holding our collar if we see an ambulance. The difference is that in miniscript we are unaware of the belief so it doesn't get updated (just as some of us are still avoiding pavement cracks without realising we are doing so).

There are five common myths that we link to OKness: we have to hurry, be perfect, please people, try hard, or be strong. These are described in detail in Chapter 6 but the key point to note here is that these are all things we can never do quite enough. However fast we go, we still feel more speed was possible. Human beings will always make some mistakes; absolute perfection is not attainable. People are sometimes displeased with us through no fault of ours. Trying hard goes on forever as we can always see yet another aspect needing our attention. And being strong requires us to show no emotions, to have no human needs, to be a robot.

These myths take on the nature of *drivers* because it seems as if we are driven by them. The resulting behaviour may well be commented on as a strength. Unfortunately, as long as we fail to 'demythologise' ourselves, we will continue to fall short of the arbitrary standards we are applying to ourselves. We may also set equally unrealistic targets for others.

When we or someone else fails to perform in the driver mode, we feel bad. We shift to the *stopper*, named because it feels as if we come to an abrupt stop. We move from believing I'm OK IF, You're OK or I'm OK, You're OK IF, into the life position of INOK–YOK. We feel emotions such as depression, guilt or inadequacy of some kind. If this is our usual window on the world, we may stay at this point for a while.

When we move on, one option is to shift to *blamer* position and blame someone else for whatever has happened. We therefore slide into the life position of IOK–YNOK. Now we can justify feelings of anger or triumph, as clearly the other person is at fault. We may or may not accompany our move here with appropriate derogatory comments spoken out

Figure 3.4: The Miniscript

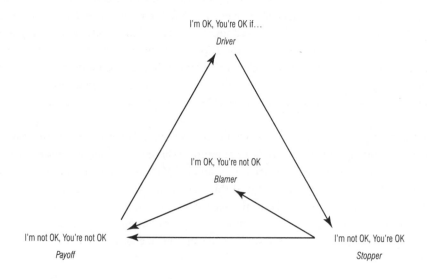

loud but we will certainly be concentrating our minds on how incompetent or inept they are. This is our way of fending off the bad feelings that arise when we think, even fleetingly, that we did something wrong. Not all of us shift to this blamer mode. If IOK–YNOK is our usual window on the world, we will make the most of our opportunity to remind ourselves how other people are so useless. If it is not our chosen window, we'll move on quickly or we may bypass it altogether.

We will then arrive at the final *payoff* from the sequence. This is where we shift to the window marked INOK–YNOK. Our feelings here are of being alone, unloved, rejected. We have 'got it wrong' again. This is sometimes known as the *despairer* position.

There is a miniscript antidote; an alternative version of the miniscript diagram which contains a positive sequence. The aim is to avoid the OK IF belief and behaviour in the first place. If we can do that, we will not go down the staircase – we will not go around the sequence of feeling bad, possibly blaming, and then feeling even worse.

We can give ourselves permissions so we can counteract the OK IF belief. Those who feel obliged to hurry need to know it is OK to take their time. The perfectionists need to be themselves, and to accept that we all make some mistakes. Those setting out to please others need to respect themselves and pay more attention to their own preferences. Instead of trying so hard, we can just get on and succeed at what we do. And rather than being strong, we need permission to be open about our feelings and to accept that we have a right to take care of ourselves.

Equipped with the relevant permissions, we can change the sequence into one of IOK–YOK all the way round, going first to effective action, then to self-affirmation about our competence in the world, and finally to elation about our achievement. Why not take an example now of a situation you find stressful and apply this framework to it:

The first step is to note down what happens when things go wrong: what do you think, feel, do at each point around the miniscript. The second step is to select the type of permissions you need from the ideas in the previous paragraph. You can then word these so that they apply specifically to you. Now you can resolve with yourself to replace the mythical belief you have with the new permission – and start being more effective in stressful situations from now on!

PSYCHOLOGICAL STAMP COLLECTIONS

Our psychological stamp collections are our stores of bad feelings. We file away the payoffs, or negative feelings we have picked up, as if they were the coupons we get in supermarkets or petrol stations. Trading stamps is the term used here because the original idea was suggested when we used to receive these in the form of stamps that had to be pasted into little books. I recall (many, many years ago!) that there were 'green shield stamps, and that the 'co-op' stamps were pink. Hence, the idea is that we paste our feelings into an imaginary book until we have collected enough to claim a prize. We then cash them in for a 'free gift', which will be some form of behaviour that we believe is justified by our collection. The 'straw that broke the camel's back' was a trading stamp.

Serious examples include nervous breakdowns when we have collected enough feelings of stress, or resigning abruptly on grounds of having been passed over for promotion yet again. Less severe, fairly common instances are temper tantrums because we feel that people have persistently been rude to us, or pretending to be sick for a day off because we are unappreciated anyway. We may also cash in our stamps for prizes such as a special evening out because we deserve it after working so hard, or an extra cake as a reward for all those boring low calorie meals we have eaten.

The stamp collecting process is illustrated well by considering what happens to an airline passenger. Let's suppose this particular passenger is a businesswoman making a trip to corporate headquarters. She starts her stamp collection as soon as she is summoned to the meeting, as she pastes in a stamp concerning her frustration at being told to make the trip just when she had planned to use the time to catch up on a backlog of work. Her next stamp is provided by a secretary who fails to book her on the mid-morning flight she wants; now she will have to get up at 5.00 a.m. to reach the airport in time. At home, her partner is annoyed that she will be away for two days, so she pastes in more frustration. She fails to wake in time (more frustration, aimed at the inanimate alarm clock that she forgot to set correctly). She rushes to dress when the taxi driver wakes her, and they reach the airport just in time for check-in. There are no porters to help, the check-in queue is long, it is too late to get a window seat, the coffee bar is closed, the aircraft is not on a jetty so she has to walk across the tarmac in the rain. She now has a full book of frustration stamps and is looking to cash it in.

At this point, the aircraft steward asks her to put her briefcase under the seat in front of her and not in the aisle. She erupts, complaining bitterly that the airline is incompetent, that there should be more overhead storage, that the steward is rude, that she will not be told what to do like that, and so on. Afterwards, she may wonder ruefully why she behaved like that, when she knows the steward was only reminding her of safety regulations. At the moment, though, she is too intent on cashing in her stamps to think rationally. The immediate outcome will depend on whether the steward understands the concept of trading stamps. If he does, he will recognise that the outburst relates to events beforehand and will tactfully deal with the safety issue. If he does not, he may well use this as an opportunity to cash in his own collection, to which the passenger has obligingly provided the final stamp.

Nowadays trading stamps have been replaced by store cards with points and sometimes with vouchers but the similarities between our collection of feelings and the way we deal with points and vouchers is still there. We may collect only certain kinds of stamps. Just as people will not want store cards for shops they visit infrequently, and will leave behind vouchers for schools if they have no school-age children, so we vary in the events which generate feeling stamps for us. Perhaps we collect green envy stamps, yellow jealousy stamps, red angry or blue depression stamps. Or we may concentrate on stamps related to people making mistakes, to being kept waiting, to perceived snubs, or to any other specific preferences we have. If an 'impatience' collector is offered a 'mistake', they may not even notice it. On the other hand, I always notice – and look hopeful - when the person in front of me at the checkout declines the computer vouchers, because I have grandchildren of school age. Just as in shops, then, a 'mistake' collector standing nearby may take the stamp for their own collection; any mistake is remiss in their eyes, even if they are unaffected by it. If we see a colleague reprimanded in public, we may decide to pick up 'angry' stamps on their behalf when they seem to 'take it lying down'.

Many of us plan in advance how to spend our collection of stamps. We look in the catalogue to decide what to save for. We will vary in the size of gift we want. Some of us cash in as quickly as we can and settle for relatively small prizes. Others save for a long time to have enough points for a really big prize. We may go for frequent outbursts of low level misery or wait until we can justify a major disruption in our life. Meanwhile, we may also spend time fantasising about the forthcoming prize, as when we imagine ourselves cashing in. We run a video in our heads as we see ourselves in action. We go over what we will say and do "if someone does that to me just once more".

Another similarity is with the bonus stamp. Just as some suppliers offer extra or double points on certain purchases, so we can collect more bad feelings in some situations. Our rackets may generate only one or two stamps at a time; if our collection is progressing too slowly we may unconsciously up the stakes by moving into more serious arguments with people as these will provide enough stamps to full whole pages in one go.

A final contrast can be drawn about positive prizes. Commercial trading points are cashed in for gifts that have some value to us. Many of our stamp collections, however, relate to unhealthy payoffs. Even a collection of gold stamps, exchanged for positive prizes, has its drawbacks. The major problem is the underlying belief that we somehow have to earn the prize. This works against our innate spontaneity. Psychological health requires that we are free to decide what to do and how to behave. As long as we operate under the illusion that we must collect enough experiences, good or bad, to justify what we want to do, we will be limiting our own potential for autonomous living.

Understanding the concept of stamps can enable us to throw away our collections. We can concentrate on dealing with each situation as it arises; when something occurs that we are uncomfortable about, we can recognise this at the time and take appropriate immediate action. Even if we decide to do nothing, we can still avoid the unnecessary stress of carrying unhelpful feelings into the future with us.

Reviewing my stamp collection
At this point, you might like to review your stamp collection:
- *How many kinds of stamps do I collect?*
- *What prize(s) do I have in mind?*
- *How many books do I need?*
- *How full are my books?*
- *When am I planning to cash in?*

and even more importantly:
- *How will I now deal with situations as they occur instead of collecting stamps?*
- *How will I scrap the books I've already filled?*
- *What 'safety precautions' will I enact so I can avoid being 'dumped on' by someone else who has a full book?*

and, in the interests of relationships with others:
- *How will I now refrain from offering stamps to others? (and I'll tackle one person at a time so I don't get overloaded with good intentions)*
- *What genuine responses will I make to them about my feelings and my thinking?*

and, finally:
- *How will I reward myself for being so aware and for giving up such unhelpful habits?*

CHAPTER 4:   PERSONAL STYLES

WAVELENGTHS

Our *personal styles* are the ways we present ourselves to others. They therefore consist of two elements: our intended observable behaviour and the effects on that behaviour of our internal systems of beliefs, thinking and feeling. Often the external behaviours and the internal systems are operating in unison, so the personal style observed by others is in line with our inner processes. At other times we use our outward behaviour to mask our internal sensations. And sometimes we intend to hide our internal reactions but they 'leak out' via body language and similar signals that have escaped our conscious control.

Imagine for a moment that people are radios. As we move around, we are tuned into and broadcasting on a particular *wavelength*. Other people pick up the signals that we are emitting and this forms their impressions of us. Each of us has preferences about the radio stations we like best so we tune ourselves in accordingly. Then as we become conscious of the wavelength emitted by another person, we make some fairly instantaneous, possibly out-of-awareness, decisions about whether we anticipate having much in common with them. Are they playing pop music while we like classical? Are they tuned into a documentary while we pay attention to news bulletins? The particular mix of wavelengths will determine the success or otherwise of any interaction between us.

Skilled communicators are the ones who quickly, and accurately, identify the wavelength of the other person and then ensure that they themselves select a corresponding wavelength. Unskilled communicators fail to identify correctly, or select an inappropriate wavelength to adopt for themselves. Poor communicators take no notice of the wavelength of the other person, or simply expect everyone else to fit in with them.

Dorothy and Paul were both progress chasers whose job involved them in a wide variety of contacts as they checked on items that went from manufacture through quality control and into packing and despatch. Normally they both selected a bright and cheerful wavelength and went about broadcasting light entertainment and amusing short stories. Most people were pleased to see them coming.

Mark was a chargehand. Unlike Dorothy and Paul, he was usually fairly gloomy – his wavelength was full of depressing news about what had gone wrong, what was even now going wrong, and what was almost certainly going to go wrong in the near future.

When Dorothy needed to deal with Mark, she switched wavelengths. She used instead a style that was the equivalent of an investigative documentary. She would ask lots of questions to get the information she needed. She made sure she concentrated only on the facts and avoided being drawn into any discussion of Mark's gloomy views of working life.

Paul was less skilled. He stayed in his cheerful wavelength when he went to talk to Mark. If anything, Paul became even more determinedly cheerful as he did his best to cheer Mark up. He failed, of course. Mark would complain even more forcefully, so that at times Paul found himself feeling depressed. And it always took such a long time to get the information he needed from Mark.

Although we all have basically similar radio equipment available to us, we do not all use it to full effect. Some people tune in to one station more or less permanently. We may well believe that this demonstrates a certain constancy; that people 'know where they are with us'. However, it also severely limits our ability to communicate competently with people. We will only get on well with those who are already in a matching wavelength, and those skilled individuals who are willing to make the effort and switch themselves into a corresponding mode. Most of us know someone who is like this – who is predictable and inflexible and expects others to accept them as they are. This is fine as long as we are prepared to make the extra effort to get along with them but says little for their interpersonal skills.

Another difficulty arises with the person who is not clearly tuned in to one wavelength. Perhaps they change stations so frequently that we cannot judge which would be best to select for ourselves. One minute they may be serious, the next humorous, then sad … how can we choose an appropriate way to respond? Can we switch fast enough to keep up with them? At times the switch may be quite dramatic, as for example when someone who has been asking us a series of rational questions about our opinions on a new company policy suddenly accuses us angrily of lacking commitment or persisting with outdated views.

Sometimes, as with a real radio, a person has set their tuning dial so that it is not correctly on a station. This means that we pick up garbled signals. We can hear more than one wavelength at a time, and none of them is clear enough to distinguish properly. Again, we are in a quandary over how best to respond.

The other common problem is the individual who stays on one wavelength during an interaction, but who opts for different wavelengths at different times. These are the people that no-one wants to deal with, because you never know what mood they will be in. One time they may be friendly, another time they ignore you. Or perhaps they respond impatiently one day and then want to chat the next time, when you are busy. We find ourselves thinking it would be easier if they stayed in a bad mood all the time – at least then we would know what to expect.

It is possible to distinguish five wavelengths, or *personal styles,* that seem to apply generally, as shown in Figure 4.1 . Check out yours with the Personal Styles Questionnaire on page 181 before you read on. The five options are:

Controlling Parent – behaving as a real parent might do when establishing rules, being firm

Nurturing Parent – behaving as a real parent might do when looking after someone, being caring

Functional Adult – behaving as an adult might do when working jointly with a colleague, acting in a logical and problem solving manner

Adapted Child – behaving in a polite way as we were taught as a child, being courteous

Natural Child – behaving in a natural way as we might as a child, being friendly, creative

The names of the ego states are labels only – they do not relate to real children, parents or adults, as you will see as you read on. To help you separate the labels from the real thing, I will put capital letters at the start of labels – so Parent is an ego state, parent is a real person with children; Child is an ego state, child is a very young person.

Figure 4.1: Personal Styles (Behavioural Ego States)

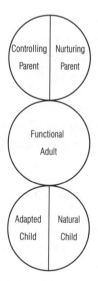

Each of us has all five ego states, or personal styles, available to us. However, we may not use them all to the same extent. Other people will judge our 'personality' on the basis of how much of each personal style we display. They build up a picture of us, as I described in chapter 2 (see figure 2.1 *Attitude Labelling*) by noting the wavelengths we are in – they may do this over a period of time so that they get a balanced picture – but they may also make a snap judgment based on the ego state we presented to them in the first few minutes of contact.

If we want to create a good first impression, and be more skilful in dealing with people, we need to increase our awareness of different wavelengths and to add consciously to our range of options when we identify any shortfalls. As you read on, relate my descriptions to yourself. You will then be able to check out whether you need to pay particular attention to developing your use of specific personal styles to have a more balanced set of approaches.

Natural Child

We arrive in the world with our Natural Child ego state. In it, we display our genuine feelings, letting people know we have needs and acting on our impulses. Our communication as babies is limited to crying and cooing but we still manage most of the time to let the grown-ups know when we want something. Soon, we add a whole range of other emotions, including contentment, a sense of humour, and frustration when we cannot get our own way. Curiosity emerges, especially as we start to move around and explore our world. We begin to show our creativity as we invent toys out of everyday items, like using saucepans as drums. We may have to be protected from the results of our curiosity and creativity, as when we want to play with matches.

As small children, we also demonstrate a considerable capacity for friendliness and affection. At this age, we like other people unconditionally; we have not yet learned to be wary. Watch how small children accept each other, strangers and stray dogs alike – they look pleased and excited as others move towards them. As grown-ups, whatever we retain of this open friendliness will be an important facet of our personality.

Natural Child is the wavelength to adopt when we judge it appropriate to let others know how we feel. We will then let them see our genuine pleasure in their company, our friendliness, our excitement about working with them. It is also the wavelength in which we let people know that we are angry, or sad – provided these are genuine reactions and not the rackets described in Chapter 3.

Our Natural Child is an especially useful attribute if we deal with customers, for instance, as we will then really enjoy serving them. There is quite a difference in the quality of a greeting from Natural Child and the pale imitation of it that comes from someone who is 'just doing the job'. This will be particularly important where service providing organisations are selecting their staff, as is shown in the following example.

The recruitment process for check-in staff for a major airline included trainability tests. This procedure involved teaching the job applicant a small part of the job and then seeing how well they could do the task. It had been found that success in the trainability test usually lead to success on the full training course, and this in turn was a good predictor of success in the job.

Applicants were therefore shown how to check-in a passenger, and then asked to do so themselves. They would read the ticket, key in the details on the terminal, attach the tag to the baggage, print out the boarding pass, and so on. Observers would note whether they got the sequence right, without any omissions. The focus was on technical competence, so they passed the test if they did everything the instructor had taught them.

In spite of this thorough selection process, the reputation of the airline for customer care was not good. Research unearthed the interesting finding that check-in staff tended to see passengers as a necessary evil – often their main concern was whether the passenger would make it difficult for them to work through the correct procedures. In order to improve the airline's customer care image, a major change was obviously required in the selection criteria. Check-in staff needed to use more Natural Child behaviour.

The trainability tests were retained but the observers changed the basis for their assessment. They concentrated on how the applicant related to the passenger. Did they smile, make eye contact, use the passenger's name? A candidate who forgot part of the sequence could be drilled until they did it automatically. No amount of training, however, could instil a genuine friendliness. Drilling people to smile only results in an obviously faked appearance. It made far more sense to recruit people with plenty of Natural Child in the first place.

In Natural Child we will also allow those we trust to know when we are disappointed, or angry that things have not worked out as we hoped. Genuine sadness at unhappy events in our lives will not be hidden or denied. This honesty allows us to form closer relationships with people, who will warm to the fact that they know how we really feel.

This is also the ego state needed for genuine brainstorming as this is when we are at our most creative and can invent ideas that are outside our experience. Many of the best new ideas come about only when we revert to a childlike way of looking at things without preconceived and rigid views on 'how it's always been done'. Other positive aspects of this mode are our willingness to ask questions and express our curiosity without feeling the need to pretend to know more than we do.

However, there is a potential problem with Natural Child. If we spend too much time in this ego state, we risk being labelled immature, childish, over-emotional. People may feel that we are unlikely to settle down to serious work instead of having fun. A forfeit of creativity may be perceived as being out of touch with the real world. Our genuine friendliness may come over as too good to be true; we may be somewhat naïve if we expect everyone to reciprocate. Also, showing our genuine emotions is not always appropriate – expecting a customer, for example, to sympathise with our sadness at the death of a pet can backfire if they simply want prompt service.

Adapted Child

Even while we are still children, we learn that Natural Child is not always appropriate. We sense that the grown-ups have certain expectations of us and we do our best to meet them. Before we can talk, we are already picking up messages from the way they hold us and through their tone of voice. Later, they tell us how they want us to behave, and may punish or reward us for specific actions. We note all these clues and set about developing an alternative Adapted Child ego state. This version of behaviour patterns then enables us to fit in with the requirements of our family and our society.

Depending on our culture, we learn to say please and thank you; to perform simple greeting rituals; to eat with knife, fork, chopsticks, right hand only; to defer to our elders; to help old ladies carry their packages. In other words, we acquire the skills of getting along politely with other people and of behaving in socially acceptable ways.

We may also acquire some of the gender-specific messages that belong in our culture. Often, boys are allowed to show anger but mocked for sadness; they may grow up determined to display only aggression and no tenderness. Girls may well receive the opposite programming, so that as women they become tearful when the genuine response would be anger. In Chapter 3 I explained how these may be rackets, or substitute feelings. Looking at our wavelengths, or personal styles, is simply using a different framework to understand what is happening.

Our parents 'teach' us these substitute patterns with the best of intentions. They know that boys who cry may be bullied at school. Girls who fight angrily may be punished while boys who fight get only a "boys will be boys" type of comment from the teachers. Unfortunately, this well-meaning programming is often picked up by small children in a way that interferes with their ability to express their genuine emotions.

When we are older, we move into Adapted Child when we demonstrate that we know how to behave. By now, much of this is automatic and we are barely conscious of it. If we are British we apologise when someone else bumps into us, we join queues, and we do not talk to strangers. At work, we are especially polite to customers and senior managers. We pay attention to the organisational norms about dress and appearance. We adapt in a variety of ways so that other people will find us acceptable and amenable.

The staff in an international hotel group needed plenty of Adapted Child behaviour. As in most large hotels they were expected to wear uniforms, and to maintain a smart appearance that upheld the image of the hotel. There were sensible reasons for uniforms. It helped guests identify the staff, both for day-to-day queries and in emergencies. In the kitchens, it protected the food – chef's hats ensured there were no hairs in the soup. Without sufficient Adapted Child, there is a risk that staff look untidy and give a poor impression, or that they omit items of clothing and may contaminate the food they are handling.

Adapted Child was also needed in most of their initial responses to guests. People want hotel staff to be helpful and polite, as if nothing is too much trouble. Especially when they are paying high prices, they expect an appropriate level of deference. Some will react unfavourably if the hotel staff behave too much like friends and not enough like servants.

If we overdo our Adapted Child behaviour, however, we may be perceived as lacking confidence. We will not then be trusted with responsibility and may have difficulty in resisting unreasonable demands from colleagues or customers. We lack assertion skills and are seen as overly submissive if we spend too much time adapting to the expectations of others. Or perhaps we grew up with the message that "children should be seen and not heard" – so now we sit so quietly at meetings that no-one recalls afterwards whether we were there or not. It is as if we are invisible; we never upset anyone but instead we get overlooked.

Alternatively, we may have learned during childhood to over-compensate so that now we appear aggressive and rebellious. This may result in a characteristic Rebellious Child version of this ego state; a distinctive subset of Adapted Child in which we seem determined to do the opposite of what is expected. In this case, we may well be seen as being difficult for the sake of it, and our objections may be dismissed as just another attempt by us to start an argument. Rebellion is still an adaptation, because we feel compelled to act in this way instead of freely choosing how to behave from our own range of options.

A common source of difficulty at work occurs when we have grown up with different adaptations about speech patterns. Some of us talk across other people to show that we are interested in what they are saying. We do not intend to stop them talking; instead our comments often come from Natural Child and are signals of our enthusiasm. However, others of us have strongly established Adapted Child patterns that require us to remain silent until the other person has finished talking. We are likely to have the belief that it is rude to interrupt. Put a 'talker' and a 'listener' together and you have the potential for farce: each time the 'talker' shows enthusiasm the 'listener' stops talking because they feel interrupted; each time the 'talker' makes a point they feel let down because the 'listener' shows no enthusiasm!

Nurturing Parent

At some point when we are small children we realise that one day we too will be a grown-up. We set out to prepare for this by copying as much as possible of what the big people around us are doing. Much of this has to do with looking after others. The grown-ups dress us, comfort us when we are hurt, prepare meals for us. So we do the same, as best we can, for our dolls or pets or younger siblings. We may notice that the grown-ups do similar things for other adults and not just for children; if not we may grow up believing that such nurturing should be restricted to babies.

As adults ourselves, we need our Nurturing Parent ego state at those times when it is appropriate to care for someone else. Perhaps a new member of staff needs to be shown around the building, or someone about to tackle a difficult task needs some reassurance. Sympathy may be called for when bad news has been received, or we may get coffee for a colleague who is overworked and needs to relax.

In many organisations, there is barely enough Nurturing Parent to go around. Often this ego state is associated, incorrectly, with being female. This is probably because we grew up seeing mothers do more of this behaviour than fathers (a situation which is fortunately changing as men and women recognise that there is no good reason for denying men the pleasure that comes from connecting with other people in this way).

This organisational lack of Nurturing Parent may be very apparent when redundancies occur. This is a time when nearly everyone needs some extra nurturing, even those who are not losing their jobs. Stress levels are high, people are likely to revert to Natural or Adapted Child behaviour, and it's as if they want a surrogate mother or father to take care of them. Caring managers organise counselling at times like this, as they recognise that some extra support is needed temporarily. Organisations that neglect this aspect generate more problems – both from the poor reputation they get once redundant employees complain to their friends and neighbours, and from the loss of morale and confidence in those employees who remain.

You will also meet people who over-use this ego state. They are likely to smother you with their concern. They may fuss over you as if you were not capable of managing alone, or even insist on doing the job for you. It is difficult to refuse their assistance when they are so clearly intending to be helpful. When this happens, people are denied the opportunity to develop their own skills.

Perhaps you remember when you first started work. You were given an apparently simple job to do that involved using a piece of equipment you were unfamiliar with. For example, making photocopies. As you did so, the copier ran out of paper. Up bustled an overdosed Nurturing Parent, who loaded more paper for you. Unfortunately, they did not show you how to do this task yourself. So, the next time it happened, you had to ask for help again. People around are surprised how slowly you are learning to operate a copier! The Nurturing Parent approach in this case was inappropriate – you needed to be allowed to practice loading the paper yourself.

Controlling Parent

In addition to Nurturing Parent, we develop a Controlling Parent ego state. We do this in the same way, by mimicking our elders. We observe that one of the ways we can take care of others is by setting down rules and boundaries for them. In this way, we keep them safe and make sure they learn the correct ways to behave. Parents do this for children when they stop them doing dangerous things, warn them against going with strangers, impose curfew times on reluctant teenagers.

This ego state is the one to use when we need to be firm. Many disciplinary hearings in organisations might be avoided if managers were to use Controlling Parent sooner – to spell out clearly what the performance requirements are and how the person must change in order to meet them. Firmness may also be appropriate with colleagues and customers who are trying to take unfair advantage. A firm refusal to do their work for them or to provide services not covered by the contract will be more skilful than resentful compliance.

Overdo this personal style, however, and you will come over as bossy and overbearing. This happens when we insist that the job is done our way, even though there are other options that would work just as well. Imposing rules based on our opinions rather than the true requirements of the task is another area for grievance. Ordering people about as if they were children will not usually fill them with enthusiasm for us or our instructions. Indeed, we are more likely to stimulate rebellion than obedience.

Again there are some gender differences that commonly occur. We seem to expect more Controlling Parent behaviour from men than from women. We even associate it with particular jobs, so that our fantasy image of a woman traffic warden is quite different to our picture of a man in the same role. We may observe identical actions, as when someone states a definite opinion, but we interpret it quite differently – the man is being firm, the woman is being pushy, and the teenager is being obstinate!

Functional Adult

Finally, we have what is called Functional Adult – the ego state that is tuned in when we are being logical and rational. As children, we begin to understand cause and effect. We drop a rattle from the pram and observe that people keep picking it up for us. We tip the bottle too far and our drink overflows the mug; we work out that we need to hold the bottle differently to avoid spilling any more. We learn that compromise may be called for: if I want to ride my brother's bike I will have a better chance if I offer to lend him something of mine for a while.

We develop the ability to think rationally on more than one level, so that we can understand both our inner and outer worlds. We acquire the skills of problem solving and decision making. All of this is clearly very relevant to us in later life. We have to balance priorities and decide between conflicting requirements and limited resources. We have to take into account our own feelings and those of others, yet still remember the objectives and practicalities.

Staff for project teams in an organisation that designed and built oil rigs needed plenty of Functional Adult behaviour. Much of their time was spent discussing strategies and solving problems. They needed to be very logical as they worked through the design stage, considering a whole range of potential hazards. During the build stage, they often had to find ways of dealing with local conditions. They could not afford to be too creative – every idea had to be examined and analysed thoroughly. The consequences of getting it wrong were potentially devastating to the environment and to the company.

A word of caution. If we spend too much time in Functional Adult we will come over as boring and pedantic. It is not always necessary to analyse a situation. Sometimes intuition or past experience will provide a better basis for our decision. Imagine the effect of Functional Adult on someone who is telling jokes, as we keep attempting to analyse the punch lines. Being logical about everything may make us seem like a robot. If we lack the characteristics of the other four ego states, people will find it hard to get to know and like us.

Ego State Availability

We each have available to us all of the five ego states, or personal styles. However, over the years we often let some of them fall into disuse. We get into 'comfort ruts', doing the same thing over and over because it worked well in the past. In this way, we limit our options unnecessarily.

If you completed the Personal Styles Questionnaire on page 181, you should now have some idea of your own profile. You can get other perspectives if you think of situations in which you now recognise the use of each ego state. Then consider how often these situations occur. In that way, you can produce an egogram – a simple bar chart that shows the relative proportions of time spent in each. If you are not satisfied with the balance between the five, you can then plan how to increase your use of certain styles by practising in appropriate situations. These two activities are described below.

Step 1: Identifying your own ego states

Recall a time when you now recognise you were in a specific ego state. Do this for each of the five personal styles, using the suggestions below as a guide.

As you recall an incident, do your best to replay your memory of it, identifying your behaviour, how you felt at the time, what you were hearing and seeing, what the other person was saying and doing, etc. The aim is to 'log' the experience so that you will be better able to identify what ego states you are adopting in the future.

Controlling Parent: recall an occasion when you have directed another person to behave in a particular way e.g. saying "you should do it like this ..." or advising them of the correct procedure
Nurturing Parent: describe a situation when you have 'looked after' or cared for another person e.g. getting them a cup of tea when they are tired, being sympathetic or encouraging over a problem
Functional Adult: think of a time when you gathered information on which you based a decision e.g. choosing a training course to attend, buying a car

Adapted Child: identify something you do because other people expect it or take it for granted e.g. holding open a door, making polite conversation
Natural Child: how do you relax and enjoy yourself; what aspects of your work are the most stimulating to do?

Step 2: Drawing your own egogram

Decide whether you want to consider your pattern of personal styles in a particular environment, such as at work or in your family.

Then draw your egogram, making the column heights reflect the different proportions of time that you estimate you spend in each ego state. You should end up with something like Figure 4.2, but with your own proportions. Be honest with yourself – you don't have to show the egogram to anyone else!

An optional extra would be to draw your egogram above and below the line – put a column above the base line for your positive uses of an ego state, and another column below the line for your negative uses of the same ego state.

Step 3: Planning a change

If you are happy with the proportions on your egogram, you have no more to do. However, most of us look at our patterns and realise we could be more effective if we reduced our use of some ego states and increased our use of others.

The most effective way to change your pattern is to concentrate on what you want to do more of. This applies even if what you want to do is actually to decrease your use of a

Figure 4.2: A Typical Egogram

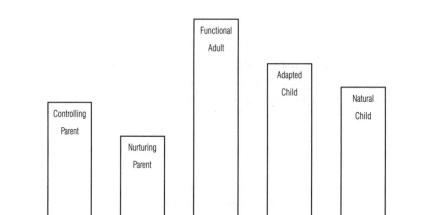

particular style. This is because human beings tend to do whatever they think about, even when they are thinking about something they don't want to do! If I say to you "Whatever you do, don't think about rabbits" you will find yourself thinking about rabbits!

Focussing on what you want to do is also effective because each person's 'combined energy total' for the five ego states is a constant; you have only so much time to spread between them. Therefore any change in one will have a corresponding effect on another. So, if you want to decrease the time spent in one ego state, plan to make a corresponding increase elsewhere. If you want to reduce your level of Adapted Child, set out to spend more time in Natural Child (or Controlling or Nurturing Parent or Functional Adult); for less time in Nurturing Parent aim to increase your use of Controlling Parent (or Natural or Adapted Child or Functional Adult); and so on. Planning to do something new is also easier than seeking to stop doing something that has become a habit.

Think also about the effect on your psychological health if you have found that some ego states are rarely engaged at work. Don't let them wither away from lack of use. If you have a particularly uninspiring job, for example, you may need to look outside the organisation for opportunities to exercise your Natural Child. If you are a junior employee in a very autocratic organisation you may be able to find scope for using your Parent ego states by joining a voluntary organisation where you can take on more responsibility.

WHAT HAPPENS INSIDE US

So far, I have only described in detail the way our ego states are exhibited to others as wavelengths on our imaginary radio. This concentrates on the identification of an ego state using behavioural clues. For many of our interactions, this will be enough to allow us to analyse the interaction and select our own ego state for good communication. However, there will be times when this is not so. It will sometimes seem as if the person is in two ego states at once, or the behavioural aspects will feel somehow out of line with our intuitive sense of what is happening.

We can use a similar diagram of three stacked circles to show *internal ego states*, using dotted lines to indicate that these are under the surface – they cannot be observed directly by others although we can speculate about them based on what behaviour and body language that we do see. You will see in Figure 4.3 that in this case Parent and Child are not subdivided, so that there are only three internal ego states: *Internal Child, Internal Adult, Internal Parent*. Again, you can check out your own profile before you read on by completeing the Internal Ego State Questionnaire on page 184.

Internal Child

As with Natural Child, we arrive in the world with the beginnings of our Internal Child already in place. Basically, it is our sense of ourselves. We have needs, wants and feelings. These include hunger and thirst, fear, curiosity, anger, wanting to be loved, and a whole range of other feelings that occur as we grow.

Figure 4.3: Internal Ego States

All of these are recorded. It is as if our Internal Child is a computer disc on which we file everything away. We are continually adding new data. We also refer back from time to time to the old files. We may do this consciously, as when we are aware that we are remembering. We may have lost the file, as when we try unsuccessfully to recall something that happened years ago. We may go back without realising, as when an incident in the present subconsciously triggers an emotional response from the past.

Another way to think about this is to visualise the Internal Child as the rings in a tree trunk, as in Figure 4.4. As the tree grows, more rings are added to the outside. The rings are hidden underneath the bark but there is always a new ring being formed just under the surface. So, every day, we add new recordings to our Internal Child. We react in a variety of ways to what is going on around us; these responses will become our memories of the future as new rings form on the outside.

Contained in some of our rings will be knots. These are distortions that are formed when significant events occur, such as when we were distressed. We took a metaphorical (or physical) knock and our mind created a damaged section just like a tree does. Perhaps a teacher criticised us unfairly and we felt helpless and angry – so we now have a knot that represents that event. In later years, we may rubberband back to such events and think we are experiencing them in the present. Perhaps we meet someone who looks rather like that teacher did, or who speaks to us in the same tone. Without being consciously aware of it, we suddenly feel just as we did years ago as a small child.

Because we are unaware of this process, we may behave inappropriately. We may respond to the other person as if they really were our old teacher, and be more upset or rebellious than seems justified. This may provoke just the sort of response that we got in the original scene! Or we may recognise that our reaction is inappropriate but not know why we feel so bad. With luck, we may recognise the origin of the reaction and be able to put it on one side. When we can spot the rubberbanding, we have more options about how to behave.

We may of course rubberband back to positive experiences, such as when the smell of a particular food takes us back to our grandmother's home. This may seem good but can still be problematic if we then behave inappropriately. Estate agents use this as a technique to persuade us to buy houses – they get the home owner to generate smells of coffee and bread being baked that lead us to feel 'at home' so we overlook any faults the house may have.

We may choose to go back to positive times rather than rubberbanding, which is an involuntary process. When we choose, we can 'borrow' positive experiences from the past and apply them to the present. For example, if we are nervous about doing a presentation, we can recall how we felt nicely confident years ago when we finally managed to ride our bicycle, or a horse, or skates… and then we can choose to replay that confident feeling as we do the presentation. I once made it easier for myself to complete a panel examination interview successfully by recapturing a sense of relaxation mingled with excitement from a time spent wandering through Kings Canyon in Australia.

Figure 4.4: Internal Child

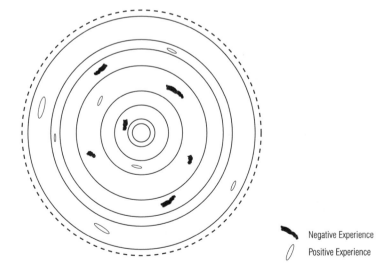

Negative Experience

Positive Experience

When we experience genuine emotions in response to current events, we also have some choices about whether to display these feelings through Natural Child. We may decide that this would be inappropriate; in that case we select a different way to behave. We may go for Adapted Child and hope that people remain unaware of our real feelings. We may use Functional Adult to describe or explain our feelings, and perhaps to review how their behaviour affects us. We may use Controlling Parent to insist on a change in their behaviour. Our Nurturing Parent might shift the focus onto someone else's feelings. In the right circumstances, however, we will let other people know how we really feel.

Internal Parent

I have already said that Controlling and Nurturing Parent are learned by copying the big people. Internal Parent is our storage system for all of these copies. Included are the opinions, beliefs and value systems that go with the behaviours. As with Internal Child, at any moment we may pull out an old recording or lay down a new one.

It is as if we have millions of miniaturised copies of all the big people we ever came into contact with, as shown in Figure 4.5. Those we saw most of will be well represented in our 'file copies'. Old recordings will emerge when we catch ourselves repeating what our parents told us years ago.

Maintaining the same beliefs as our parent figures may be a problem if, as is very likely, things have changed since then. We may share our parents' political views without question

---

Figure 4.5: Internal Parent

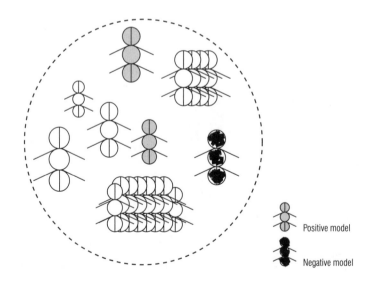

Positive model

Negative model

and yet be leading a life that depends on economic policies they would disapprove of. Racial prejudices are often the result of old recordings from a time when people had insufficient information and exposure to other cultures.

At work our earlier models based on our parents may not be relevant. We may never have seen our own parents in an organisational environment. There is a risk that we then pull out examples of how they behaved that were suitable in a family setting only. We probably have alternative copies based on previous managers we have worked for. Again, if we have not experienced good managers we are at a disadvantage when we need to manage people ourselves. The same old ineffective patterns get recycled and may serve as models to other people who also lack exposure to good management practices.

Sometimes we rubberband just as I described for Internal Child – except that now one of our parent figures seems to pop out. We speak to someone as if they are a child and we are their parent, or to our real child as if we are a clone of our own real parent. For example, we meet someone from a country where please is not used as frequently as it is in the UK, and struggle not to say out loud "What's the magic word then?" when they request something without saying please. (Apart from offending them, the danger is that they may tell us the magic word is "Now.")

Our development as individuals requires that we can update our Internal Parent. We need to have easy access to the contents of the file for scrutiny. Then we can archive those aspects which are no longer relevant. As we meet more people, we can observe and copy the things they do that are effective. We can then add these new options to a part of our filing system where they will be readily accessible.

Internal Adult

Our Internal Adult is like a computer programme that we use to access our memory banks and to process and store new data. I diagram this as shown in Figure 4.6. It takes in information from the outside world, such as who is talking to us and how. It monitors our reactions in Internal Child and checks whether these seem relevant to the situation. It scans through our Internal Parent for any recorded ways of responding that would be appropriate now.

When our Internal Adult is functioning well, we are continually making choices about what to do. These selections may take only fractions of a second, yet we manage to weigh up probabilities and make balanced decisions. Doing this does not prevent us from behaving instinctively; rather it paves the way for more spontaneity by ensuring that we have considered the consequences first.

Imagine for a moment that you have gone in to speak to your manager about an idea you have that would save money for the organisation. You are full of enthusiasm for your idea and looking forward to some well-earned praise because you have also worked out the

Figure 4.6: Internal Adult

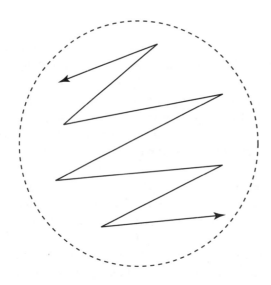

details of implementation. As you walk into the office, you see that your manager is frowning. As you begin to describe your idea, the frown gets fiercer. Now your manager is looking distractedly through a pile of folders. Slowly your enthusiasm seems to be slipping away in the face of this reaction.

If your Internal Adult is 'switched on', you will process this event. You will note the signs that tell you your manager is not in the best ego state to receive your exciting news. You will therefore reassure your Internal Child (inside your head!) that it is still a good idea but that this is not the time to present it. You will promise your enthusiastic inner self that patience will be rewarded. You will then check your Internal Parent for ideas on how to deal with a distracted boss. Perhaps there is a model there of how to be reassuring or concerned. You can use this to ask your manager what is wrong, is there some way you can help, or just to say that you will come back later.

PUTTING IT TOGETHER

We can now combine the concepts of external and internal ego states to give us a model for understanding the elements of our personal styles. Figure 4.7 shows the two sets of circles. Often, we will need to consider only the external, behavioural evidence. However, in some situations the internal ego states will be significant and we will need to take them into account. We can of course only speculate about these for someone else but even this will add to our skills at communicating. The next chapter includes a number of examples of how you might use this framework.

Figure 4.7: Inside and Outside

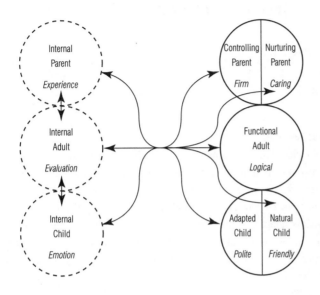

We may rubberband sometimes, so that a response comes directly from our Internal Parent or Internal Child. This may or may not be constructive. When our Internal Adult is functioning well, we evaluate and choose which behaviours are most appropriate. This still allows us to select from Internal Parent or Internal Child and makes it much more likely that our behaviour will stimulate the type of response that we want.

To recap, in the working environment the following are probably the main ways in which we need to use our five behavioural ego states:

- Controlling Parent - when **firmness** is appropriate
- Nurturing Parent -when **caring** is needed
- Functional Adult - for a **logical**, problem solving approach
- Adapted Child - when we need to be **polite** and fit in
- Natural Child - for showing our genuine **friendliness**

On the inside, we have available:

- Internal Parent - our store of **experience**
- Internal Adult - where we **evaluate** the situation
- Internal Child - our **emotional** reactions

CHAPTER 5: INFLUENCING AND BEING INFLUENCED

APPROACHES TO INFLUENCING

We all spend a lot of our working lives influencing others, being influenced, or both. The more we understand what makes people tick, the better we can communicate skilfully and therefore the more effectively we can influence. The frameworks already described will all help you to increase your awareness of what happens during the influencing process. The personal styles concept is especially relevant, as this gives us the tools for enhancing our success rate at communicating. The windows on the world model adds important additional information, as this enables us to understand why we get into situations where someone has to be the loser, when we could just as easily have opted for a win/win outcome.

In this chapter, therefore, I am going to take each of those models and show how they can be related specifically to influencing. I will give some examples of using personal styles to handle conflict, to deal with complaints, and to work more effectively within a hierarchy. I'll then show briefly how the windows on the world model gives insights into problems with being assertive. As you read, I'll invite you to plan how to deal with a selection of situations in which you feel your current behaviour may not be as skilful and constructive as you'd like.

To start with, let's expand what you've learned about yourself from the previous chapters. Check back to your results from the Windows on the World, Personal Styles and Internal Ego State Questionnaires and the other suggested activities.

Using your increased self awareness, pick a specific situation and think about your responses to the following questions:
- *Which personal styles, or behavioural ego states, do you find hardest to use?*
- *Which do you think are most liked by others when you use them?*
- *Which do you think are least liked by others?*
- *What does each ego state contribute to your overall effectiveness?*
- *What more might each ego state contribute?*
- *How does each ego state cause problems?*
- *How else might each ego state cause problems?*
- *What real life instances can you now understand better?*
- *How can you apply what you have learned from answering these questions?*

Here are some ideas of possible answers if you apply the questions to the task of chairing a meeting:

- Controlling Parent   - structuring the meeting to the agenda
  - controlling interruptions
- Nurturing Parent   - making sure everyone is heard
  - being reassuring when people are anxious
- Functional Adult   - initiating problem solving
  - identifying compromises
- Natural Child   - introducing an element of humour
  - encouraging enjoyment of the task
- Adapted Child   - demonstrating courtesy and respect
  - talking to people politely

Problems may include:

- Controlling Parent   - being bossy
  - insisting on doing it your way
- Nurturing Parent   - fussing
  - worrying about taking care of everyone
- Functional Adult   - dispassionately demolishing every idea
  - ignoring people's feelings
- Natural Child   - making silly jokes
  - bringing personal problems into the meeting
- Adapted Child   - not participating
  - waiting to be asked

CHANNELS OF COMMUNICATION

This example of chairing a meeting shows that our process of choosing an ego state needs to include consideration of the effect we want to have on the other person. Although in theory you can pair any ego state with any other, some combinations just fail to connect. In practice there are four channels that are especially likely to result in good working relationships:

Functional Adult – Functional Adult: when we want to have a logical, rational conversation, such as for joint problem solving. This channel is particularly useful with people who like to focus on work issues and 'get down to business'.

Nurturing Parent – Natural Child: when we want to be nurturing, encouraging, reassuring. This channel is especially liked by people who respond well to an interest in them as people, who like us to notice their appearance, ask after their family, and spend time in establishing a relationship with them before we get on with the task.

Natural Child – Natural Child: for having fun, being creative, and playing together. The most effective channel for people who like to share their enthusiasm with us, who may have unusual hobbies or exciting ideas to talk about, and who appreciate the chance to tell us about these as long as we respond in a child-like way (not childish) that matches their own level of enthusiasm.

Controlling Parent – Adapted Child: for giving instructions and telling people what to do next. Although our interaction is targeted at Adapted Child, it connects also with their Internal Adult as they think about what we said. This channel is preferred by people who are more comfortable if they receive clear instructions, and who then like to be left to get on with the job.

As you have seen, each of us has a preferred channel. We will probably be reasonably comfortable with one or two of the others, and somewhat uncomfortable with the fourth. What most of us do is use our own preferred channel most of the time. This is not particularly skilful – we will have more success if we match the channels we use to each recipient. Paying attention to the channel they use themselves will give us a good idea of the best way to initiate contact with them.

Lani was Research Director in a detergent manufacturers. She was very work-orientated and preferred the Functional Adult – Functional Adult channel. However, her research role meant she needed to gain the support of other directors. She found that she needed to use all four channels: the Managing Director was the only one who responded best to Functional Adult – Functional Adult; the Marketing Director liked to talk about exciting new promotions and publicity stunts that were being planned, so preferred Natural Child – Natural Child as Lani shared his enthusiasm; the Financial Director reacted best to Controlling Parent – Adapted Child when Lani told him how she wanted her budget allocations dealt with, and the reverse when he told her that her staff were completing their expense claims incorrectly; the Personnel Director used Nurturing Parent – Natural Child to encourage Lani to set up training courses for her staff and clearly enjoyed talking to Lani about his children.

There are other options that will enable us to communicate adequately but these will not necessarily have the added benefit of building a close working relationship through using the preferred channels. Instead, they involve some element of shared reaction towards other people that may sometimes be unhelpful.

Nurturing Parent – Nurturing Parent: for discussing how to care for others, as when two managers review a subordinate's progress.

Controlling Parent – Controlling Parent: when agreeing on what rules should apply to others.

Adapted Child – Adapted Child: being compliant or rebellious together, as when we 'whinge' about the management or obey instructions.

Some combinations of ego states are very unlikely to lead to good communication. Miscommunication is likely to occur if we use Functional Adult to address someone in any of the Parent or Child ego states. Conversely, we are unlikely to get an appropriate response if we use Parent or Child with someone who is clearly tuned into Functional Adult and expecting a logical discussion.

Such crossed transactions are only useful when you want to make a significant change to the communication. Even then, you are more likely to be successful if you select one of our four preferred channels before you attempt the change. By doing this, you will establish an initial contact in the way the recipient expects. They will then be more likely to follow your switch in ego states so that they can maintain communication with you.

We can gain even more insight into the effects of various ego state combinations if we analyse our transactions in terms of whether they are *complementary, crossed* or *ulterior.*

To do this for complementary and crossed transactions we need consider only the behavioural aspects – the observable uses of ego states. Complementary transactions occur when the ego state addressed is the ego state which responds. If I use Controlling Parent to address your Adapted Child, and you reply from Adapted Child to my Controlling Parent, we have a complementary transaction. If you opted instead to respond from Functional Adult, and sought to interact with my Functional Adult ego state, we would have a crossed transaction. Figures 5.1 and 5.2 give examples of each type of transaction.

Ulterior transactions involve 'hidden' messages – we seem to be in one ego state but somehow another ego state is also involved. Perhaps I sound Functional Adult but frown as if from Parent. Figure 5.3 shows an ulterior transaction.

Complementary Transactions

A very simple complementary transaction may consist of little more than one person asking for something, from Controlling Parent, and the other acquiescing from Adapted Child. No surprises, the matter in hand is dealt with, and the conversation ends. Bank and building society counter staff often interact in this way with customers, who expect little more than polite responses when they hand in their paying-in books or want to withdraw money.

Longer sequences may also occur. An entrepreneur asking the bank manager for an overdraft facility may involve several complementary sequences: starting with Adapted Child – Controlling Parent as they establish their relative roles in the conversation; moving on to Functional Adult – Functional Adult as they check through the facts and establish whether the business can justify an extension of credit; finishing perhaps with Natural Child – Nurturing Parent as the entrepreneur shows feelings of relief and the bank manager makes reassuring comments about the future (or is it that the bank manager shows signs of anxiety and the entrepreneur makes reassuring comments about the future!).

Figure 5.1: A Complementary Transaction

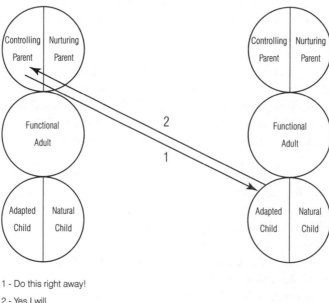

1 - Do this right away!

2 - Yes I will.

It has been said that the recession in the UK was partly caused by the banks encouraging people to take out loans they could not afford. Whether this is true or not, the easier climate for granting loans certainly meant there were complementary transactions. In those cases the bank manager may well have been in Nurturing Parent and the entrepreneur in Natural Child. The absence of Functional Adult in both parties had a lot to do with the failure to consider the future implications, and the subsequent business collapses when the economic situation changed.

Complementary transactions, therefore, are not necessarily 'good' – it depends on the circumstances and the specific context. Someone yelling from Controlling Parent to another person's Adapted Child is complementary and decidedly negative.

Crossed Transactions

In a crossed transaction, the response comes from a different ego state to that which was addressed. Telling Adapted Child to do something and getting a reply from Functional Adult means that the conversation may shift course into a discussion about the deadline - with a consequent delay in getting the job done. Or perhaps the Controlling Parent end of this particular conversation will persist, with a comment such as "You already know the deadline is today. Just get the job done now!" Or they may even say "Don't question my instructions. If I say now, that's because I mean now."

Alternatively, asking about the deadline may prompt the other person to move to Functional Adult also. It will then be possible to review how realistic the deadline is and maybe do some joint problem solving if it really isn't appropriate to do the job immediately.

With a complementary transaction, therefore, it is as if the communication can continue indefinitely. With a crossed transaction, some form of a break in communication will occur. This does not mean that we stop talking after a crossed transaction – but we will change the topic of conversation.

Perhaps your complementary transaction is a highly unsatisfactory one, with an angry colleague shouting at you from Controlling Parent about a mistake you have made. You have begun with a complementary transaction by apologising from Adapted Child. However, they are ignoring your apology and are still shouting at you. It will not be appropriate to keep apologising while they keep shouting. You need the break in communication that a crossed transaction would provide; shift to Functional Adult for some problem solving discussion, or use your own Controlling Parent to tell their Adapted child firmly that they may not talk to you like that.

Keep in mind, though, that even if we have to cross a transaction, we will still need to attain some matching of ego states for the communication to proceed at any length.

Figure 5.2: A Crossed Transaction

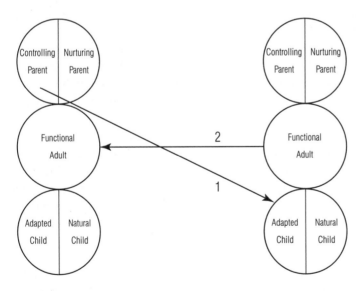

1 - Do this right away!

2 - When is your deadline?

Ulterior Transactions

Sometimes we have what appears to be a complementary transaction but we sense there are undercurrents. This will be an ulterior transaction – one where communication is taking place on two levels. We then have to extend our analysis to take account of both levels – the social and the psychological. In other words, our outward behaviour may not match what is happening within our internal ego states.

If we are both engaged in an ulterior transaction, we may not realise that our communication is unsatisfactory until afterwards. There is a well known selling technique that involves 'hooking' the purchaser's Internal Child by telling them something is too expensive for them. Often they will then spend more than they should through bravado, and not realise the problem until later. This is why it is so helpful to have the 14 day 'change of mind' period the UK law allows when you buy something within your home.

At other times, our Internal Child will be intuitive enough to pick up the underlying signals from someone else's internal ego states whatever they may be doing behaviourally. Take the example in Figure 5.3 of the manager who asks a subordinate whether the report will be ready by the deadline. This may be phrased as a logical, rational question. However, the manager may really be convinced that the subordinate will be late with the report, as has happened in the past. The manager's Internal Parent is therefore holding some fairly derogatory thoughts about the subordinate's performance. These are liable to 'leak'; there may well be small indicators of them through the manager's body language and tone of voice.

Any reasonably intuitive subordinate will pick up these small signals, as if they have secret 'antennae' attached to their Internal Child. They may choose to say nothing but will now believe that the manager does not trust them. This can be enough for them to justify a late report – why bother if it's not expected on time anyway? Or they may respond directly to the signals and accuse the manager of lacking trust. This is more likely if the comment has reactivated the stored feelings in Internal Child that they acquired during previous bad experiences.

With an ulterior transaction, the behavioural outcome will be determined by the psychological, or ulterior, level of the interaction. The unspoken intent will have more impact than the overt, social comment. Whenever our inner and outer messages conflict in this way, the secret agenda will carry the most weight, even if we both pretend it does not exist. It will be difficult to build effective relationships with people unless we address their underlying concerns.

Sometimes we will use an ulterior transaction to convey positive messages or to allow people to save face. We may tease someone outwardly by reacting negatively to them when our real message is that we are pleased to have them around. Or we may change the subject when someone seems uncomfortable, with the hidden message that we don't want to embarrass them. Sometimes an ulterior will be the appropriate way to deal with a situation

Figure 5.3: An Ulterior Transaction

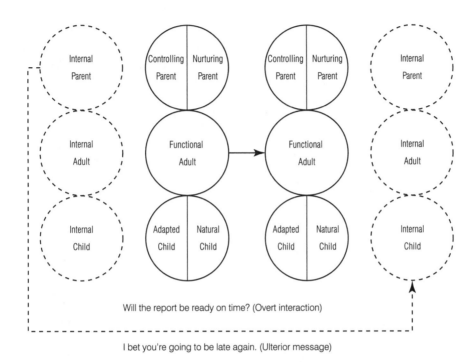

Will the report be ready on time? (Overt interaction)

I bet you're going to be late again. (Ulterior message)

but keep in mind that there is always the risk of being misunderstood. The person may think we really are not pleased to see them, or that we just don't care about their problem. And even if they do know what we mean, those observing may get the wrong impression.

HANDLING CONFLICT

Figure 5.4 shows how a conflict develops. Often, this sequence will begin with an ulterior transaction. At other times an individual's frame of reference will lead them to believe that there is an ulterior when none was intended. The result may be the same, whether the ulterior is real or not.

Chris picks up or imagines that Pat is criticising. Chris's Internal Child makes contact with an old experience of being criticised, and feels threatened. Chris's Internal Child then does what any small child does when scared – goes to fetch Mother (or Father). In this case, Mother is handily stored away as a copy in Chris's Internal Parent. Chris simply sifts through to find the best version of Mother when she was telling someone else to leave her child alone. Chris's Internal Adult has been bypassed in this process so Chris is not considering any other options. Instead, Chris selects a copy of Mother and uses external Controlling Parent to criticise Pat.

Figure 5.4: Stages of Conflict

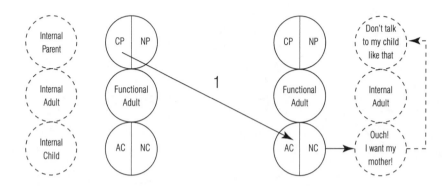

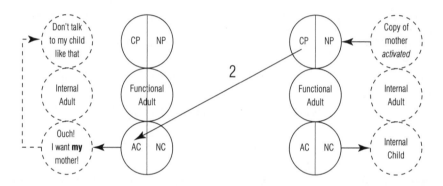

1 - Change this report

2 - No. It's correct as it is.

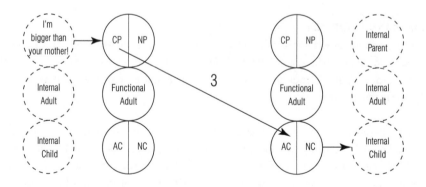

3 - I insist that you change it

At this point, Pat does the same as Chris has done. Pat goes back into an old experience, feels scared, fetches Mother, puts a copy of Mother into Controlling Parent, and zaps Chris. And so it goes on, with each 'mother' becoming increasingly aggressive on behalf of her offspring, and each 'child' feeling even more scared. If they get scared enough, they may even bring their grandmothers into the fray!

Knowing about internal ego states can help us to avoid conflict. As we are criticised, we can:

- Make a point of investing extra energy into Internal Adult.
- Count to ten and keep thinking.
- Remind ourselves that we are likely to react by re-experiencing an old hurt.
- Check how much of the pain is really related to the current comment.
- Consider the consequences of responding angrily.
- Review what other options we have.
- We can then use our external ego states in various ways:
- Natural Child could be used to let them know that we are hurt by the criticism. They may not have realised they have said something unkind.
- Adapted Child could accept the criticism as justified and ask how they want us to be different.
- Functional Adult could be employed to question the basis of the criticism and discuss what we might decide to change.
- Controlling Parent could tell them firmly that they are criticising unjustly or unhelpfully.
- Nurturing Parent could reassure them that our action will not cause a problem for them.

Several of these options are aimed at the internal ego state in the other person. Used in a genuine attempt to avoid conflict, they are likely to be perceived as constructive and will help build a closer relationship.

DEALING WITH COMPLAINTS

The way we deal with conflict has relevance for handling complaints. These are, after all, the sort of situations which often finish in conflict. Any of the suggestions above may be better than getting annoyed with a customer or colleague.

There is also a specific sequence of behaviours which can be particularly effective, as shown in Figure 5.5. This takes account of the probable dynamics of the person who is complaining. Although there may be times when you judge that an alternative method would be more appropriate, the steps outlined below will serve to defuse most conflict and complaint situations.

Response Part 1

We start our complaint scene with the customer or colleague in angry Controlling Parent, telling you off. You will therefore need a polite Adapted Child response to make an initial connection with them. Any other ego state will be perceived as inappropriate by them and you will not make any contact. Make sure this is an honest comment, such as "I'm sorry

Figure 5.5: A Complaint Handling Sequence

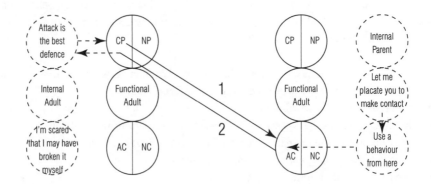

1 - I demand a refund.
2 - I'm sorry you're not satisfied. Sir/Madam.

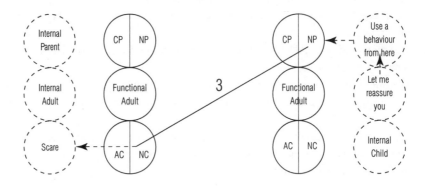

3 - I'm sure we can sort this out.

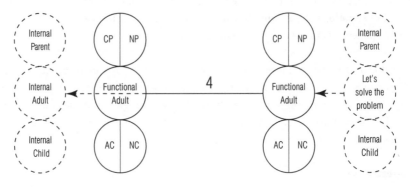

4 - Where is the broken part?

you are not satisfied, Sir/Madam." But – don't say "I'm sorry. We'll give you your money back." unless you already have enough facts to justify a refund.

Response Part 2

We now speculate about what is happening inside them. They are most probably in scared Internal Child because they are afraid you may refuse to deal with their complaint. Perhaps someone at home, or their manager, will tell them they should have known better than to spend money on your goods. You now need a reassuring comment from Nurturing Parent to soothe their Internal Child. Do not commit yourself to specific action at this stage. Tell them that you are sure you will be able to sort things out.

Response Part 3

With luck, they are now ready to solve the problem. Use your Functional Adult to ask for details of the problem. Make it something straightforward and factual to start with, such as asking to see the item.

It is essential to use this 3-part sequence without pausing – polite response, reassurance, problem solving question. If they are still angry, repeat the sequence. Sometimes when we are very upset we fail to even hear what the other person says to us. It is as if we knock the olive branch from their hand before we realise what it is. Somehow, it never seems feasible to pick it up at that stage, although we will often wish they would offer it again. If they do, we will usually accept it on the second occasion.

However, if you have repeated the sequence with no effect, perhaps they have no real investment in solving the problem. Maybe today is one of their off-days; those days we all have sometimes when we wake up feeling cross with the whole world. If you suspect that is the case, let them continue to yell at you until they run out of steam. Meanwhile, have an internal conversation in which your Internal Parent reassures your Internal Child that this is not your fault.

EGO STATES IN A HIERARCHY

Within organisations there is a tendency for a common, generally unhelpful, pattern of ego states to occur. This is particularly likely when there is a strong hierarchical structure. What happens is that managers use mostly Controlling Parent ego state while subordinates opt for Adapted Child. In other words, the managers tell the workers what to do, and the workers do it. This communication format is repeated through the different levels of the hierarchy; senior managers tell junior managers what to do, and junior managers tell first-line supervisors. This conjures up the amusing, but unfortunate, vision shown in Figure 5.6 – those in the middle doing an about-face in ego state terms as they move from junior to senior contacts. They control and instruct those below them – then go in to be controlled and instructed by those above them on the organisation chart. This pattern is repeated all the way to the top of the organisation – perhaps up to someone who then goes home to an even more Controlling Parent!

Figure 5.6: A Hierarchy of Ego States

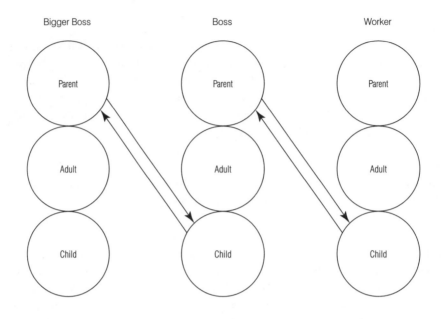

What has happened is that we have held onto patterns of behaving that we learned at home and at school. When we were real children, we spent a lot of time in Adapted Child, doing as the grown-ups told us. Generally, this made sense because they were older than us and knew more of the world. (This was not always true, and even when it was we did not always believe it but we acted as if we did). At work, we subconsciously put managers into the slot we have reserved for those who know more, and so we expect them to tell us what to do just as our parents and teachers did. (Again, we may not believe it but we act as if we do.) When we in turn get promoted, we simply switch across to the Parent ego state side of this equation.

Effective managers and competent subordinates do not fit into this pattern. They recognise that we need all our ego states in use for the range of situations we will face. They realise that a subordinate using only Adapted Child will not display the creativity of Natural Child nor the problem solving ability of Functional Adult. Such employees are unlikely to be firm when faced with unreasonable demands, and may commit themselves unadvisedly; their lack of nurturing may give a poor image of the organisation. The wise manager acts so as to encourage their subordinates to keep all ego states in good working order.

Managers who use only Controlling Parent will be perceived as bossy and uncaring. On the other hand, too much Nurturing Parent may seem overwhelming. Lack of Functional Adult ego state will limit their consideration of options when problems arise. Lack of Natural Child will cause them to appear unfeeling, with no sense of humour. Lack of Adapted Child will mean that polite pleasantries are missing. They are unlikely to motivate and enthuse their subordinates; rather they will encourage staff to avoid risks and to check first instead of using initiative.

A very extreme version of Controlling Parent management occurred several years ago in a fire station. When fighting a fire no-one expects the fire chief to call the team together and engage in democratic discussion while the building is in flames. Controlling Parent – Adapted Child offers a quick channel of communication; each fire officer follows orders and in that way their actions are co-ordinated (they do of course use Internal Adult to think about what they are doing).

However, when Maurice was promoted to fire chief he based his behaviour on permanent Controlling Parent. He never relaxed, and was just as controlling at the fire station as he was out on a call. The fire officers eventually became so incensed that they actually went on strike until senior officers recognised the problem. Maurice was posted elsewhere on a lower grade.

Refracted transactions

Another way of understanding what is happening when managers interact with subordinates is through the notion of a refracted transaction. Just as objects under water appear to be in a different place because the light is refracted, so also do we sometimes think that someone is addressing us from a different ego state to the one they are really using.

Imagine a scene where a new, young, keen to learn employee has just started a new job. The boss tells the employee to do something. The employee asks why it is done that way – meaning to learn and understand. The employee speaks from Functional Adult, or maybe Natural Child if they sound very curious. The boss, however, is expecting a new employee to address them from Adapted Child. Asking 'why' from Adapted Child sounds challenging and cheeky? The boss therefore feels annoyed and gets even more definitely Controlling Parent and says something like "Don't question what I tell you. Just do what I say."

At this point, if the employee has any sense, they switch to Adapted Child and do as they are told – and decide not to bother asking questions or learning more – and also not to bother suggesting any improvements they can see in the future.

Figure 5.7 shows how a refracted transaction operates. It is as if the Functional Adult-Functional Adult intended communication from the employee hits the boss's frame of reference and this acts like the surface of the water – so it refracts the transaction and makes it seem to the boss that it is coming from Adapted Child.

Refracted transactions have long term negative effects within organisations because they discourage new employees from asking questions or thinking for themselves. This means that employees settle into Adapted Child mode and don't bother to think about what they

Figure 5.7: A Refracted Transaction

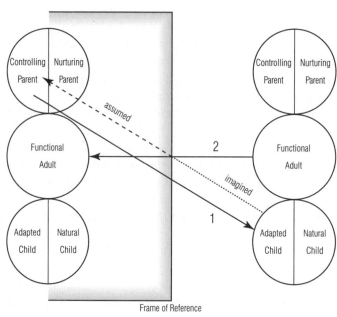

1 - Do this right away!

2 - Why do we do it like that?

are doing. Managers may later complain that employees lack initiative because they act by rote even when the circumstances have changed, or that employees are not clever enough to put forward suggestions for improvements. These managers are unaware that they 'created' employees like this through using refracted transactions.

ASSERTIVENESS

We may lack assertiveness because we do not have the social and persuasive skills we need to deal with others. The previous ideas about ego states and channels of communication are useful in identifying a wider range of options that we can practise and develop. However, there is often a further, underlying cause associated with our individual ways of thinking and perceiving the world. Without an understanding of our internal processes, we sometimes find it difficult to apply the skills we know we should use. It is as if we do not believe we can behave in the way proposed. This is the result of our window on the world, or life position.

Provided we are looking through the I'm OK, You're OK window, we will be confident of our ability to use what we learn. Generally, we will not lack assertiveness because we are interested in other people and have therefore developed appropriate communication skills.

We will not be aggressive because we do not believe that we have the right to force our choices onto others. We will not be submissive because we know that they likewise have no right to force their decisions on us. When conflict occurs, our thinking will be directed towards problem solving and compromise.

However, if we opt for I'm not OK, You're OK, we will spend our time admiring the skills of other people and insisting that we are incapable of such effective behaviour. We will do our best to get someone to be assertive on our behalf instead of tackling the situation ourself. Each time they succeed, we re-confirm our own inadequacy as we think how hard it would have been for us to match their performance.

With the I'm not OK, You're not OK window, we get nowhere with any attempts at learning assertiveness. We doubt our own ability to change, we doubt the goodwill of other people, we even doubt the whole notion of assertiveness. We assume that, even if we did the right thing, other people would not respond accordingly – so why bother.

And if we adopt I'm OK, You're not OK, we are convinced that we are already perfectly assertive. Others may describe us (more accurately) as aggressive but we reject this and blame any problems on them. We are unlikely to accept any need for change unless we are given very specific feedback (and even then we probably believe it's just because no-one is clever enough to appreciate our virtues).

You can check out your own tendencies towards adopting the unhelpful life positions by working through the following situations. Take a sheet of paper, list any of the examples that are relevant to you, and add any others where you have doubts about your ability to be assertive. Leave spaces so that you can write a brief description of your typical behaviour in each situation.

A colleague approaches you with a sponsorship form. Their children have entered a fun-run to raise money for a charitable cause that you are not particularly interested in.

You call a supplier about a faulty item of equipment and they say "You must have used it incorrectly; one's never gone like that before."

A stranger comes up to you in the canteen when you are part way through eating your meal, and says "Would you mind moving to that smaller table so my group can sit together."

Your manager, or a customer, says "This is not good enough. You'll have to do it again."

A colleague asks for a favour. The last time you asked them to help you they were too busy.

At a meeting, someone keeps having side conversations when you and others are speaking. The chairperson appears not to notice this.

A colleague who is also a close friend says something that annoys you.

You feel ill when there is an urgent job to be tackled. Your colleague could do it but you know your manager really wants you to do it.

Now go back over each description, deciding which life position it reflects. You might like to check these out with a colleague you respect and trust. Use four small columns down the side of the sheet, so you can enter IOK–YOK, IOK–YNOK, INOK–YOK and INOK–YNOK as appropriate. Then do a tally to see which windows on the world predominate.

Finally, decide in which situation you would most benefit from a new approach. This may be your top priority or you may want to practice first on something a little less significant. Use the personal style model to identify some alternative ways for you to behave when you are next in this situation. If possible, arrange to rehearse your new behaviour with a colleague. If you can't arrange this, at least rehearse in your head, by visualising the scene, imagining yourself using your new options, and fantasising the other person responding exactly as you would like them to. This preparation, although it may sound strange, will have a positive effect on your ability to handle the real situation when it next occurs.

Once you have used your new approach a few times you will find it becomes automatic. This is the time to repeat this exercise, so that you can choose another situation to work on. In this way, you can continually add to the range of approaches you use to influence the behaviour of other people. You will also be building better relationships, and putting yourself in a good position for using the ideas in Chapters 7 and 8.

CHAPTER 6:   WORKING STYLES

There is a Working Styles Questionnaire at page 186 that you might like to complete before you read this chapter.

Could this be you?

Chris gets through a lot of work, by doing everything very quickly. Chris moves fast, thinks fast, talks fast, and seems to do everything so much more quickly than most people.

However, every so often Chris makes a mistake through rushing so much - and then it takes twice as long to put it right - especially as Chris seems intent on finding a shortcut instead of taking time to work it through again.

Chris also has a bad habit of arriving late at meetings, and of needing to leave early to get to the next meeting! And during the meeting Chris is quite likely to be openly impatient and interrupt a lot, so that people feel pressured and hurried.

Pat, on the other hand, expects to arrive at and leave the meeting on time. Pat brings the correct files and makes sure that proper minutes are kept. Meetings with Pat progress slowly as everything must be considered in great detail.

Pat is meticulous. Laid down procedures are followed to the letter - even when you are begging Pat to make a minor exception. Everything Pat deals with is double checked and even insignificant errors are corrected carefully and painstakingly.

Other staff sometimes complain that Pat is nit-picking, especially when their own mistakes are pointed out. And Pat misses deadlines through taking too long to collect every single piece of information which could be relevant.

Vijay is nearly always willing and helpful; nothing is too much trouble. Vijay can be very pleasant to have around, making sure that everyone on the team is comfortable. Work gets accepted from just about anyone and sometimes Vijay does things without even being asked.

However, this means that Vijay exercises little control over workload or priorities, so that jobs get left undone when someone else needs help. Vijay sometimes gets tired and emotional from being so helpful and complains about being misunderstood.

Vijay also gets very anxious and upset by criticism, even when it is offered constructively. And Vijay has been known to keep quiet instead of pointing out problems - for fear of offending anyone!

Robin is enthusiastic and interested in all aspects of work. Robin is generally the first to volunteer when new tasks are being allocated. In fact, Robin is involved in some way in just about everything that is going on in the department and even outside it when opportunities arise. People tend to ask for Robin's help in their section because they know the answer will be an enthusiastic yes.

However, Robin quickly gets bored with some tasks and this often means that the work never quite gets finished - there always seems to be another important part of the job left to do. It is not uncommon for projects to be handed over to someone else to be completed because Robin's time is taken up with other new work. This sometimes leads other people to complain that they have to pick up work which they feel Robin should have done.

Lee works steadily and produces work at a regular pace. Even when the pressure is on, Lee stays calm and continues to work at the same steady rate. Lee never appears to worry about the workload, and won't be hurried.

Lee seems to ignore how people feel and doesn't understand the need to be flexible to deal with those sudden emergency jobs - everything can just take its turn.

Lee prefers to work alone and never asks for help. Somehow, Lee appears aloof and almost unfriendly - it's as if there are no real feelings there. Sometimes the work is not being done after all; Lee has tidied it away to give an appearance of coping.

WORKING STYLES

These five people have rather extreme versions of five typical working styles. There are many people who have similar characteristics, although most of us have more of a mix of styles. You may not match one of the patterns exactly but you probably recognise aspects of a couple of them that are uncomfortably close to you. Check out your Working Style Questionnaire results or your responses to the following prompts:

Think about what is important to you as you do your work. What aspects keep you energised and motivated?

*Do you enjoy having lots to do, like Chris? Are you usually in a hurry? Can you pull out all the stops when urgent work comes up? This is the **Hurry Up** style.*

*Or are you more like Pat? Do you pride yourself on your accuracy? Does it worry you when you see mistakes? Do you enjoy the challenge of bringing order into the world? In that case, you have a **Be Perfect** style.*

*Is your priority to get on well with people? Are you intuitive about how people are feeling? Are you happiest working in a team where everyone's views are taken into account? If you are like Vijay, your style is **Please People**.*

*Are you motivated by almost anything as long as it's new? Do you enjoy most the early stages of each new project or task? Is it a challenge to explore different areas of work? This is the **Try Hard** style, like Robin.*

*The fifth style is called **Be Strong**. If you are like Lee, then you pride yourself on your ability to cope. You may even welcome pressure because it gives you the chance to show how well you can deal with it. You stay calm when there is a crisis.*

In the real world, people don't always fit into the neat categories of a framework like this. However, most of us still fit more into some of the categories than others. We fit even more closely when we are under stress as this seems to emphasise some of our weaknesses.

Alan had the task of responding to a large volume of customer complaints. Alan's manager, David, suspected that the workload was too high for one person to deal with. David was puzzled that Alan's desk always seemed clear but the more he questioned Alan the more insistent Alan was that everything was under control. Offers of help were treated with suspicion, as if Alan thought his job was at risk.

Alan worked longer and longer hours and then he got the 'flu - probably because he was run down through overworking. At that point, David finally discovered that there was a considerable backlog of complaints. Alan had been filing them neatly away to maintain the appearance of coping. Like Lee, Alan was reluctant to admit problems or ask for any help, even though the workload was in fact excessive. Instead he had struggled on. David, for his part, was a bit like Vijay - afraid to confront Alan for fear of hurting his feelings.

Knowing the effect of stress on working styles means you can plan better ways of working with people. You can take care that you do not unintentionally make the situation even more stressful. Had he known about working styles, David could have insisted on monitoring the workload himself. If he'd demanded to see the complaints and the responses, instead of being so afraid of offending Alan, he would have known that more staff should be allocated to this task. As it was, Alan simply got more stressed the further behind he got, and the more stressed he got the more determined he became to prove he could cope on his own.

There are a number of other ways in which understanding more about our working styles can be of use. These styles affect everything we do. They show up in the ways we organise our work, manage our time, how we function alongside others, our contribution to the team, our style of communication, even our sentence patterns. They have an impact whether we are alone or with others. Greater awareness can help us build on the strengths of our style and minimise any problems. We can also develop alternative approaches so that our range of options is increased.

Drivers

As you have read, each working style has a number of benefits. Unfortunately, each style also has drawbacks. These drawbacks are known as drivers, so called because they have a 'driven', or compulsive, quality when we are under stress. They are subconscious attempts by us to behave in ways that will gain us the recognition we need from others. Drivers are also programmed responses to the messages we carry in our heads from important people in the past. They start the unhelpful miniscript sequences described in Chapter 3.

So a driver is rather like a superstition. When we were little we used to believe that if we avoided the cracks in the pavement, or crossed our fingers when we were afraid, then we would be spared from some awful impending occurrence. In the same way, we operate as if a certain style of behaviour will ward off problems and earn us the respect of others. Unfortunately, this is a myth. The reality is that we can never do quite enough of whatever our driver calls for. In seeking to be more and more as we believe we should, we create problems. These in turn lead to us feeling more stressed, so we put even more energy into our driver behaviour, create more difficulties, and get yet more stressed.

On the other hand, our driver characteristics are often the things we did when we were children because they seemed to satisfy the grown-ups. When our stress levels are acceptable, the driver will appear as a strength. It is probable, therefore, that we will be known to others in terms of our working style and how effective it is. If they have a different style, they may wish they were more like us – put them, or us, under pressure, however, and they may see only our negative aspects after all! If they share the same style, they will probably regard us even more highly. Bosses are likely to value subordinates more when there is a good match of working styles.

One important point to note is that drivers occur outside our awareness. We can recognise our working styles when they are described, and even accept that the drivers also occur. However, at the time that we move into the unhelpful aspects of our working styles, we are not conscious of doing so. We believe that we are still operating within the effective band of the style. We need, therefore, to review our behaviour from time to time, especially when we are under stress, so that we can avoid the problems that driver behaviour brings.

Hurry Up

Let's look now at each style in more detail. As you have read, if we have Hurry Up characteristics we work quickly and get a lot done in a short time. Our major strength is the amount that we can achieve. We respond particularly well to short deadlines, and our energy peaks under pressure. We actually seem to enjoy having too many things to do. The saying "If you want something done, give it to a busy person." was probably coined with us in mind.

Our underlying motivation is to do things as quickly as possible. We feel good if we can complete tasks in the shortest possible time. Like organisation and methods specialists, we look for the most efficient way to do work in the hope of shaving even a few minutes off each task. These few minutes can add up to significant time savings across the week. We also spend less time preparing than others do, giving us chance to meet more people and contribute more to the team.

However, give us time to spare and we delay starting until the job becomes urgent – then we start work on it. This can backfire because in our haste we make mistakes. Going back to correct the mistakes takes longer than doing the job right first time, so we may miss the deadlines after all. At the least, the quality of our work may be poor because we have not left enough time to check it over or improve it.

Our urge to save time may be inappropriately applied to everything we do, instead of being reserved for those tasks where it will make a real difference. Our ability to think fast may lead us to appear impatient. We speak rapidly and have a habit of interrupting others. We may even finish their sentences for them, sometimes incorrectly so wasting time. Our body language reflects our impatience through fidgeting, tapping with our fingers or toes, looking at our watch, and perhaps even sighing or yawning ostentatiously.

Our appointments get planned too close together, so we rush from one to another, arriving late and leaving early. We are likely to turn up at a meeting having left the necessary paperwork in our office; we may even fail to arrive because we didn't stop to check the location of the meeting. When we do arrive, others must wait while we are given a summary of what we missed. Our constant rushing may prevent us from really getting to know people, so that we feel like an outsider.

A typical event for a Hurry Up is the time we approach a door that opens towards us, while we are carrying two cups of coffee. Most people would put one cup down, open the door, go through, put the cup down and then return to fetch the second cup. Not a Hurry Up, though. We juggle! Usually it's quicker. Every so often, it's a lot slower because we have to stop to clean up the coffee we spill. (If you never get the coffees, imagine an armful of files to be picked up from the floor, or the pulled muscle from carrying too many bags of groceries in one trip from the car, or the piece of wood that is too short because you didn't check the measurement carefully before you sawed!)

Be Perfect

Be Perfect people are as unlike Hurry Up's as can be. Our motto is: "If a job is worth doing, it's worth doing well". Be Perfect characteristics involve a quest for perfection – no errors, everything must be exactly right, first time. Our major strength is our reputation for producing accurate, reliable work. We check the facts carefully, we prepare thoroughly and we pay attention to the details. Our written work will look good because we aim for perfection in layout as well as content.

This working style means we are well organised because we look ahead and plan how to deal with potential problems. In this way, we are not taken by surprise but have contingency plans ready to put into effect. Our projects run smoothly and efficiently, with effective co-ordination and monitoring of progress.

Unfortunately, we cannot be relied on to produce work on time because we need to check it so carefully for mistakes, and this checking takes time. Because of our concentration on how something looks, we are likely to call for a whole series of relatively minor changes to layouts. Our concern about being seen to be wrong means we are reluctant to issue a draft rather than the final version, so opportunities for incorporating the ideas of others may be lost.

We are also likely to misjudge the level of detail required. We include too much information and have the effect of confusing the recipient. Our reports become lengthy; our sentence patterns also suffer whether we are writing or speaking. We have a tendency (as demonstrated here) to add in extra bits of information in parentheses; not so difficult for the reader (who can always glance at it again) but hard for a listener to follow. We choose our words carefully and may therefore use long, less familiar words or technical terms that others do not understand.

There is a danger that we end up doing everything ourselves because we do not trust others to do it right. We apply our high expectations constantly and fail to recognise when a lower standard would be appropriate and acceptable. This makes us poor delegators and may earn us a reputation for demotivating criticism. On the other hand, when we recognise the errors in our own work we may well feel worthless and not good enough even though others are satisfied with our performance.

The Be Perfect carries the coffees on a tray! The really Be Perfect even has a napkin on the tray to mop up any spills. And they never saw the wood too short; they check the measurements several times with a range of different measuring tapes, find they get different results, and postpone cutting the wood at all while they write to complain to the manufacturers of the measures!

Please People
Please People are the good team members. We enjoy being with other people and show a genuine interest in them. Our aim is to please other people without asking. We work out what they would like and then provide it. This working style means we are nice to have around because we are so understanding and empathic. We use intuition a lot and will notice body language and other signals that others may ignore.

We encourage harmony within the group and work at drawing the team closer together. We are the one most likely to invite the quieter members into the discussion so that their views are shared. This is especially useful when someone is not airing their concerns and might otherwise remain psychologically outside the group. At the same time, we are considerate of others' feelings and will not embarrass or belittle them.

Unfortunately, this style can have serious drawbacks because of our avoidance of the slightest risk of upsetting someone. We may worry so much about earning their approval that we are reluctant to challenge their ideas even when we know they are wrong. We may be so cautious with criticism that our information is ignored. Our own opinions and suggestions are so wrapped around with qualifying words that we seem to lack commitment to them.

We spend a lot of time smiling and nodding at people to indicate our agreement with them. Our own views are presented as questions only, with us ready to back off if they do not like what we are saying. Our facial expression is often questioning, with raised eyebrows and an anxious smile. We may be seen as lacking assertiveness, lacking critical faculties, lacking the courage of our convictions. When criticised by others, we may take it personally and get upset even when the comments are worded constructively.

Because we are reluctant to say no, we let people interrupt us and we are likely to accept work from them instead of concentrating on our own priorities. We hesitate to ask questions because we feel we should somehow know the answer, only to find out later that we've not done it the way they wanted. Our attempts to read people's minds often result only in us feeling misunderstood when they do not like the results.

Please People fetch the coffees frequently. They also open doors for other people who are carrying coffees, even those with only one cup to carry who could open the door themselves. Please People rush to open the door long before you reach it with your coffee - or offer to carry the coffee for you anyway. And they want to know if you approve of the way they are about to saw the wood!

Try Hard

The Try Hard working style is all about the effort put into the task, so we tackle things enthusiastically. Our energy peaks with something new to do. People value our motivation and the way we have of getting things off the ground. We may be popular with colleagues in other sections, and with customers or clients, because of our enthusiastic approach to problem solving. Managers especially appreciate the fact that we often volunteer to take on new tasks.

Because of our interest in anything new and different, we may well be noted for the thorough way in which we follow up on all possibilities. Given a project to undertake, we will identify a whole range of ramifications and implications that should be taken into account. The result is that we pay attention to all aspects of a task, including some that other people may have overlooked. We get a reputation for showing initiative because we go beyond the obvious.

However, we may be more committed to trying than to succeeding. Our initial interest wears off before we finish the task. Managers begin to realise that we are still volunteering for new projects even though we have not completed any of those tasks given to us previously. Our colleagues may come to resent the fact that we do the early, exciting parts of a project but then expect others to finish off the boring, mundane, detailed work.

We may fail to finish also because we spread our interest over too broad a range. Our attention to so many aspects makes the job impossibly large. Even if we complete most of it, we may still think up yet another angle to pursue before we can really agree that the job is done. Thus a small straightforward task may be turned into a major exercise, creating havoc with the time schedule. We miss the deadline or hand in a report full of items that are largely irrelevant. It is as if we are secretly making sure we do not succeed, so that we can just keep on trying.

Our communication with others may be pained and strained, as we frown a lot while we try to follow them. Our own sentences are likely to go off at tangents because we introduce new thoughts just as they come to mind. The listener becomes confused, both around the constantly changing content and about judging whether we have finished speaking. Sometimes we string questions together so the listener has to 'try' and sort out what to respond to. When asked questions, we may well answer a different question – a skill used deliberately by politicians but not so useful when it is outside our awareness.

Try Hards forget they were going to collect coffees because something more interesting occurs on the way. Or they stop to oil the door when they hear it squeaking - so the coffee gets cold. They change their mind about what the wood was for anyway – they may have several half-built items. Or they decide to redesign the saw or build a better workbench. They end up with lots of unused wood with saw marks!

Be Strong

Be Strong people stay calm under pressure. With this working style, we feel energised when we have to cope. Because we are so good at dealing with stressful situations, we are great to have around in a crisis. We are the ones who will keep on thinking logically when others may be panicking. We seem to be able to stay emotionally detached from the situation, enabling us to problem solve around difficult personal issues and to deal efficiently with people who are angry or distressed. We are able to make 'unpleasant' decisions without torturing ourselves with guilt about the effects of those decisions on others.

Because we are so good at staying calm and dealing with all that the job throws at us, we are seen as consistently reliable, steady workers. Our strong sense of duty ensures we will work steadily even at the unpleasant tasks. We get a reputation for being conscientious. As supervisors, we are likely to handle staff firmly and fairly. We will give honest feedback and constructive criticism. We stay even-tempered so that people know what reaction to expect from us.

One problem with this style is that we hate admitting weakness - and we regard any failure to cope as a weakness. So we get overloaded rather than asking others for help. We may disguise our difficulties by "hiding" work away; often our desk looks tidy but correspondence is filed away in a rather large pending tray. We may be highly self-critical about our shortcomings, as well as seeing it as weakness if other people ask for help.

Colleagues may feel uncomfortable about our lack of emotional responses. This may be especially pronounced in those situations where most of us would feel the strain. They may suspect that we are robots rather than human beings. It can be hard to get to know us when we seem to have no feelings. Occasionally, someone with this style will appear to be very jovial and friendly. However, this will be a mask that prevents anyone from getting to know the real person beneath the superficial layer of jokes.

Our communication may reinforce the barriers to getting to know us. We are likely to use passive rather than active voice – "It occurred to me..." rather than "I thought...". We may depersonalise ourselves – "One often does..." rather than "I often do...". Our voice may be monotonous or dispassionate; our face may be expressionless. The observant person will spot that our smile does not extend from our mouth to our eyes. Deep down, we fear that we are unlovable so we avoid asking for anything lest it be refused.

Be Strongs are very matter-of-fact about having coffee. They get coffee when they are thirsty. They carry only one cup because they get it for themselves. This means opening the door is not a problem. Neither is sawing a piece of wood. Be Strongs never have problems - they specialise in coping with anything. If the saw breaks and cuts them, they apply a tourniquet and finish what they were doing before driving themselves to hospital!

WORKING STYLES AND RELATIONSHIPS

Different combinations of working styles will have different effects on relationships. We are likely to have a higher regard for people who share our own approach. We find it easier to understand them, and to empathise with their problems. Even our sentence patterns will match. You can check out your key relationship with your manager using the Manager Working Styles Questionnaire on page 189 and comparing the results to your own. Think about how alike or different your styles are and what that means as you interact.

Mary and Harry were both Hurry Ups who were sub editors in a busy corporate newspaper office. They spoke rapidly to each other, interrupted each other, and made quick decisions together. Each thought the other was quick-witted and decisive; the interrupting did not bother them as they hardly noticed it in their rush to sort out which stories to print.

Ernest and Mike, on the other hand, were Be Perfects. Each of them spoke carefully, with plenty of long words and specialist jargon. They arrived at carefully considered decisions together. Mike was Ernest's boss; as they worked in a pharmacy their careful attention to detail was also seen as reassuring by doctors whose prescriptions they dispensed.

Please People are very polite to each other, keep checking that the other party is comfortable with the discussion, and aim to find compromises. Mervin and Gloria were like this. They were employed as care assistants in a residential home for old people. Their courteous and caring approach was also much appreciated by the residents in the home, who felt they showed good old fashioned values.

Try Hards explore many alternatives, go off at tangents, fail to finish their sentences, and make decisions enthusiastically. Shipra and Catriona worked for an advertising agency, where they sparked each other into increasing levels of innovation. Between them they produced many workable ideas for the rest of the team to implement.

Carol and James were Be Strong professional buyers for a large local authority. They spent their days behaving rather like poker players, giving little away about how they felt. This meant that they got good deals from salespeople, who would increase discounts for fear of losing the business. Carol and James respected each other's skill at making logical, pragmatic buying decisions.

Unfortunately, we do not always attain the benefits of complementary styles. Instead, we are just as likely to have relationship problems when our styles differ. Our incompatibility generates stress; stress sends us more deeply into driver behaviour; the more locked in we get, the more stressed we get. The more stressed we are, the less we are able to tolerate the differences in others. The scene is then set for problems.

Elena was a Hurry Up boss who had a Be Perfect subordinate, Peter. Peter had a report to produce. The deadline had arrived (it was a short deadline anyway because Elena did not think the job should take long!) but Peter had not finished the report. Indeed, he wanted another week to double-check some of the data in the appendices, to amend the layout and run off a reprint, and to have the diagrams produced professionally. Elena was expecting a draft report, which would be combined with the work of others to form a final proposal to a customer. Elena was expecting to take the report to a meeting at which senior managers would determine the content of the final document.

Imagine the conversation which took place. Elena asking impatiently for the report; interrupting when Peter tried to explain the need for more time; complaining that it has taken too long already; and finally demolishing Peter by pointing out that only a rough draft was needed. Peter, meanwhile, concluded that Elena clearly had no interest in quality; was incapable of allocating a realistic time to an important task; was bad-mannered and was refusing to listen to a reasonable request for more time; and, horror of horrors, was proposing to show imperfect work to senior managers who would get a totally wrong picture of Peter's standard of work.

In another case, Michael was a Try Hard design engineer who joined a quality circle led by Dennis, who was a Be Strong. Michael showed typical Try Hard characteristics and enthusiastically raised several ideas in the quality circle meetings. He became increasingly frustrated with Dennis' apparent lack of enthusiasm. Dennis, on the other hand, thought Michael's ideas had not been thought through and were impractical. However, neither knew how to explain their misgivings to the other, with the result that Michael become disenchanted and left the quality circle. Dennis had no one else in the circle who generated ideas and after a time senior management closed it down. Had they been able to work together, Dennis might have added a useful element of practicality to some of Michael's better ideas.

Other instances of the problems that arise when styles do not match include Please People trying desperately to read the mind of a Be Strong so that they can please them; Be Strong observing uncomprehendingly the anxiety of Please People about doing the right thing; Be Perfect's frustration at the tendency of Try Hards to leave jobs unfinished; Try Hard's resentment at Be Perfects who insist they do the boring part of the task. I'm sure you can think of more examples!

A major danger with compatible working styles is omission. We need a variety of styles to compensate for the potential negative elements of each.

A Hurry Up will add necessary urgency for a Be Perfect who is in danger of missing a deadline, and prompt a Be Strong to request help to save time. A Be Perfect will stop the Hurry Up from rushing into an expensive mistake, and encourage the Try Hard to finish what they started. Please People will stop the Hurry Up from pushing others into hasty decisions. Try Hard will provide Be Strong with the animation they fail to show, stimulate the Hurry Up to consider more options, and respond enthusiastically to the tentative ideas of Please People. Be Strong will highlight the need to complete the mundane tasks that the Try Hard tends to overlook, invite the Hurry Up to be less frenetic, and the Please People to be less anxious.

Les, like Elena, was a Hurry Up. When Peter transferred to Les' section, he found that his Be Perfect style was treated quite differently. Les made it clear that he appreciated Peter's attention to detail. He made a point of commenting favourably on Peter's thoroughness, and asked Peter to check reports that Les had drafted. Les did not make all the changes Peter suggested - that would have taken too long - but he did explain how he decided which were important enough to incorporate. He also told Peter clearly how he made his decisions about which corrections to ignore. Once Les was sure that Peter felt valued, he then began to set clear timescales for work. He also gave Peter guidelines about what he wanted included and what he felt could be omitted. In this way, he gradually coached Peter into being able to make his own decisions about the level of detail to include. And Les found that his own manager soon noticed the improvement in Les' reports, which had previously tended to be a bit sparse sometimes!

Fiona was a Be Strong accountant whose relationships with line managers in a manufacturing unit were very rational and rather formal. She handled their budgets and often needed to query payments.

When Steven joined her team, she saw how his Please People style led him to notice when managers were uncomfortable or annoyed that their requests had been rejected. Steven would then check out his impressions and encourage the managers to clarify their concerns. Even when he was still unable to help them obtain financing, they understood why and there were fewer complaints made about 'inflexible accountants'.

WORKING STYLES AND TIME MANAGEMENT

The five working styles give us invaluable insights into what happens to our management of time. We can then identify specific actions to redress the balance. It may be that we need to select from more than one style to create our own time management plan.

If we are **Hurry Up**: to avoid mistakes, we need to plan sufficient time for tasks, especially the preparation that we are so inclined to skimp. To avoid appearing impatient, we should consciously slow down so that other people have time to absorb the information. We must stop interrupting them and concentrate on listening. It can be very helpful to remember to ask about their needs instead of making assumptions, and to paraphrase back to check our understanding. If we feel we lack real contact with others, we could plan our arrival or departure times to allow us to join in the socialising that goes on before and after meetings.

If we are **Be Perfect**: we need to relax more and accept that human beings, including ourselves, are not capable of total perfection. Making mistakes is an important source of learning. Prioritising is required so that we can decide which jobs really warrant such high levels of accuracy. We must also understand that deadlines are important to others and that we should keep sight of the objective. We need to plan to finish on time instead of using too much of the time to plan. Check how much detail is enough; then give the key information and stop before we bury people in facts and figures.

If we are **Please People**: to avoid being dumped with unrealistic requests and unimportant tasks, we need to learn to say no skilfully. It is important that we set our own limits and our own priorities if we are to be respected by others. How much credibility will our "yes" have if they never hear us say "no"? Basic assertiveness techniques will help us to handle customers and colleagues - a firm refusal, said politely, is often all that is needed to maintain reasonable boundaries.

If we are **Try Hard**: we need to control our tendency towards boredom with the later stages of projects. We, even more than the other styles, can benefit from positive programming into our diary of all aspects of the task. Once we finish a project, we can usefully spend time enjoying the feeling of success so that we will want to repeat it. Sometimes we can find creative ways of making mundane tasks more exciting. Sometimes we simply need to get on with them in spite of our boredom.

If we are **Be Strong**: we may have the hardest working style to identify in ourselves. Our potential weaknesses may be well hidden. Before we take on new tasks, we should review the potential requirements and check we have access to the appropriate resources. We also need to recognise that there is nothing wrong with asking for help sometimes. Others may well have relevant skills, knowledge, time or enthusiasm for the tasks we are doing, and will welcome the opportunity to contribute.

Using a Time Management System

Our working styles have a direct bearing on the way we use a time management system.

Hurry Up people are usually too impatient to get the full benefit from such a system. They start using the system before taking time to work out the most appropriate way of setting it up to match their work. Without clear sections, they record items hastily and then cannot find them again. Hurry Ups are also the ones most likely to keep lots of scraps of paper with notes on that they have been too rushed to transcribe into the system.

Hurry Ups are probably better off with a very simple system that allows them a quick sort into a few categories, with no need to transcribe. If you have this style, carry a pad of stick-it sheets for making notes - then you can attach them simply to the correct page. Avoid computerised systems unless they are very quick; otherwise you'll find even logging in takes too long for comfort.

Be Perfect people have 'perfect' time management systems. They keep them so accurately and neatly that it uses up a lot of time just making the entries. One problem is designing the 'ultimate' category system. A Be Perfect will be reluctant to use the system at all until they are certain they have made it foolproof. They may spend an inordinate amount of time on this. If they subsequently realise that their arrangement is not quite perfect, they may feel compelled to start all over again and spend hours transferring their data across.

Be Perfects need to review the available systems before choosing one that fits their needs best. You could also look for a system that allows customising. You will probably enjoy a computerised system that automatically amends and updates every time an entry is made. If you operate a manual system, use a pencil so you can erase when things change instead of having to write out pages again.

Please People worry about whether they are using their time management system in the way they are supposed to. They look at other peoples' systems to check if their own is all right. They have real problems using pre-set pages or templates for anything other than the original intention, so they are limited in how far they can personalise a system.

Please People need to stop worrying about what other people think is right. Choose a system only because you like it yourself; don't adopt one just because everyone else has. Once you have a system, feel free to do just as you like with it. If you choose a manual system, use coloured pages or stick cartoon characters on it to help reinforce your right to be individualistic.

Try Hard people are likely to go from one time management system to another. Each system lasts only until they lose interest. They may be very enthusiastic at first, demonstrating their great new system to everyone else. However, they somehow keep not quite getting around to the mundane aspects of deciding how to operate the system in detail. So then they discover another, better system and start again, and again...

Try Hard people need variety in their time management system. A system which allows you to add new features from time to time will maintain your interest. You also need a system with the minimum of detailed recording. You will probably benefit from computerised project management systems that prompt you to cover all significant aspects of the task.

Be Strong people are likely to wonder why anyone needs a time management system in the first place. They may secretly believe that a good memory should be enough. If their work is very involved, then a straightforward system will be seen as appropriate. Having got a system, then entries must be made regularly and conscientiously, regardless of the circumstances; they may delay an urgent task while they update what has already been done.

Be Strong people should select a system that is very practical. If manual, you will prefer something in a plain yet serviceable cover. If computerised, you will not want too many enhancements to the basic system. Any instructions for the system must be clear and logical, so you do not have to ask for any assistance in setting up.

GETTING THE BENEFITS OF WORKING STYLES

You may well have recognised bits of yourself in each of the styles. Look more closely, though, at the one or two styles that have most impact for you. Consider what matters most to you: to be quick, to be perfect, to get on with people, to tackle new tasks, or to be calm. How have you approached the task of reading this chapter about working styles: have you skimmed through in a hurry; considered each slowly and carefully; been most interested in ways to improve your relationships; been keen to see if there are new ideas in it; or wondered what all the fuss is about?

What can you do with your increased awareness? The next step is to set out to obtain the advantages of your preferred working style(s) without the potential problems. What is needed is a conscious choice of options, followed by a period of practice as you become competent with additional techniques.

If you are Hurry Up:
- *plan your work in stages, setting interim target dates*
- *concentrate on listening carefully to others until they finish speaking*
- *learn relaxation techniques and then use them regularly*

If you are Be Perfect:
- *set realistic standards of performance and accuracy*

- practice asking yourself what the consequences really are - do this whenever you find a mistake
- make a point of telling others that their mistakes are not serious

If you are Please People:
- start asking people questions to check what they want instead of guessing
- please yourself more often, and ask other people for what you want
- practice telling other people firmly when they are wrong

If you are Try Hard:
- stop volunteering
- make a plan that includes finishing a task - and then stick to that plan through to a conclusion
- check out the parameters of a task so that you do only what is expected

If you are Be Strong:
- keep a task and time log so that you can monitor your workload
- ask other people to help you
- take up a spare time activity that you can really enjoy

A word of warning, however. When we want to make changes to the way we behave, we need to remember that our boss, colleagues and customers may like us just the way we are. And we get lots of recognition for being like that. When we change we can help ourselves by being aware that we may miss some of the recognition we are used to. Others may resist our changes so we need to plan to deal with these barriers. We need to make sure that we get our new behaviours reinforced by ourselves and other people. Here are a few ideas:

Hurry Ups get praised for being quick; so set out to get recognition for accuracy as well.

Be Perfects get praised for accuracy; look for recognition for meeting deadlines and appropriate levels of detail.

Everybody thinks Please People are nice; aim for recognition for being assertive.

Try Hard people score points for enthusiasm; get recognition for finishing tasks - successfully.

Be Strong people often get low key recognition for not needing help; watch how relationships improve when you let people help you.

Remember also that it may be useful to acquire some of the other working styles if you recognise you are heavily into one or two only.

CHAPTER 7:   BUILDING RELATIONSHIPS

Working in an organisation means working with other people. The quality of our relationships will therefore have considerable impact on how well we are seen to do our work. However technically competent we are, we are of little use to an organisation unless we can communicate effectively with others; communicating on any long term basis depends on us having acceptable relationships. Much of the time, our relationships also have to exist within groups and teams – we need a range of interlocking alliances so that getting along well with one person is not done at the expense of our relationship with another.

We also have basic human needs to be in contact with people. This is why solitary confinement is such a severe punishment. It is also why babies left without attention and stimulation, as they were years ago in Romania, fail to develop normally. Although as individuals we vary in the amount of recognition we need, we must all get at least some attention from others if we are to function as healthy human beings.

STROKES

Any form of interaction with others is an exchange of recognition. A term often used for this is stroking – a *stroke* is a 'unit of recognition'.

To stroke someone, we may touch them, speak to them, or simply catch their eye and look away. Even the glance has shown we know of their existence and is therefore a stroke, though it is one that has very low recognition power. People who lack sufficient contact with others will respond disproportionately to a minor stroke, such as when we nod politely to a stranger in a lift and then find ourselves listening to their life story.

At the top end of the scale is touching, which research has shown to have major impact even when we are not aware consciously that we have been touched. One candid camera type study found that, if you touched their arm gently, people were far more likely to admit to finding and pocketing your money when it had been left (deliberately) in a telephone box they had used. Those not touched in this way were prone to claim that the money must have gone before they came along.

As babies, physical strokes are also necessary because we cannot yet understand what people tell us. Once we grow older and acquire speech, we learn to accept our strokes in non-physical ways as well. As adults any form of recognition serves as a stroke: being smiled at or frowned at; having a conversation; having an argument or a cuddle. We recognise that our society places restrictions on how we touch each other so the majority of strokes at work are conveyed through sight and hearing. We see a smile or a frown; we hear the comments made and questions asked of us. In the UK our strokes via touch tend to be restricted to shaking hands, although in other countries it may be customary to have much more physical contact with colleagues.

Handshakes also demonstrate how we appear to treat strokes as if they were money. Watch what happens when a group of senior managers and their subordinates are gathering for a meeting. Quite often, a pecking order of handshakes appears! The senior people shake hands with other senior people. The junior people are expected to shake hands with other junior people. It's as if we are signalling that our handshakes have a certain value and can only be given to people who will return a stroke of the same value. We know we've arrived when the top managers are prepared to shake hands with us.

Incidentally, this was one of the ways in which sexual discrimination commonly showed (and does so less now). Male managers would often fail to shake hands with female managers on the same level. This was because they were making assumptions – female equals lower grade, lower grade does not get one of my high value, high status handshakes. Women sometimes compounded the problem inadvertently by not expecting to shake hands, and therefore neglecting to initiate such contact themselves.

If you doubt the truth of this, think about how you feel when someone neglects to shake hands with you. Our response to this is usually quite dramatic – we may feel snubbed, put-down, angry, bitter or despairing. We will generally not want to interact with that person in the future. This is because the touch element is so significant to us. Indeed, this same significance of touch is what leads to some complaints of sexual harassment; we are willing to receive such powerful strokes only from people with whom we have an appropriately close relationship.

Positive or Negative

As well as varying in their level of intensity and mode of communication, strokes may be *positive or negative*. Positive strokes invite us to feel OK about ourselves and others IOK–YOK window. Negative strokes invite us to feel not OK about ourselves, about others, or both – the SHNOK window.

Complimentary remarks about our work, our appearance, our family, our hobbies, will all be positive strokes. Questions are also strokes; paying attention to someone by asking for their opinions, their concerns, their ideas, or their latest news, is a powerful way of recognising their existence as a human being.

Positive strokes are not always 'nice' comments; a positive stroke may also consist of constructive criticism even though we may not feel it is positive at the moment we receive it. When phrased in a way that tells us how to improve, such criticism carries with it the implication that we are OK – and can therefore do still better than we have – and will only be offered by someone with our best interests in mind and who is therefore also okay.

Negative strokes, too, are more complex than simply saying something unpleasant. In addition to interactions aimed at inviting us to feel bad in some way, there are also negative strokes involved when we are encouraged to feel that we are one-up. Being invited to look through the I'm not OK, You're OK or the I'm OK, You're not OK window is not a psychologically healthy way to maintain our sense of self-worth. We may also experience strokes that leave us feeling that no-one is OK. These are the cynical comments along the lines of "Whatever makes you think the idiots will listen to you of all people!", so that we shift to the hopeless I'm not OK, You're not OK life position.

Our classification of positive and negative strokes is sometimes confused by the use of sarcasm. Although it would seem that sarcasm is negative, this form of interaction is used commonly between young men. When they talk in this way to people they like, they are generally exchanging disguised positive strokes. A 'macho' culture inhibits us, especially if we are male, from being too open with our feelings of friendship and caring. We learn to hide behind jokes and comments such as "Oh no, not you again!" when really we are pleased to see someone.

A difficulty with sarcasm of this type is that we use a similar technique when we wish to disguise a negative stroke. Perhaps we are angry with someone but feel that it is too risky to tell them so – maybe they are senior to us, or noted for their bad temper. So we make a joke of what we want to say to them. Then, if they react too strongly, we can deny any negative intent and accuse them of lacking a sense of humour. True experts in this manoeuvre can say this in such a hurt tone that the victim finishes up apologising!

As recipient, it is easy to get confused about the true message when sarcasm is employed. We get a mild case of paranoia – did they really mean that as a joke; was there evil intent under the surface? Our communication will be much clearer and our relationships will improve if we take the risk and say in a straightforward way what we really think. If we phrase our comments as positive strokes even our criticisms will be constructive.

Conditional or Unconditional

Another way of classifying strokes is by whether they are *conditional* or *unconditional*: given for doing or given for being. The traditional view of organisations implies a conditional form of stroking – recognition is something that results from performance of the task. Conditional strokes cover the range of things that we can control: how we do our work, how we dress, how we exercise our skills. They may be positive or negative: "that was a good report"; "this needs changing"; "your shoes are the wrong colour"; "what a stupid idea". If we are fortunate, we receive a regular diet of positive conditional strokes in a mix which both reinforces our strengths and gives us feedback for our development.

Unconditional strokes add an important dimension; such strokes do not have to be 'earned' through work achievement or appearance. Asking someone about their family or their spare time activities is a powerful form of stroking that involves relating to aspects of them which may otherwise be neglected during worktime. Being told that someone enjoys our company is a potent stimulus to most of us to become energised and enthusiastic. The increasing attention being paid in organisations to the 'whole person' is a reflection of this need for unconditional strokes. We spend too many hours at work to limit ourselves to conditional strokes only.

There is no clear dividing line between conditional and unconditional strokes. It is more like a sliding scale. At one extreme is the totally unconditional stroke, positive or negative, such as "I love you" or "I hate you." At the other, the very specific conditional such as "You've chosen the best/worst colour to wear today." In between come a range of options, including strokes that are partly both. The examples above of asking about families and hobbies may fit here. Enquiring after the health of someone's parent will seem more unconditional; showing an interest in their children may be picked up as conditional – especially if your comment refers to how their children behave and is therefore seen as related to the way they brought them up. Hobbies are similar: we may be paying attention to their excitement and enthusiasm for the activity or we may be stroking their prowess and performance of a skill.

It is useful to keep this idea of a scale of conditionality in mind. If you make the effort to notice how people respond to the strokes you offer, you will be able to identify where on the scale they prefer to be. Too conditional a stroke and they react as if you are being impersonal, or a workaholic. Too unconditional and they may respond as if you are invading their personal life. Just as with a musical scale, if they don't appear to like the sounds you are making you can move up or down the keys until you get the effect you are seeking.

STROKING PATTERNS

Our personal *stroking pattern* consists of the strokes that we give and receive. We develop patterns of interactions between us and the people we are in contact with so that we receive a supply of strokes to match our needs. It is not random. We will unwittingly establish relationships with people who are likely to provide the levels and types of strokes that we became used to during our childhood. These have become integral to our way of being in the world; if our customary balance is upset we feel uncomfortable and seek to re-establish it. Unfortunately, this applies even if we have become used to a preponderance of negative strokes.

We will of course vary in our sources of strokes. Being part of a team means that strokes are available to us from many directions. Working mostly alone yields fewer strokes. Depending on our own preferences, we will therefore opt as far as possible for the situation that is most likely to produce the pattern we want. Hence some of us thrive in open plan offices while others like to shut ourselves away. We may be uncomfortable if our working situation doesn't match these preferences.

We will also differ in the groups of people with whom we choose to exchange strokes; it may be our work group, our family, our friends, the people at night school, the local amateur dramatic society, and so on. And we will operate different intervals between strokes; some of us want frequent strokes while others can go for long periods provided we can 'stock up' occasionally.

The intensity of a stroke can be measured by the effort the giver puts into it. However, the impact on us will be influenced by the value we place on it. This will depend on the nature of the interaction, our feelings about the stroke giver, and our personal preferences for which aspects of our personality or behaviour get stroked. Some of us like our recognition to be about work performance and achievement: others are more comfortable with strokes about families and personal relationships; yet others get more of a kick when people show a keen interest in our exciting spare time activities.

The structure of an organisation can have a significant impact on our options for obtaining strokes. For instance, working closely with customers may lead us to rely on the customer instead of our colleagues for our recognition, so that our loyalty to our own organisation is weakened. Site engineers working on large projects, for instance, often find that they develop closer relationships with the customer's staff than they can with their own head office, who may be little more than voices on the phone. Problems then arise if there is a conflict of interests; an engineers' loyalty will tend to go where the best strokes are.

Morarji and Angus were site engineers working on the installation and commissioning of automated product lines. They had support teams back in Headquarters but spent at least four days a week on the premises of their major customers. They rarely saw their colleagues, had little contact with their managers, and met each other only occasionally at the quarterly departmental meetings. Both therefore got their work-based strokes from the employees who worked for the customers.

In Morarji's case, this was not a problem. Morarji was a fairly quiet person, who actually preferred to work alone. He played badminton weekly with some friends who lived near him, attended an evening class to learn Spanish, and otherwise was content to watch television or read. His personal stroking pattern was relatively low key so he didn't mind the lack of contact with colleagues.

Angus was very different. He had moved away from his friends and family to take the job as site engineer, and very much missed the strokes he'd been used to. Because he had so little contact with his colleagues, he looked to the people on the customer site for his recognition. He was most comfortable with strokes for work performance so he put his effort into producing the sort of results the customer wanted. This might of course have been highly appropriate but unfortunately the customer staff wanted more than was included in the contract. Angus cost his own company quite a lot of money by providing extra services without charge.

Stroke swaps

Many of us develop a tendency to operate a kind of *stroke exchange*, 'swapping' or returning a positive or negative to match whatever we receive. I've already mentioned how this may happen with handshakes; it occurs in many other ways too. Someone compliments us on our appearance, so we tell them that they look good too. Or they admire some aspect of our performance, only to have us respond with an instant but somewhat artificial remark about the equivalent for them. Done without thinking, this is inauthentic. When it happens, the initiator of the interaction is left feeling that their stroke has somehow been cancelled by a less than satisfactory return stroke.

There is another way in which we appear to swap strokes. In this case, though, we are seeking to maintain our stroke balance by matching the quantity of stroking rather than the subject matter. Let's take a typical example – our interactions with a fellow employee who we meet regularly on the way in to work. We know they work in the same organisation because we habitually walk into the building together each morning.

Every day without fail, for weeks and months, we say "Good morning." to each other. Nothing more; this may not be someone we wish to become closer to. One morning they are not there. We do not see them for two weeks. Then they reappear, just as before. Only the social incompetent would say "Good morning." again as if nothing had happened.

Instead, we remark on their absence and return. "You're back. Good to see you. Have you been away?" And they tell us about their holiday or their spell in hospital, while we make suitably envious or sympathetic comments. The next morning, we probably pass a few more remarks, such as asking how it was at work on the previous day. So they talk to us briefly about that. On the third day, we are ready to revert to our usual "Good morning." format and so are they. And so it continues until the next time one of us misses a few days.

What has been happening is that we were maintaining our stroking exchange over time. Every day, each of us expects to give and receive one stroke as a contribution to our balance. But if one of us is absent, we miss out. Somewhere mysterious inside us is a special calculator that clicks up the deficit. 2 weeks without seeing them, 5 days per week, so we have missed 10 strokes. On day 1 of their return we manage to exchange about 7 strokes by chatting to each other. Our calculator registers that we are now 3 down from last week, plus we have to catch up with the 2 days of the current week. So on day 2 of their return, we need 3 plus 2 equals 5. Provided we make these up on day 2, we can go back to the one-a-day ration from day 3.

This type of exchange runs through many of our relationships, with different quantities involved. Perhaps we have a former colleague who has become a good friend. We now meet up with them once a month and have a great time comparing notes on our respective careers or gossiping about mutual acquaintances. In this way, we each contribute a number of strokes to each other's pattern. Miss meeting one month and we have a lot of catching up to do (and that is often the phrase that we use.). We make up the deficit by spending longer with them next time, by telephoning between times, by being a lot more animated when we do meet, or by a mix of all three.

Contrast this with what happens if we bump into them before the month is up. We will spend about the right energy to reflect how long since we last met, and will 'deduct' this at our regular date. If we continue to see each other more frequently, the pattern will gradually adjust and they will take their place as a more significant contributor/recipient within our stroking structure. If we continue to miss seeing them, we will probably relegate them to that part of our stroking pattern that handles intermittent contacts. If that happens, we will probably also replace them partially by having increased contact with another friend who is more often available.

Stroke pattern analysis
You might like at this point to take time out to consider your own stroking patterns. If so, take a sheet of paper and divide it into 5 or 6 columns. At the top of each column put the name of someone you have regular contact with – perhaps the members of your work group or some regular customers. Think about the kinds of strokes you give and receive when you are with them. Use the columns to make notes so you can compare your responses for each person.

- *How intense are the strokes you exchange with them? (just greetings, talking shop, significant praise or criticism?)*
- *Do they give you positive or negative strokes?*
- *What strokes do you give them?*
- *How often do you give each other strokes?*
- *Are you operating your stroking on an exchange basis?*
- *What are the strokes about?*
- *Are they conditional or unconditional?*

When you have a set of responses, look for patterns:

- *Are you offering everyone the sort of strokes you prefer, regardless of their preferences?*
- *Are you only giving positive strokes to a few special people?*
- *Does a lack of stroking coincide with those relationships that are not as good as they might be?*
- *Is the person really difficult to get on with or is it because you keep giving them the wrong sort of strokes? (or because they are doing that to you?)*
- *Are you behaving differently towards some people so that you seem to have favourites?*
- *What could you change in order to have better relationships more of the time with more of the people?*

Finally, consider the total picture:

- *Do you have an overall pattern in life or are there distinct trends for work, social, family?*
- *Do you rely on a few people for high intensity strokes or a large number of people for low level stroking?*
- *Do the same problem areas occur in several places?*
- *What stroking pattern exists between you and your boss? (are you falling into the trap of only giving the boss negative strokes of complaint – or none at all because bosses "don't expect it"?)*

Stroking Problems

Because our stroking patterns and preferences are determined largely when we are small, we fall into some common traps. We then grow up with a range of unhelpful beliefs about how stroking should be conducted, and some programmed responses that lead us to react illogically to strokes. We can identify some myths, or arbitrary 'rules' about strokes that we are likely to believe to some extent. These are like parent messages inside our heads. Although we may not be consciously aware of them, they reflect the views that our parents had about the correct ways to behave. Just as each family is different, so too do individuals vary in the degree to which they operate under each rule. You can check yours out with the Stroke Myths Questionnaire at page 191 - as usual, I suggest you do this before you read on.

Don't Give: we may hold back specific comments or strokes in general. Perhaps we worry that the person will become complacent if we praise them, or upset if we criticise. So we see someone achieve a difficult task but act as if nothing unusual has happened, or we claim that there is no need to make a fuss when someone is "just doing the job they get paid for".

Don't Accept: sometimes you can actually see the movement as a person shrugs off a stroke. At other times the rejection may be verbal, when we make comments about the credit (or blame) belonging elsewhere. Our manager compliments us on an excellent report – and we say that our colleague should really get the praise as they did most of the work (when they didn't).

Don't Reject: we feel obliged to accept whatever is offered, even though it is not what we wanted. We may even come to resent the strokes yet give no clue of this to the giver. Women may smile politely as they accept strokes about their appearance instead of their competence; men may settle for comments about their decisiveness instead of their sensitivity.

Don't Ask: this is a common difficulty in organisations, where we feel embarrassed to ask for feedback. In personal relationships, we may give this an added twist by declaring that strokes "don't count if I have to ask for it." We feel disappointed and demotivated when our special efforts and skills go unnoticed but we don't know how to draw attention to ourselves without showing vulnerability.

Don't Stroke Yourself: this is even more of a problem in organisations. Our fear of being thought boastful prevents us alerting people to our strengths and achievements. This false modesty may lead to us being overlooked for tasks to which we are suited. So we go for a job interview and fail to sell ourselves properly. Or we sit through a poorly structured meeting instead of offering to use our skills to chair it effectively.

Another way in which we build in problems to our stroking patterns is through a tendency to settle for negative strokes when we think there are no positive strokes available. Any stroke, even a negative one, is better than being ignored. Imagine a young child, playing on the floor. Few parents would go up to them, interrupt the play, and provide positive strokes for being so good. Instead, most of us would think this was a good opportunity to put the kettle on and have a few moments break from childminding. The small child, therefore, may well come to associate amusing themselves with the momentary absence of the parent. Even when they behave as parents want them to, they still cannot be sure that positive strokes will follow.

Contrast this with a scene when mother is talking to a neighbour. Small child tries to get her attention, only to be told to go away and play. After a couple more unsuccessful attempts to get positive strokes from mother, the child does indeed go away to play. The plaything selected is something breakable, mother hears the crash, and guess what she does! She promptly leaves the neighbour and rushes in to give the child some negative strokes about breaking things. The child notes that strokes were forthcoming, albeit not nice positive ones.

We all experience these typical scenes when we are small. Many of us come to the 'logical' conclusion: we know how to stimulate negative strokes without fail but there seems little connection between our behaviour and the receipt of positive strokes. Schools obligingly continue the pattern; teachers generally pay far more attention to pupils who misbehave than to the average performer. Behave badly enough and you even get to talk directly to the headteacher, a privilege denied to most of your classmates.

Now, as grown-ups, we can replay the unhelpful sequences when our stroke balance is running low. Organisations know the routine too – managers call in for interview those who perform poorly or have high absence levels. Good performance and consistent attendance, on the other hand, is so often simply taken for granted.

ORGANISATIONAL STROKING PATTERNS

It can be enlightening to do a quick analysis of the stroking patterns in your organisation. The following questions will give you some ideas of what happens.

What characteristics earn recognition? (remember that both positive and negative strokes will reinforce the behaviour that is stroked)

long service	*creativity*	*being caring*
absenteeism	*accuracy*	*customer care*
risk taking	*calmness*	*quality*
making mistakes	*working hard*	*speed*
politeness	*being friendly*	*enthusiasm*
appearance	*being firm*	*teamwork*

What recognition processes operate within the organisation?

suggestion scheme	*employee awards*
customer letters put on notice boards	*celebrations*
payment for results	*quality circles*
publication of results against targets	

Think about the impact of these processes. How do they link with your own stroking patterns? Does the organisation reinforce your behaviour and attitudes in a healthy way? Do you need to make any changes – either within the organisation if you are in a position to do so – or to your own stroking patterns if you need to make adjustments in some other way?

Check your own stroking balance. If you feel that there are more negatives than positives, consider what you can do to change the pattern. The questions I listed earlier will give you some ideas. You may also need to change some of your activities, or some of your friends, in order to create more opportunities for positive stroking. Set out to meet new people who will recognise your good points, take up an interest in which you can demonstrate your competence, plan activities where you can enjoy yourself with other people so that there will be plenty of positive strokes around.

Joining a new team

Joining a new team requires a major change to our stroking patterns. This is why it can be so stressful, even when we have initiated the change ourselves. It takes some time to recreate the whole range of patterns across areas such as new boss, new colleagues, new procedures, new customers, new tasks, new products. First, the boss may not know you well and will therefore find it harder to provide the sort of strokes that match your preferences. If you place high value on personal contact, there will be a delay while your new manager and colleagues get to know you; if your usual strokes are for competence and success, there will be a delay until you demonstrate these qualities.

The new team may already have stroking patterns established between themselves. In that case they will need time to incorporate you, and to do that effectively they have to get to know you. In the meantime, strokes from your former team may have abruptly ceased, especially if you have changed organisation or location as well. Sometimes we take care of the stress around a job change by 'visiting with' our old group for a time. We go back to see them; they stop whatever they are doing and ask us about our new job; in this way they provide us with a quick top-up of strokes to keep us ticking over. As we gradually get absorbed into the stroking patterns of the new team, we find less and less reason to keep going back – and eventually we can't remember why it seemed so important to us to stay in touch!

GROUP IMAGOES

The ways in which we join and co-operate in teams, and therefore establish new stroking patterns, are influenced by our mental images, or imagoes. An *imago* is a picture we create in our heads of a group of people. We are not usually consciously aware of the imago but it influences our actions. Thus, before we enter a room to join a group, we already have in our minds an imago of them and us. This is likely to be based on a mixture of past events, preconceptions, rumour and fantasy. The imago will be personal to each of us, so that we enter a group with different expectations, leading in turn to different perceptions.

Simply knowing that we start our involvement in a team with a pre-existing imago can be useful. Recognising this phenomenon means we can unpack our mental baggage and decide how much of it is relevant, how much is assumption, how much we should discard if we are to meet people with an open mind. However, the concept has additional advantages when we realise that our imago stays with us and is updated as we spend time in the group. Constant monitoring of its content will enable us to relate more effectively to others in the team.

As we become involved in a group, we collect more information about our fellow group members. We are able to develop our imago, with separate slots appearing for individuals as we get to know them and to differentiate between them. We build up increasing amounts of detail in the slots we have for each person. We can identify four stages in this development of our imago, from the time we first enter the group until the point at which we are as integrated into – or are as alienated from – the group as we will become. These phases are not separated by clear boundaries; we gradually move through them. However, the characteristics of each are recognisable and knowledge of them can help us with our teambuilding process.

Anticipatory Group Imago

We begin with a *group imago* or mental picture like that shown in Figure 7.1. Typically, this will contain little more than a slot for ourself, a slot on a higher level for the leader, and an undifferentiated slot for everyone else. If we already know some of the group members, these people are likely to have a slot of their own within our mental picture.

The detail contained within the imago cannot be shown in a diagram on paper. In our head there will be a rich pattern of our ideas, opinions and expectations that make up each slot. Into the slot for ourself we will have incorporated aspects such as our recollections of previous group experiences, our views of the task, our personal objectives and hidden agendas, and our opinions of our own competence and confidence in such situations. These may or may not be relevant to the situation we are now in!

Figure 7.1: Anticipatory Group Imago

For the leader slot, there will be an amalgam of previous leaders we have known, selections from the comments made and rumours put about by others, all merged with any experience we have acquired personally of this current leader. If no formal leader of the group has been announced, we will still have a slot into which we put our attitudes and memories of previous leaders. We will then be waiting for a body to insert into the slot, and will unconsciously study the group members for likely candidates – or perhaps we will decide that the leader slot should belong to us.

Slots for other group members will vary depending on what we already know about them. Existing colleagues will be well differentiated, with detail on how we expect them to react based on our observations in the past. Similar to our aim in the board game of Scruples, we will be able to predict their likely responses to a range of events – something we cannot do with new acquaintances. We may be less accurate in our slot content for those we worked with in the past; although we believe we know them, we may have missed out on important changes they have undergone since we last had contact. This is why we sometimes find to our surprise that we now get on well with someone we disliked intensely in the past.

Group members we do not know will be compounded together into one conglomerate slot, perhaps labelled in our minds as 'the others'. Or we may have separate, but still relatively undetailed slots, for males versus females, or managers versus staff. Another common division is into departments, as if we believe that anyone from sales will be one sort of person, and different from people who work in accounts, who are not like those in production, and so on.

Our behaviour and attitudes as we join the group will be structured by our anticipatory imago. We will gain a certain level of satisfaction if we can confirm our anticipations. At least the world is how we expect it to be. However, if our original imago is depressing, we will be hoping to be proved wrong. Unfortunately, we may well invest our pattern with so much power that we create a self-fulfilling prophecy. It is worth taking the time to sketch out our anticipatory imago before we go into a group. We can then be on the alert for potential problems caused by our own preconceived ideas.

Adjusted Group Imago

After we have been in a group for a while, we update and augment our picture into an *adjusted group imago*. We can begin to differentiate between individuals who were formerly grouped into one slot, so that our imago comes to resemble that in Figure 7.2. A major contributor to this process is the pastiming and superficial working together that we do. As we converse, we are collecting data about each other and about how we will fit in.

Our personal approach to rituals, pastiming, playing and working will be important here, as this will be the basis on which others are judging us. If we fail to demonstrate

Figure 7.2: Adjusted Group Imago

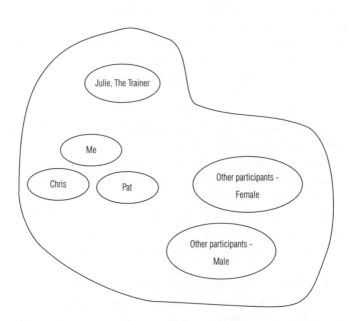

acceptable rituals such as greetings, their imagoes may finish up with a slot for us that includes detail about our lack of social graces. If we have no small talk to offer, the other group members will become uncomfortable around us. Without realising why, they will react negatively because they cannot acquire the data they need to flesh out a proper slot for us in their imago. After initial attempts to engage us in suitable conversation, they may well retreat and ignore us. If we fail generally to respond, it will seem as if we do not belong in the group.

This stage in the life of a group is a time of testing, to see what the others are like, and to think about whether and how we might fit in. Our behaviour will provide the others in the team with the evidence about us that they are needing. They may also have expectations about us in their own anticipatory imagoes and it will be important that they confirm or change these appropriately and accurately.

Adapted Group Imago

In the third stage we develop our *adapted group imago*, which concerns our relationship with the leader. We need to sort this out before we can decide how to behave towards other members of the group. This is similar to being a child in a family; we needed to know where we stood with our parent(s) in order to deal appropriately with our siblings. Now we interpret the behaviour of our manager as a guide to how we should deal with our colleagues. The positions of the slots in our imago, vis a vis the leader's slot, take on more significance, as in Figure 7.3.

A clear organisational structure will help here, as will consistent indicators from the leader. Power plays are likely to occur at this stage, as we seek to establish the level of control that will apply. In addition to bids for the leadership, we may also be jostling with colleagues to see where we fit in the pecking order.

Whoever is leader will still have a leader slot in their imago. This may be filled with detail about themselves. However, it may instead contain information about other leaders they have known. This will mean that they model their own behaviour to suit a fantasised leader. In effect, they will be transacting with a phantom, with the obvious difficulties that may lead to. They may respond to an internal dialogue with some previous manager or parent figure who must be satisfied, or insists on compliance with outdated requirements. Organisations in which each manager seems like a clone of the managing director are operating on this basis.

Within this adapted imago stage, we will be working at the tasks of the group. We are also likely to engage in some repetitive and unhelpful interactions as we move into our habitual patterns for transacting with other people. I will say more about dealing with these problems in the next chapter – basically we are in danger of seeking to confirm our unhelpful life positions; of getting and giving negative strokes to fit our patterns; and maybe even collecting stamps to cash in for prizes.

Figure 7.3: Adapted Group Imago

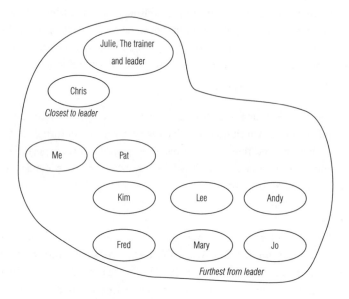

Attached Group Imago

Finally we will develop our *attached group imago*. We will enter this stage with a clearer view of individual members of the group. There will be enough detail for us to have decided which people we want to work closely with, who we would prefer to lose from the team, and who we will tolerate provided we do not have to spend much time with them. They will of course have made the same decisions about us. We have also decided the leadership issues, or have determined to continue our struggle for control. Our imago may well look like that in Figure 7.4.

Each of us may have come to different conclusions but now we have some shared expectations about how the group will function. The worst case result will be a group that is sabotaged by gamey behaviour, with conflict and power struggles – in which case maybe we have an *alienated* rather than an attached imago. The best case will be a group in which we are close, open and trusting and work together to achieve our shared objectives. Either way, our imago now contains sufficient data to guide our interactions with each other.

Recognising Your Imagoes

You might like at this point to experiment with your own imagoes. It can be very useful to sketch out all four stages as you become part of a new team. However, you may not be about to join such a group. You can still use the framework to increase your understanding of your relationships with others. Imagoes will apply to any groups, so you may think about teams at work, groups of friends, groups you share hobbies with, etc.

Figure 7.4: Attached Group Imago

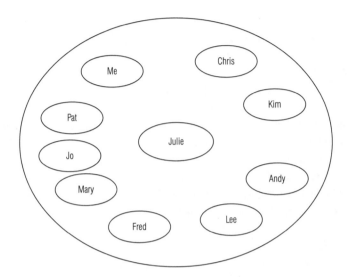

Think back to a time when you joined a new group or team. Start at the beginning or at the end – i.e. start with your anticipatory imago and work forwards or start with your attached imago and work backwards. Your aim is to track the various developments as well as you can recall them:

Anticipatory
- What preconceived ideas did you have?
- What did you already know about people?
- What assumptions did you make?

Adjusted
- What did you conclude about people?
- How did your views about the others change?
- What evidence did you rely on?

Adapted
- Who did you decide was the leader?
- How did you relate to the leader?
- Where did you fit in the pecking order?

Attached(or alienated)
- How close did the group members become?

- *Did you have any particular allies or enemies?*
- *How did the group objectives get met?*

You can change these questions to the present tense if you are using this framework to consider your imagoes in a group now forming.

IMAGOES AND STROKES

Whenever we need to build new relationships, whether one-to-one or in a team, awareness of our stroking patterns and our imagoes will be helpful. Knowing our previous stroke patterns gives us a target to aim at. We can also consider alternative stroke sources while we establish new relationships. Family, friends and previous colleagues will usually be happy to give us extra strokes during that time if we let them know what we need. This will minimise the potential stress associated with the change and give us an easier transition. Understanding the effect of our imagoes can add to this by enabling us to avoid some of the pitfalls of preconceived ideas about others in the team.

We can also link the two:

1. *sketch your current imago for a particular group you are in*
2. *draw up your stroking pattern for the people in the imago*
3. *Use a coloured pen to draw in lines between you and each person to represent the positive strokes you offer them. Use different thicknesses of line to show the relative intensities of stroking to different people i.e. thick lines for lots of strokes, thin lines for not many*
4. *repeat this, using a second colour to represent negative strokes*
5. *review the resulting pattern and decide what you might do to improve it*
6. *use a third colour to indicate what extra positive stroking you now intend to do.*

CHAPTER 8: LEADERSHIP AND MOTIVATION

Much of what you've read already will be useful when you need to lead and/or motivate people. It will have helped you understand how you prefer to be led and how best you can be motivated.

In this chapter, which has been added for this second edition of this book, I intend to draw together some of the earlier material and provide you with a simple framework for assessing people. This will help you to choose the most appropriate personal style to suit them, rather than expecting them to adjust to you. It will prompt you to target in line with their stroke preferences rather than your own. And it will give you a quick way to assess which leadership style will work best.

However, before I present this framework, I need to emphasise some caveats. It will seem as if you can slot people into boxes – this is obviously not the case. The boxes are there to simplify things but any classifications you make must be treated tentatively. Think of them as hypotheses which you still need to check out. Behave towards people in line with the hypotheses but be prepared to change if you don't get the reaction you're expecting. People are individuals and will not always conform to our theoretical models.

Having said that, the framework I am going to describe can still be very useful. This is partly because people do often behave in line with a limited number of styles and partly because people have a tendency to 'climb into their boxes' when they are stressed so they become even more like the stereotypes. And when they are stressed, it becomes even more important that you interact with them in the way they find easiest to handle.

AP³ – THE ASSESSING CUBE

I call the framework AP³ because it has three dimensions that are each labelled with A and P. These are active versus passive, alone versus people and acceleration versus patience. Figure 8.1 shows it as a cube - hence I also refer to it as the Assessing Cube. It is not easy to show a cube on paper in two dimensions so please use your imagination. Note that the third dimension does not go neatly from the back to the front; instead it goes from the upper right-hand corner at the back to the lower left-hand corner at the front. This is because the model was developed based on real people and that is how the categories worked out. There are proportionally more people clustered in the active/alone/patience and passive/people/acceleration combinations than in the other corners.

Figure 8.1: AP³ Basic Dimensions

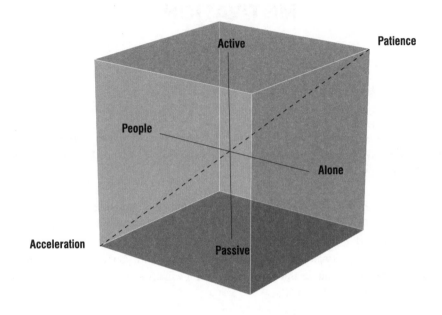

The labels for the dimensions are fairly self-explanatory. Acceleration/patience refers to people who do things fast (and sometimes faster and faster!) versus those who operate slowly and patiently. Alone/people sorts us out in terms of whether we prefer to be alone, or maybe with just one or two people, or like to be within a group of people, whether that be on the periphery or as the centre of attention. Active versus passive refers to whether we initiate interactions and goals or wait for others to initiate contact with us and for goals to present themselves to us – either because a goal seems appealing in some way or through someone telling us what to do. Active/ passive should not be confused with physical energy levels – both may apply to people who dance on tables and to those who sleep under the tables...

Figure 8.2 shows that we can discriminate between five main types on AP³. Note that we really need three dimensions to show it properly as a cube. Because this printed page is only two-dimensional, an extra box has been added in the bottom left corner for the acceleration aspect. We do not need one at the top right because this corner is just the more extreme version of the active/alone box.

I am going to add a lot of details into each box and this will be Figure 8.4. However, before I do that, I want to explain how to use the framework in a sequence that takes into account how well you know someone already. This means that you can use the framework to classify (tentatively) someone you are meeting for the first time; to analyse someone you already know well; and to work out what leadership style is likely to match their preferences, so

Figure 8.2: AP³ Overall Classification

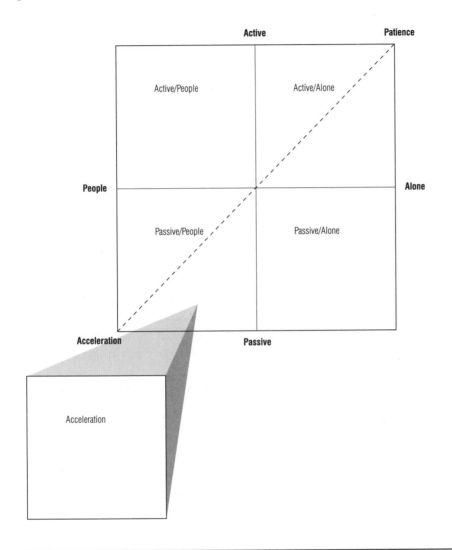

you know how to lead them or how they are likely to lead you. The sequence is shown in Figure 8.3 and has four stages. For fun I call these ABC, CCC, S&S, and CLS.

The initial stage in the overall sequence is what I call the ABC of AP³– appearance, behaviour and concerns. This is a great mini-sequence to apply when you meet someone for the first time. What are they dressed like: businesslike, accessorised, unusual, scruffy? How do they behave: do they seem to be in a hurry, do they walk towards you or wait for you to approach them, start talking or respond when spoken to – and given a choice, do they seem to prefer to interact with one or two people only or with a group? When they do

Figure 8.3: The AP³ Sequence

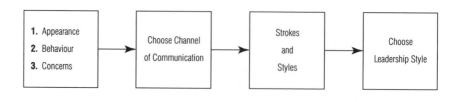

talk, what concerns them: the work, personal matters, how they 'play' (inside and outside work), or do they talk just enough to be polite or seem in a hurry to get on?

Once you've had chance to assess their appearance, behaviour and concerns, you can choose which channel of communication is likely to suit them best. They may of course demonstrate this anyway if they are at the 'active' end and start talking before you do.

By channel, I mean which combinations of personal styles, or ego states. I explained in Chapter 5 that there are four channels that are most likely to lead to effective communication. Hence we have one for each of the four AP³ boxes, with any of them possible for the acceleration box provided we talk fast. These are shown with details in Figure 8.4.

As you get to know someone better, you can move on to consider their stroke preferences and working styles. For people you already know, you can of course start here in the sequence although it can be fun to see how well their ABC fits with what else you know about them.

You might want to refer back to Chapters 4 and 5 for a reminder of personal styles and channels of communication, Chapter 6 for working styles and Chapter 7 for stroke preferences.

The final step in the sequence is to choose the most appropriate leadership style. If you are not the officially-appointed leader, you might still use the ideas here as prompts for how to get people to do what you propose. You can also apply this part of the sequence to understanding whoever you regard as your leader – and perhaps changing your own response to them in order to develop a better working relationship (or at least to convince them that you are an ideal subordinate).

THE CLASSIFICATIONS

Figure 8.4 contains key words as reminders of what you are likely to notice as you work through each stage of the sequence of getting to know someone. Each 'type' is also described in more detail in the text.

Before you read on, however, let me repeat the warning I gave earlier. This framework is a simplification, albeit of some well-founded research within a psychotherapeutic context. Simplifying the material means that we lose some of the detail and focus instead on stereotypes. So although you will recognise people you know, especially when they are stressed and therefore 'climbing into the security of their familiar box', you must still treat your classification as a hypothesis only. Be ready to notice and respond appropriately when people act 'out of character' – don't insist on pigeon-holing them.

Active/People

Appearance – they will look pleasing to the eye, colourful, often wearing jewellery, scarves, etc. to look even better. Men may be limited about colours at work so this may only show in small ways (e.g. ties). Likewise, male jewellery may be restricted to rings and watch bracelets (rather than plain straps) – some men may also have medallions on chains or cufflinks but earrings on men will tend to indicate passive/people.

Behaviour – they will walk up to a group of people and instantly become the centre of attention, will greet group members with pleasantries and show genuine interest in them.

Concerns – they will talk about personal aspects such as asking about someone's children or aged parents, will ask how you are and really listen to the reply, will also respond with personal information when questioned about themselves.

Channel of communication – they will be likely to interact from Nurturing Parent and invite (and expect) Natural Child responses. If others are more senior than them, this channel may be reversed and they may expect you to nurture them.

Stroke preferences – strokes about them, and you, as a person will be most significant for them. Expect to check out how they are feeling before you attempt to discuss work.

Style of working – this is usually Please People, so they will put effort into creating a harmonious atmosphere, will be great team members who check everyone is happy – but may become over-anxious and avoid letting people know when decisions being taken will lead to problems.

Leadership style preferences – they will prefer a caring leader who will know them on a personal level and show an interest in them outside work. They will be such a leader themselves. A potential drawback is that they may smother people by taking too much care of them. They may also confuse the boundaries between nurturing as a manager (e.g. encouraging before a presentation) and behaving as if they are your mother.

Impact of acceleration/patience – some of this group may tend towards acceleration so will hurry to please as many people as possible. Others will take their time.

Figure 8.4: The ABC of AP³

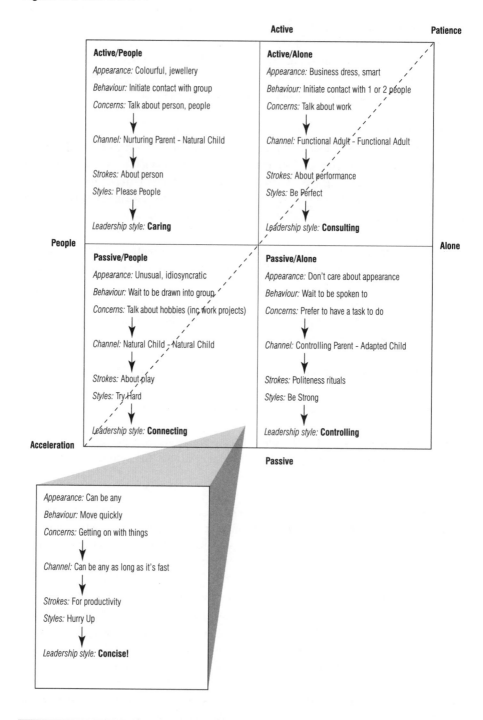

Active/Alone

Appearance – they will look very smart and business-like, with everything polished and pressed. You may suspect they look just as carefully dressed even when relaxing at home.

Behaviour – they will walk up to one or two people and initiate conversation.

Concerns – they will talk about work. If they know you, they may ask about your response to their recent email. If this is the first meeting, this will typically give their name and occupation and expect you to do the same and then to talk about work.

Channel of communication – they will prefer their conversations to be Functional Adult – Functional Adult. This is ideally suited to rational discussions and logical problem solving.

Stroke preferences – their preferred strokes will be about performance, especially when about how perfectly they have done something. They will tend to stroke others about performance also, with a tendency to notice how things could have been done better.

Style of working – this will be Be Perfect, so they will typically check their work – and yours – carefully, will plan ahead well and will ensure that tasks are completed properly. Watch out for delays caused by over-zealous double or triple checking and some reluctance to let others see drafts because these are less than perfect.

Leadership style preferences – a consulting style is needed, so that leader and subordinate discuss what is needed rationally and make joint decisions.

Impact of acceleration/patience – they are most likely to be at the patience end of this dimension, sometimes so much so that they take too long. Occasionally you will encounter an active/alone, Be Perfect type who also exhibits Hurry Up acceleration. These two working styles may conflict but may also give them two very useful strengths of accuracy and speed.

Passive/Alone

Appearance – they may well look as if they don't care about appearance. Shoes may be unpolished, clothes creased – or garments may be inappropriate such as jeans in a formal business setting. Occasionally they may look smart because someone at home took care of their clothing but as the day progresses they may become increasingly scruffy-looking.

Behaviour – they will prefer to avoid contact, especially with groups. They may act like a wallflower or find a task that eliminates the need to interact. They will wait for others to initiate conversation.

Concerns – their preference will be that someone gives them a task to do. They may lack the inclination for small talk and just want to get on and do something. If they are the senior person, they may tell others what to do.

Channel of communication – depending on level in the hierarchy, they will prefer one end of Controlling Parent – Adapted Child interaction. One gives instructions and the other obeys.

Stroke preferences – they will prefer not to receive too many strokes. Just enough to be polite will be fine. This is usually all they will give, too.

Style of working – these are Be Strong. Conscientious, do even the unpleasant aspects of the job, calm in a crisis, focus on the task regardless but may seem aloof and will not ask for help even when they are hopelessly overloaded.

Leadership style preferences – they will expect a controlling style and will use this themselves – they may find it hard to respect a manager who asks for opinions instead of telling people what to do. For them, the traditional, autocratic style of management is how it should be – the manager gets paid more so should make the decisions.

Impact of acceleration/patience – Be Strong style is about working steadily. Some may be influenced by patience to work rather slowly and carefully (perfectly) whilst others may have the combination of steady and fast.

Passive/People
Appearance – they are likely to wear something unusual. It may be minor if they work in an environment with strict dress codes; perhaps sandals or moccasins instead of business-style shoes. Or they may wear very unusual clothes, or earrings in one ear only, or prominent tattoos.

Behaviour – they will approach a group but wait for someone to draw them in to the conversation. They may seem as if they are keeping open their options about joining other groups. Or they may interrupt by speaking about something that is only tangentially related to whatever the group is talking about.

Concerns – they will prefer to talk about play; this may be their hobbies but may also be about work projects, which they will enthuse about in the same way as hobbies. If you already know them, you may find that their hobbies and work projects change frequently as they move on to new interests.

Channel of communication – these are the enthusiasts so they will prefer a Natural Child – Natural Child mode, during which you can both become energised about the topics of conversation.

Stroke preferences – they will value most strokes as if from a child about the exciting things they are doing, especially when the activities are unusual, challenging or even dangerous. Parental-style nurturing strokes may be seen as boring.

Style of working – these are Try Hard. Enthusiastic, energetic, set out to cover all the bases but may then go off on tangents and 'forget' to finish each project. They will show initiative but this may lead to tasks being expanded way beyond the expectations of management.

Leadership style preferences – they will enjoy a connecting approach, where employee and manager both 'roll up their sleeves' and get actively involved in the work. However, they may volunteer to start new projects whilst finding excuses not to complete projects already started.

Impact of acceleration/patience – empirical studies have shown that people/passive types are often also at the acceleration end of that dimension. When this is the case, they may rush around starting lots of new projects and not finishing them – but they may also have the ability to work fast and hence juggle several balls in the air at once.

Acceleration

This may be combined with any of the previous four but may also exist as a type in its own right. In the latter case, many of the other indicators will be irrelevant because it will be their speed of speech and movement that will indicate their style.

Appearance – could be as for any of the above styles but may also show signs of dressing in a hurry, such as odd socks or earrings, blouses or shirts not properly buttoned or not tucked in, garments chosen for how fast you can dress in them.

Behaviour – again, they might approach or wait, opt for one person or a group – but they will hurry into the room and will quite possibly arrive late and in a rush. They may also hurry out again before a meeting or event has finished because they are late for another appointment.

Concerns – they will want to talk hurriedly, about what needs to be done, how they, or you, need to get on with things, how much they have to do.

Channel of communication – they will be in such a hurry that any channel will probably work. The main thing is that whatever you say in Nurturing or Controlling Parent, Functional Adult or Natural Child, you say it quickly. Otherwise, they may interrupt you or may even have rushed off before you finish speaking.

Stroke preferences – they will prefer strokes about their productivity, and will give strokes to others for the same – assuming they pay attention long enough to notice how much has been achieved.

Style of working – these are the ones who Hurry Up. So they get lots done but may make mistakes. They may not bother to do anything until the deadline is approaching, and as managers they may set unrealistically short deadlines for others to meet.

Leadership style preferences – to maintain the donkey bridge of same initial letters, I call this the concise style. Basically, you have to manage them with as few words as possible, said quickly, so they don't rush off and start action based on hearing only the beginning of your request or instruction. They are likely to lead others in the same way, with abrupt-sounding comments and an expectation of immediate activity.

APPLYING THE FRAMEWORK

You may already have worked out where you fit as you've read this chapter. However, few of us fit nearly into one category. A colleague of mine said that we are more like clouds floating within the cube. Our cloud may be any shape; it may be mostly in one place but tendrils of it may stretch in several direction even though the main part of the cloud stays in the same place.

- *Check back to the previous chapters where you've worked on your personal styles and your stroking patterns for clues about your preferences. Think about how you dress, how you behave when you arrive at a meeting or conference session, what subjects you most like to talk about.*
- *Then think about someone you find it hard to interact with. The one you might label 'dipper' as in 'difficult person from hell.' How do they dress, behave at a gathering, what topic do they talk about? Where do they fit within the cube? How does this affect the way you interact with them?*
- *Think also about a range of colleagues, or people who report to you if you are in a leadership role. Slot them into the cube also. If you don't know them well enough to do this, plan to pay more attention and get to know them better in the future.*

Cross check the above by reviewing how many people you know that you can fit into each area of the cube. Aim to find two or three names for each of the main boxes and for the extra section.

- *If possible, find names for each section according to whether they are a 'pure' version of the style or are influenced by elements of the next box.*
- *Can you also find names to complete Please/People with Try Hard and Please/People with Be Perfect*
- *Can you confirm that you are interacting effectively with a wide range of people 'types?*
- *Do you now realise that some are also classified as likeable, or intelligent, or worth being with, whereas others are in the 'don't want to know them' or 'too difficult to talk to' sections.*

Where you have gaps:
- *Is it because you lack the skills to interact with some types of people?*
- *Could you be overlooking people you find it hard to interact with?*
- *How can you develop the skills so you can interact effectively more widely?*

Repeat of the Caveat!

Finally, the caveat again! Presenters are taught that people hear only one-third of what gets said, so important points should be said three times. Although you are reading and not listening to this, I am going to repeat the caveat for the third time.

This framework is a simplification and must be used with care. It will often be extremely useful, allowing you to choose the best ways to motivate and lead others. It can also be very unhelpful if you become too dogmatic over the content.

Even if you have correctly assessed where someone fits within the cube, people are infinitely variable and will not conveniently stay within a stereotype. So use your analysis tentatively and be prepared to change your approach whenever necessary.

Another potential drawback may be your own limitations. Few of us can naturally move between all of the options within the cube. You are likely to find it easier to get on with people who are like you, and hardest to interact with those who occupy the opposite corners. For example, controlling leaders and nurturing leaders may regard each other negatively, as may also consulting and connecting leaders. Use the ideas throughout this book to initiate changes that will add to your repertoire of skills so you will be able to interact effectively across the range.

CHAPTER 9: AVOIDING PEOPLE PROBLEMS

STROKE FILTERS

A common response to the idea of strokes is for someone to go straight out and start giving out positive strokes. With most people, these have the desired effect – the person responds positively and another relationship improves and develops. With some people, however, the stroke seems to be picked up as negative. This can be disheartening and demoralising, leaving you with the suspicion that the theory does not work in real life.

We can understand what is happening here if we combine the ideas of strokes and life positions. If you offer a positive stroke consisting of praise to someone who is looking through one of the unhelpful windows on the world, it will seem as if they 'filter' it and convert it into something negative.

If they are:
- IOK–YNOK: they accept it conceitedly (they already know they're wonderful), managing also to imply that your opinion is of no interest to them (it's a fluke that you're right about them).
- INOK–YOK: they tell you they don't deserve your praise, they did nothing special, although "it's very kind of you to say so".
- INOK–YNOK: they look at you very suspiciously and wonder cynically what you are after as that is the only reason they think you'd be nice to them.

How about constructive criticism. If they are:
- IOK–YNOK: they tell you you're wrong, and that you're incapable of judging good performance anyway.
- INOK–YOK: they agree with you – they know they are incompetent, and thank you for pointing it out (but they don't act on it).
- INOK–YNOK: they tell you about your faults too, and blame you for their own shortcomings.

So what can we do about this? One strategy is to keep in mind that they appear to be looking through an unhelpful window on the world at the moment. If we go away and come back another day, hopefully they will be in a better frame of mind to receive our positive strokes. Linked with this is the need to stay away from our own unhelpful life positions. It is all too easy to shift across to our own version of Not OK when our well-meant attempts are brushed aside. Counting to ten before responding is very old and still very wise advice - that short pause should be enough for us to choose a better option.

Their response may also be an indication that we are offering them the wrong kind of stroke – perhaps conditional when they want unconditional, about work instead of family, about their Adapted Child when they believe a different ego state is best, or maybe about Hurry Up when they are Be Perfect! It's worth checking our stroking patterns for this type of 'error', especially if we repeatedly seem to get it wrong.

The other reason that people respond in these ways is that they are actually trying to get negative strokes, in the same way that they learned to do when young when positive strokes were not forthcoming. This notion that we will settle for negative strokes is particularly important in understanding why some of our relationships incorporate pain and stress as well as positive aspects. In our efforts to get enough strokes, we engage in repetitive transactions with others that lead to negative payoffs. The more we need strokes, the more often we are likely to engage in such unhelpful interactions.

GAMES PEOPLE PLAY

These repetitive but unsatisfactory transactions with others are known as *psychological games*. The time period encompassed by a game if flexible. We may spend minutes only in an interaction which contains the complete sequence: perhaps we start to argue with someone almost as soon as they walk through our door. Games may instead extend over a lengthy period as we move through the steps during a series of contacts. In this case, we may appear to be working well with someone, only to realise later that we have a major misunderstanding.

For example, *Harried* involves one person rushing about earning the right to mutiny or collapse as a martyr, while someone else sets themselves up to be disappointed and let down. One of us accepts any work that needs to be done, adding it to an ever increasing array of tasks and responsibilities. If we are a manager, we are likely to be a poor delegator. Our ulterior message here is that we are the only person capable of doing so much work, and doing it properly.

We may have several partners in this game who collude with our efforts to do everything. On the surface, they may well encourage us to further excesses by commenting in awe about the prodigious amount of work we absorb. Their secret agenda will be to reassure themselves that no-one is actually that capable, as will be proved when we become ill or lose our temper through overwork.

Lunch Bag has similar characteristics to Harried. We bring our lunch to work (in a bag) so that we do not need to take a break for a meal. We then offer to answer the telephones while our colleagues go out to lunch. We refuse their invitation to join them, explaining that we do not want to waste the food we already have with us.

When they return happily from lunch, we complain in an aggrieved tone about the length of their absence and the number of interruptions we have had to deal with on their behalf. We end up feeling righteous and taken advantage of; they end up feeling guilty and annoyed with us for spoiling their pleasant mood.

The Drama Triangle

An easy way to understand and analyse the dynamics of a game is to use the *Drama Triangle*. This uses the similarity between psychological games and theatrical drama; the scenes which capture the audience's attention best contain the elements of a game. As in drama, the players also take on the roles of *Persecutor*, *Rescuer*, or *Victim*, as shown in Figure 9.1. The Drama Triangle. Note the use of initial capital letters, as was done with egos state labels, so we can differentiate the drama triangle roles from real persecutors, rescuers and victims.

Take for example the well-known James Bond films. Repetition is there in abundance; the sequence of events repeats itself through each episode in the film, and is even repeated with different villains in different films. This adds to our excitement because we know there is more to come. Predictability comes in the form of knowing that whoever is winning (persecuting) now will be losing (victim) later in the film. We also know that James Bond will emerge as victorious persecutor at the end, unless the producers want to show his comeback in a sequel.

The director makes it easy for us to spot the ulterior transactions. The viewer is allowed to see the hidden agenda because we watch the actors preparing their trap and discussing their motives and their plans with henchmen. James Bond is smarter than the villain; or is the villain smarter than James Bond? There are many switches in such a film. Indeed, the quicker the switches follow each other, the more exciting is the action. Suddenly the

Figure 9.1: The Drama Triangle

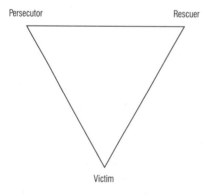

villain is persecutor and gloating openly while Bond the victim swims with sharks, then James Bond regains control and persecutes the villain, then again the villain gains the upper hand. And this happens all the way through the film.

The payoffs are clear. The villain is punished, maybe by death. Bond is able to relax, with his payoff of smugness and glory, until the next time.

Yes but ....

The results of organisational games may be less extreme but they still follow a pattern around the drama triangle. Figure 9.2 shows the moves of a typical organisational game of *Yes, but,* a sequence in which helpful suggestions are countered with reasons against. Typically, someone mentions a problem they have. When solutions are put forward, they

Figure 9.2: A Game of Yes, but…

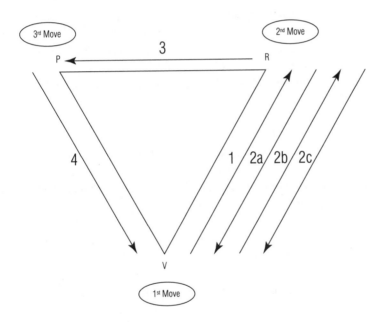

1.	Lee sighs, acts victim
2a.	Andy rescues with "Why don't you…"
2b.	Lee responds "Yes, but…"
2c, 2e, etc.	Andy offers more "Why don't you…"
2d, 2f, etc.	Lee continues "Yes, but…"
3.	Andy shifts to Persecutor and complains/vents frustration
4.	Lee feels worse than at the start

respond by pointing out why each idea would not work, beginning with the words 'Yes, but...'. Eventually, one of the 'players' becomes exasperated and makes derogatory comments about the other person.

The underlying communication here is about who is cleverest. The problem-holder is reinforcing a belief that they have thought of every possible solution, and that they know more about the pitfalls of the job than anyone else. The solution-offerer takes the attitude that they can easily improve on whatever has already been considered. Only one of them can emerge from the interaction feeling they have been proved right.

In our example, Lou would sign deeply, Victim-like. Ainslie, a keen Rescuer, would ask what was wrong. Lou would mutter something about having a lot or work to do, and needing to leave on time that day. Note that Lou may not have asked directly for help from Ainslie to solve this problem.

Ainslie would however begin to offer solutions, usually beginning each sentence with the phrase "Why don't you ....". Lou would point out the flaws in each suggestion, using the phrase that gives the game its name – "Yes, but last time I tried that it didn't work"; "Yes, but asking them for help was a waste of time"; "Yes, but I can't concentrate on priorities only because it's all equally urgent"; "Yes, but my manager won't agree to me delegating any of it ...." And so on.

Several solutions would be offered by Ainslie and demolished by Lou. Eventually one of them would switch to another position on the triangle. Sometimes Lou would shift first, moving from Victim to Persecutor and complaining that Lou had been wasting time making stupid suggestions. Ainslie would promptly move to Victim, and say something like "I didn't ask you to help. You were trying to interfere again."

At other times, Ainslie would shift first, by moving to Persecutor and accusing Lou of not really wanting to solve the problem. After all, Lou kept dismissing Ainslie's ideas without really considering them. Ainslie now feels smug, while Lou stays in the Victim role and feels doubly put down – the problem with the workload still exists and now Ainslie is annoyed into the bargain.

Elements of Psychological Games

We can identify several elements of a psychological game; the more of these present the more likely that a game is actually in effect rather than a simple miscommunication.

Repetition – is the sequence something that we recognise as being common? Do we get the sensation of 'here we (or they) go again'?

Predictability – can we, or an observer, predict how things will turn out? Is there a certain inevitability in the sequence?

Ulterior transaction – do we suspect that there is a hidden agenda? Are there unspoken messages beneath the overt behaviour?

Switch – does there come a moment when the interaction seems to shift? Do those involved switch to addressing the ulterior message instead of the initial subject?

Negative payoff – do the parties end up feeling bad? Is there an element of win/lose, or lose/lose apparent at the end of the interaction?

Out of awareness – this is the most significant aspect of psychological games. We do not realise at the time that we are engaged in such an unhelpful interaction. Indeed, we may not realise afterwards either as we will assume that the negative payoff is a normal part of the pattern of our life. We will have experienced it many times before; we can also see similar unsuccessful episodes happening to everyone around us.

Gotcha!

Using this list and the drama triangle makes it easy to identify other organisational games. Ainslie, for example, also engaged in Gotcha! This was played with Indira as it was not a behaviour pattern that Lou seemed to get involved in.

Gotcha consists of asking questions until we can catch the person out. This is a popular game in meetings. As we explain our ideas, we realise that someone is showing great interest. We feel flattered as they raise many queries and encourage us to expand our comments. We are enjoying the attention so much that we begin to lose track of what we are saying, and we may even start to embroider a bit rather than have to admit that we don't know everything! Then, just as we are congratulating ourselves on how well the session is going, they pounce on an apparent contradiction in what we have said. We feel confused and embarrassed; the onlookers conclude that our ideas are unsound.

The underlying dynamic in Gotcha is about being one-up. We have a high opinion of ourselves and are aiming to demonstrate how much more we know than others. The person who takes us on has an equally high opinion of their own capabilities and wants to make sure the other people see how clever they are. In a sense, we are using cunning in a battle for the hearts and minds of the audience and only one of us can win.

In this game, Ainslie would put forward various suggestions about how the staff might compete against external tenderers. Each time, Indira would look excited and ask a lot of questions. Usually, Ainslie would reach a point where more information was needed. What would be involved in a management buyout; would such an approach be allowed; would the external organisation agree to employ them; what would happen to their pension rights ...? Instead of admitting lack of knowledge, Ainslie would start to fabricate. Shortly after this, Indira would pounce, with a comment such as "But didn't you say xyz." or "You don't really know that, do you!"

Indira would have shifted from Rescuer, helping Ainslie explain the ideas, to Persecutor, showing Ainslie up as a fool. Ainslie would stay in Victim, and feel cheated that the chance to move out of Victim with Indira's help had somehow turned into such an embarrassment.

Rebuff

Meanwhile, elsewhere in the Agency other games were continuing as they had long before the changes in organisational structure had been introduced. Gordon and Saroj, two section heads, played Rebuff.

Rebuff moves from an apparent invitation into an affronted refusal. This may have sexual connotations, as when we flirt with someone and are then offended if they overstep a boundary which we have not made clear to them. Legislation about sexual harassment has reduced the instances of this, although the dynamic is still there for those playing for higher stakes. The negative payoff of a slapped face has now become litigation.

Rebuff is also played, however, around non-sexual issues. We may offer the services of our section or organisation, only to complain bitterly that we are being taken advantage of when we see the scale of the resulting request. Our colleague or customer is baffled by our reaction – they believed there were no limits on our offer of help.

Our payoff is to retain our cynicism about how people rip you off if you try to help them. Their payoff is to remain cynical about the lack of any genuine desire to help.

Gordon and Saroj played Rebuff around the work of their sections. Both were short-staffed. Gordon would suggest that one of his staff might spend some time in Saroj's section. However, Gordon would be vague about which employee, how much time, and what work would be involved.

Saroj, apparently forgetting previous interactions like this with Gordon, would once again feel hopeful that help would be forthcoming. He would suggest the name of a particular employee who had experience relevant to the section's current workload. He would also talk as if the person would move into his section on a part-time basis.

At this point, Gordon would appear affronted. He would complain that Saroj was totally unreasonable. Of course he hadn't meant that person; of course he didn't expect them to physically leave their own section; surely they could have done work for Saroj where they normally worked; and he'd only intended occasional help anyway.

Three Handed Games

It takes at least two people for a game to take place. Three handed games also occur, such as when a third party attempts to intervene. This is why police officers dread domestic disputes; like arguments at work it is hard to take action without becoming embroiled yourself. Consider the scene. Husband is beating wife (or vice versa). Neighbour calls the police. Police officer attempts to restrain husband. Wife then attacks police officer to stop the action against the husband. In this sequence, the police officer goes from Rescuer to Persecutor to Victim. The wife goes from Victim to Persecutor of police officer, Rescuer of husband. The husband goes from Persecutor to Victim. For added piquancy, the husband may then switch to Persecutor again, but this time to attack the police officer who is now attempting to arrest the wife for assaulting a police officer.

The equivalent scene in industry might involve three colleagues. Two are arguing loudly. One appears to be losing the argument and is being insulted. In wades number 3 on their behalf, making it clear that they will not stand by and listen to the insults to their colleague. Instead of being grateful for the rescue, the insulted party now persecutes by telling them to mind their own business. All three are now arguing loudly and switching rapidly around the triangle, when along comes a fourth person...

This is *Uproar*, a discussion proceeding to a formidable argument. We begin gently enough to have a sensible sharing of views. Gradually the psychological temperature increases. Eventually, we stop being polite and start telling the other person what we really think of their ideas. Our insults escalate as we get into an argument. Uproar becomes even more energetic if we involve more than two players, especially if we start taking sides.

Like Gotcha, Uproar's secret agenda is about winning and losing. If we customarily end up on the losing side of the argument, we may recognise this game better under the alternative title of *Kick Me*.

Why Play Games?
Games have different outcomes, on a scale from mild to severe. In mild games we end up with little more than a feeling of discomfort. These are the unsuccessful interactions we have with colleagues, for example. Next come games which significantly detract from our performance; people become unwilling to co-operate with us to achieve tasks. Further up the scale are games where the consequences are apparent to third parties; our colleagues complain to the boss about us, perhaps. As the seriousness increases, we move through verbal warnings into disciplinaries. In extreme cases, we get fired or walk off the job. In even more severe cases, the law is breached and we end up in court. Or we take risks with safety and finish up in a hospital or morgue, or being sued.

Why do we play psychological games? It seems strange to think that we keep repeating interactions that lead to us feeling bad. A major part of the problem is lack of awareness; we look around and see everyone else behaving in similar ways and believe that this must be the way life is. Games will be one of our habits.

There are also apparent 'advantages' that accrue from playing psychological games. Because of this, we find it hard to stop the repetitive sequences, even when we become aware of them. There are six different advantages - we get strokes, reinforce our attitudes, get out of doing something, avoid an issue from the past, get to tell our friends and also get a (negative) kick out of recalling the game. Quite a collection but once we know hat the benefits are, we can plan wider changes than simply altering the transaction. This gives us far more chance of dispensing with the unhelpful sequences and the negative payoffs that accompany them.

As I mentioned earlier when describing strokes, we all need at least a minimal level of attention from other human beings if we are to stay alive. Games generate only negative strokes but these are better than being ignored. If we work alone a lot, we may find that we row with our colleagues when we do see them. We may, for instance, be using Uproar as a way of getting a large supply of strokes during our occasional contacts.

Games also provide reinforcement of our windows on the world, or core beliefs. If we believe we are better than others, we will play games where we finish one-up. We play Uproar to win, or Gotcha to prove the other person is incompetent. If we believe others are better than us, we play Kick Me to get kicked, or Poor Me in which we claim dispensation for failing at tasks because we lack the advantages that others take for granted. If we doubt the value of ourself and others, we play games where no-one wins, such as Yes, but with a payoff of frustration for both players when they cannot solve a problem. In these ways, we reinforce IOK–YNOK, INOK–YOK or INOK–YNOK.

There will usually be something in the current situation that we avoid doing by playing a game. With Yes, but, for example, we do not have to get our work done on time if we can prove to ourself and others that no-one can find a way of doing so. Uproar may be used as justification for storming out of a meeting. Lunch Bag gets us out of going to a smoky pub and pretending to enjoy our colleagues' jokes.

A game is also a way of avoiding an original pain. It is as if we repeat a sequence from the past that we developed then to protect us from something. By doing so, we do not have to deal with the issue in the present. This maintains the psychological stability we have achieved by learning to think and feel in customary ways.

We get another 'advantage' from being able to spend time telling our friends and acquaintances about the game. We give a blow-by-blow account of what happened – what we said, what the other person said, what we said then – to the accompaniment of appropriate commiserations or admiration from our audience. Games with lots of switches sound especially exciting when described, so we may even be able to develop a reputation as raconteur and so widen our circle of acquaintances.

Finally, we can also replay a game in our heads to generate more excitement. We go over the steps again in fantasy, re-experiencing the feelings through a sort of internal pastiming with ourselves. We may repeat the game phrase to ourselves, as when we think "If it weren't for them, I could have …"

Stopping Games

In order to stop playing games, we need first to be aware of them. Once we learn about game playing, we start to recognise what is happening – but this is usually when we are in the middle of a game, which is not a good time to make any changes. Suddenly changing the subject to announce you've just spotted a game is more likely to offend the other person than to stimulate a more constructive interaction. And it may mean you just shift to another game, which is called transactional analysis and means you are attempting to show how clever you are because you can analyse what is going on, and they feel put down so do their best to prove you wrong.

A more structured approach is needed. First, check you are getting enough positive strokes generally. If not, see the ideas below about time structuring – or find some new friends, or be clearer about how you prefer to interact with your existing friends.

Then set aside an hour or so to identify and review your game playing.

Think about those times when you come away from someone feeling negative, whether this is one-up or one-down (or both down as losers). Check for examples where the pattern feels repetitive, with the same dynamic even though it may be with different people.

Check also for any elements of predictability – now you think about it, do the interactions follow some predictable steps such that an observer could predict what will happen next at each stage. Then check whether you suspect there are 'secret messages'. Do you think you and the other person(s) are saying some fairly normal things but are secretly thinking very negative thoughts? Remember that such thoughts may be buried below our consciousness.

Once you've identified occasions when all of the above seem to apply, you're ready to analyse it and plan changes.

Start by writing down everything that gets said and done. What do you say or do? What do they say or do? What do you say or do then, and so on, all the way to the final negative payoffs.

Then add in what you feel at various points during the sequence, and what you think the other person feels. The aim of this review process is to bring into your own awareness as much detail of the game dynamics as you can. What happens at the end? Who says or does what? Do you finish up feeling one-up, one-down, both down? What is your payoff from playing the game? What do you think their payoff is?

Now check you've captured the beginning of the sequence. Have you gone back in time far enough? Some games are complete within one sequence of interaction but others are run over quite a long timeframe so they start in one meeting but may not end with the final payoff until several meetings later.

Once you've analysed the game thoroughly, you can set out to avoid starting it up again with anyone in the future. Work out what you can do differently before the game begins. Maybe you need to avoid certain people, or leave the room once you become aware of the game trigger, or react in a way that is different to what you've done in the past. Or perhaps you could talk to the other person involved when you and they are feeling relaxed, so you can review together how to change the ways you interact.

Here are some brief examples:

Leaving the room – maybe the game starts up when the two of you take a coffee break, so try staggering break-times or say you have to run an errand (note – this technique is for acquaintances but not your friends).

Reacting differently – change the subject, ask them questions about something else, use a different style of interaction such as teasing them if you would have previously been serious, or vice versa.

Reviewing at another time – say you've been thinking about your own behaviour and want to improve it, or mention learning some interesting theory about what sometimes happens in relationships – and make sure they are willing to have this conversation before you go any further.

The Potency Pyramid

Another option for stopping games is to shift to an alternative to the drama triangle, the *potency pyramid*, as shown in Figure 9.3. For this, I have flipped the triangle vertically to emphasise that it is different. I have kept the PRV as the initial letters for each corner of the triangle but now these letters stand for positive elements: powerful, responsible and vulnerable. They no longer need capital letters.

Being **powerful** means using your power when it is appropriate to do so, such as when someone who really can't defend themself is being ill-treated. Bullying at work might be an example where you should intervene, especially if you are more senior than the person being bullied.

Being **responsible** means only taking actions that fit with your genuine responsibilities. You are not responsible for the decisions or actions of another person, unless you are a manager and the other person is acting on behalf of the organisation. Hence, you are responsible for making sure people follow safety regulations, that they avoid discriminatory behaviour, and so on – and you may need to use the power invested in your organisational role to achieve this.

Being **vulnerable** means admitting when you need help, being open about your own shortcomings, and asking clearly for help when you need it rather than expecting others to notice without you saying anything.

Figure 9.3: The Potency Pyramid

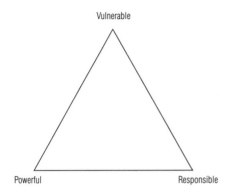

Vulnerable

Powerful   Responsible

TIME STRUCTURING

Yet another way we can set out to avoid game playing is by more careful *structuring* of our *time*. By this I do not mean time management – I mean the ways we use our time as it relates to different categories of strokes. Our natural human desire for recognition from others causes us to move through a sequence of behaviours in order to exchange strokes of ever increasing intensity. There are seven options for time structuring that form a rough ladder up which we may climb towards a closer relationship.

Alone

Time in *Alone* may be spent in many places: at the desk planning, in the car driving to appointments, in the swimming pool, sitting in front of the TV. We may be thinking about work or pleasure, be feeling cheerful or sad or angry, be engaged in physical activity or sedentary. We may also be amongst a group of people yet still be alone, as when we daydream or mentally withdraw.

When we structure our time as alone, we are not receiving strokes from others. We may be remembering strokes received previously, or stroking ourselves mentally, but this is not the same as recognition from other human beings. However, all of us need some time alone. It gives us chance to think, relax and recharge our batteries. Too little time alone may lead to stress and indicate an unhealthy over-reliance on stimulation from others.

Individuals who spend a lot of time alone may be perceived as especially self-contained, or even as unfriendly. This can become a problem when the real reason for such minimal contact is a lack of social skills. Someone who does not know how to make small talk may act as if they do not want company whilst secretly longing to socialise more. Similarly, an overly pessimistic or critical view of life may interfere with our ability to make contact with others.

Conversely, those who cannot tolerate being alone will become stressed if they lack company. In organisations, they are likely to leave their workplace to go on artificial errands in order to find someone to talk to. Open plan offices are preferred by those who dislike being alone, and hated by those who want time to be alone.

Rituals

Rituals include any interactions where we know exactly what socially acceptable remarks are expected from us. In addition to relatively lengthy rituals such as wedding and funeral services, there are the everyday greetings that we exchange. These provide an interesting reflection of cultural differences – depending on our nationality we may bow politely, shake hands, kiss cheeks, or hug. The UK greeting of "How are you?" is fascinating for its illogicality: it would be a major mistake to really answer the question instead of responding with an echo.

Our ritualised greetings to each other provide fairly low intensity strokes. Our comments are automatic so they involve little real recognition or interest in the other person. We miss them if they are omitted but do not get major reinforcement from them. However, they are an important prelude to more powerful forms of stroking. If rituals are omitted, we may decide that the person is not someone we wish to have further contact with.

Rituals form an important part of organisational life. As we meet new people, we are expected to greet them in ways that match the corporate norms. Using an informal mode of address in a formal organisation, for example, may put us at a disadvantage. Forgetting someone's name may undermine the impact of our stroke; the other person may even interpret this as a deliberate negative stroke. Not knowing the hierarchical status of the other person can leave us floundering in some organisations. I recall many years ago, as a junior member of staff, being teased about the way I had chatted causally in the lift to someone who turned out to be the Managing Director.

Pastimes

After rituals, we often literally 'pass time' with others. This *pastiming* involves small talk, as when we discuss the weather, our holidays, the prices in the shops, and so on. We pastime whenever and wherever we chat socially. Once a subject has been mentioned, we pay sufficient attention to the conversation to be able to add our own views or information. Our conversation is partly ritualised, in that we obey some intuitive rule about not changing the subject until we judge others are ready to do this also. However, it is only the subject that is controlled in this way; within the current topic we are free to say whatever we decide.

The strokes from pastimes are a bit more powerful than from rituals because of the need to pay closer attention to what the other person is saying. If we only pick up the general topic we may inadvertently repeat what they have already said. We have to listen and select our own comments so that the conversation will flow. We also have to judge when it will be appropriate to change the subject - too soon and people will think we are not really interested in what they are saying. This deeper listening is experienced as a somewhat more intense form of stroking.

Pastiming is often an important prelude to a meeting. We use this time to 'get a feel' for the other people and to establish some rapport. Those who complain about alliances at meetings have often neglected to arrive in time to join in the pastiming. Workaholics who try to move straight into the business of the meeting fail to realise that many people appreciate the opportunity to chat casually beforehand so that they will have some point of contact aside from the task.

Working

Working as a way of time structuring means performing tasks with others in order to achieve goals and produce results together. We may be discussing needs with a customer, having a meeting, reviewing ideas with a colleague, or any of the many activities we engage in with others on behalf of the organisation. We also work with family and friends, to accomplish objectives such as decorating a house, producing an amateur play, fundraising for charity, serving as a school governor.

Strokes that arise from working are medium to high intensity. We require a good degree of involvement and attention in order to stroke appropriately when we are working with someone. It is worth remembering that questions are also strokes, and can be very powerful as they indicate a strong interest in what the other person has to say.

Playing

When we *play* we spend time with others engaged in activities which we are doing because we enjoy them. The obvious examples are sports and hobbies (although some of us become so achievement-orientated that we turn these into work). Less obvious instances of play occur when we brainstorm, before we worry about whether the ideas are any use. Genuine brainstorming is play, which we follow with work as we review the practicability of our suggestions.

Play-generated strokes are medium to high intensity, depending on the energy that we put into the activity. The more enthusiastic we are, the more impact our strokes will have on each other. Joint laughter is an especially strong contributor to our stroke bank. The effect of play strokes will also be enhanced as we develop deeper friendships.

Playing in organisations is often centred around sports teams or social events. The more these are encouraged by the organisation, the more employees are likely to 'play together' and hence develop closer relationships which will enable them to work together well. An increasingly common form of playing in organisations is the involvement of groups of employees in charitable events; these also stimulate more contact inside the organisation as the arrangements are made and the results publicised.

Games

The next stage in the time structuring pecking order may well be *psychological games* like those described earlier in this chapter. These will occur when we fail to establish a good relationship. It is likely that games are actually an unconscious substitute for becoming close to others. Unless we have satisfactory relationships with others, we will not receive enough positive strokes. Just as when we were young, we will turn to negative strokes to make up the deficit. Depending on the degree to which we play the game, the strokes thus generated may be very powerful indeed.

Within a team, it is sometimes as if we have special antennae which can identify the very person who is most likely to play a corresponding game hand to our own. As we move through rituals, pastimes, playing and working, we seem to register subtle signals that tell us who wants to be one-up, who one-down, and who will join us in the repetitive, predictable sequence of game moves that we believe to be normal behaviour.

Closeness

As we get to know people, we hope that we will be able to relax and be ourselves when we are with them. Often, we do not believe this is possible so we maintain a façade behind which we shelter our strongest emotions and censor our opinions. *Closeness* as the term is used here means genuine intimacy which occurs when we establish sufficient trust to feel able to share our true feelings and express our views candidly. We are then able to give honest feedback about our likes and dislikes, and we expect others to do the same. Doing this in a caring and respectful way strengthens our relationship and allows us to depend on each other for honesty in our communication.

Closeness yields high intensity strokes which reinforce considerably our sense of well-being. Thoughtful, well-intentioned constructive criticisms are just as valuable to us as direct expressions of love and affection. The significant factor is that we feel truly close to another person, with whom we can be open and trusting.

I believe that more and more people are now recognising, and demanding, that organisations be run in ways that enable people to attain closeness with their colleagues. Training courses are often structured specifically to encourage participants to be open and supportive. Management styles are changing to reflect this move. However, it is important to remember that we need to work through the stages from alone via rituals, pastimes, working and playing, toward closeness. Expecting people to move too quickly into closeness is more likely to lead to game playing.

It may also be enough that we reach the stroke intensity level of working and playing. We may prefer to establish closeness with friends and family rather than work colleagues (although some colleagues may also count as friends). With some exceptions (such as where we depend on colleagues as in the fire service, for example) it is inappropriate for organisations to seek to create such strong connections between colleagues that they become like substitute families. We can usually perform our work roles quite adequately based on the stroking levels associated with working and playing together. We may then want only occasional closeness at work, preferring to get most of that in our private life.

TIME STRUCTURING AND RACKETS

As I mentioned in Chapter 3, we sometimes engage in rackets. Like games, rackets may be repetitive, unsatisfactory sequences that lead to us feeling bad. Unlike games, rackets may be internal processes only, requiring no real contact with another person. On bad days, therefore, when we feel determined to see the world as a cold and unfriendly place, we may slip unknowingly into rackets when there is no-one around to play a psychological game with.

We can relate this concept to each of the ways of structuring time except closeness, which is a way of interacting that is free of rackets or games.

Alone: the target of our racket response may not even be in contact with us. However, for some reason they come to mind and we imagine them making derogatory comments about us to a third party.

Rituals: two people deep in conversation fail to notice us as they hurry by, although we say hello. We conclude that they deliberately ignored us.

Pastimes: someone changes the subject when we are telling the group about our new car. They do this because they are so excited by the birth of their grandchild that they cannot wait to break the news. We feel offended and decide they were really signalling boredom with our comments.

Working: we are asked a genuine question about the progress of our work. We interpret this incorrectly as an expression of dissatisfaction and hear it as a negative stroke.

Playing: the other person wins the golf match. We suspect they cheated.

Games: rackets can be a mini-game. We have the repetition and predictability of a game, as well as the negative payoff. However we do not have a switch so the impact will be less. It may be that we escalate to a game when the negative stroke from the racket is not sufficiently powerful.

Closeness: now that we are close and trusting, we have no need of our rackety sequences.

The more we remove rackets and games from the ways we spend our time, the fewer negative strokes we will generate and the more opportunities we will have to get truly close to others and exchange healthy positive strokes. Unfortunately, games and rackets occur out of our awareness so we need some clever detective work in order to spot them in ourselves (we can usually see what other people do much more readily!).

The following sequence of questions will help you identify situations in which you may be engaging in unhealthy and ineffective interactions.

Think of a repetitive situation that ends with you feeling dissatisfied, uncomfortable or upset in some way.

- *How does it begin? Think carefully about the start as it may be before any words are spoken. Perhaps the trigger is the look on someone's face, or an action by you which stimulates a comment.*
- *What happens next? Note down the sequence of interactions as if you were writing an acting script.*
- *How does it end? What happens to finish the interaction?*
- *How do you feel when it ends?*
- *How do you think the other person feels?*
- *What underlying message are you sending the other person?*
- *What underlying message are you picking up from them?*
- *How might you behave differently at the beginning to change the dynamics and get a positive outcome?*
- *What else can you change in your life so that you no longer need the negative strokes that you collect from this type of situation?*

CHAPTER 10: CREATIVE PROBLEM SOLVING

I read somewhere that a problem is when you have a goal but don't know how to reach it. This needs to be interpreted a bit – sometimes it's not even clear to us that we have a goal, and that itself is part of the problem. So we may have a problem that 'presents itself' clearly to us; we may foresee a problem looming in the future if we don't change what we are doing now; we may forecast a problem by imagining a different future and then recognising we need to change to make it happen. We may also be the problem in other people's eyes – I remember a notice I saw in a negotiator's office which said "Are you working on the problem – or are you part of it?"

The link between creativity and problem solving occurs because of the need to create new ideas to solve problems. I define creativity as 'having an insight which enlarges understanding'. By this I mean we are able to see something that we could not envisage before. We may be creative simply for the sake of it but generally the stimulus is because we recognise one of the problem formats I've just described.

Thus, the problem itself may be a direct one, as when a process fails to produce the required outputs. It may also be indirect, such as the 'problem' a customer has when no suitable product or service exists yet to satisfy their particular need. If we generate a creative idea on its own, we then set about identifying a corresponding problem that it will solve – if we can't find a need it's difficult to get other people to pay attention to our idea!

DISCOUNTING

One of the reasons that we may lack problem solving ability is our tendency to discount. Discounting in this context is an internal process whereby we minimise or ignore, without realising it, some aspect of ourselves, others or the situation. In other words, we fail to recognise that is actually there or what is possible. There are several ways in which we may do this; they form a series of levels where each level means that all levels above it are also discounted:

- the **stimulus** - the evidence of what is actually happening or is about to happen
- the **significance** -- the fact that the stimulus is an indication of a problem
- the **solutions** - the availability of any options we have to solve the problem
- the **skills** - our own or other peoples' abilities to identify, solve or take action on problems
- the **strategies** - how we might plan to implement action
- **success** itself – we don't believe we (or others) can achieve a successful outcome.

If we miss the *stimulus*, we fail to notice that something is happening. Perhaps there are occasional raised voices within our work group, which are the result of tensions between colleagues with different opinions. If we are engrossed in our own task, we may simply fail to hear the remarks even though they are said more loudly than the general conversational level. Many of us overlook clues to what is going on in this way. This is especially likely when we have become very used to the stimulus, such as when we don't really listen to what the office bore is telling us.

If we miss the stimulus altogether, we certainly won't recognise the *significance* of it. However, we may notice the stimulus and still fail to recognise that it indicates a problem. We may see someone pacing up and down but not suspect that they are stressed and anxious. Perhaps we pace because we find it easier to think that way, so we assume they are doing the same. We are unaware of the significance of whatever data we have observed.

We may notice the stimulus, realise that it is significant and represents a problem, but cannot imagine that there are any *solutions* for dealing with it. For example, a busy supervisor may see that a subordinate looks unwell, by noticing their flushed face, sneezing, etc. The supervisor who spots these signs may decide that this is significant; it is a heavy cold that will interfere with the employee's ability to do the work. However, the supervisor may even then believe there is nothing that can be done. They know there is no easy cure for the common cold and it does not occur to them that there are options about what to do now. So they do nothing, when they might have shown concern for the individual, suggested ways of minimising the discomfort, or even considered alternative means of getting the work done.

Next, we may notice a stimulus, recognise the significance, identify some solutions, and yet still take no action because we believe that people lack the *skills* to implement any solutions. An example of this stage occurred in the UK when smoking was banned within organisational premises. Many employees who were smokers believed they lacked the skills to give up smoking, even though they accepted that smoking was a significant problem and that there were strategies that other people had used to break the habit.

Having accepted that we or others do have the skills we need, or can acquire them, we may then baulk at the notion of implementing any kind of *strategy*. The smoker may complain that they are too busy right now to add in any non-smoking activities such as joining a support group, or too stretched financially to pay for patches, ignoring the fact that they would have the money usually spent on cigarettes – and that they might get state funding. Discounting is not logical!

Finally, the last level is all about *success*. Some of us seem struck in a belief that we are not a successful person. So we notice the situation, realise the significance of it, can identify solutions, have the skills and have put together a strategy – and then we just don't do anything. Maybe we'll do it next week!

Discounting by Management

In Chapter 7 I mentioned the ways that managers inadvertently stroke, and hence reinforce, the behaviour of people who have poor attendance records. We can use discounting as an alternative way of understanding what happens. I will explain later in this chapter how we can present information to managers in order to overcome discounting at whatever level it is occurring.

At the *stimulus* level, we have managers (and sometimes whole organisations) that have no attendance records. Hence, there is no information (evidence) that would alert them to the fact that some people fail to come to work regularly. City trading houses are an example of this – their highly paid staff are not expected to sign in each day. Some small companies also overlook this because they avoid having too many administrative systems.

At the *significance* level, there may be attendance records but they are not easily accessible. Perhaps they are kept in the wages office, where they are used only to calculate payments. Managers may assume that the levels are reasonable, without ever checking the statistics. In some organisations, even when managers are shown the absence figures they merely take it for granted that these are industry norms and not worth worrying about.

At the *solutions* level, management recognise that absence levels are a problem. However, they do not believe there are any viable strategies for dealing with it. Even if they are advised of methods used in other organisations, they may dismiss these as irrelevant in their particular industry.

Then, at the *skills* level, management may conclude that they themselves lack the ability to implement the solutions, or that the employees are incapable of learning to come to work regularly, or that the trades unions or works councils would never agree, or that senior management would never support them.

At the *strategy* level, the rationale is likely to be about having too many initiatives already on the go, or there is not enough money in the budget, or no-one with the time to be the project leader.

Finally, at the *success* level, management may not want to face up to the fact that they must lead from the front and may be unwilling to deal with the absenteeism of one of their colleagues, or a senior manager's secretary.

Discounting by Individuals

An instance of discounting by individuals occurred in a group of hospital pharmacists. The hospital was introducing total quality management and wanted to set targets for patient care. The pharmacy group were required to look at the way they treated patients who were collecting prescription items prior to leaving the hospital. A consultant from the personnel section had been allocated to help them think this through.

What the consultant found was that patients often waited a long time for their medicines. They were not always dealt with in order of arrival, but had no way of knowing that this was because different staff handled different groups of drugs. A small survey of patients found that many of them were baffled by the system, felt they wasted time waiting because the pharmacists were too busy, and were resigned to low standards of care.

When the survey results were discussed by the pharmacists, the following reactions were apparent:

Stimulus discounted: Peggy was surprised. She had always thought they were doing a reasonable job and all the patients she had dealt with herself had seemed satisfied. Peggy had not noticed any signs of impatience – she had discounted even the impatient body language that was evident to most observers.

Significance discounted: Todd knew the patients were unhappy but didn't realise it had anything to do with the service from the pharmacists. He thought it was because the patients were in discomfort due to their illnesses. Todd discounted the significance of what he saw, by overlooking the fact that these patients were leaving the hospital and were therefore unlikely to still be in a great deal of physical discomfort from their ailments.

Solutions discounted: Zoran had realised that the patients were dissatisfied with the pharmacy service. However, Zoran reckoned that all pharmacies had the same problems. As far as he was concerned, there were no solutions to this lack of resources; the way they allocated the drugs between them could not be changed; they had the best system it was possible to devise in the circumstances.

Skills discounted: Maria had plenty of ideas about how the system could be improved. She had never bothered to suggest them because she didn't think anyone would listen to her. She was the junior pharmacist and doubted her ability to influence the others. Even if she did, she was sure that they would not be able to interest senior management in their ideas.

Strategies discounted: Valentyna knew about the problems and thought Maria's ideas were excellent. However, although she was a Senior Pharmacist, she had little confidence in management and assumed they would simply reject any strategies on the grounds of cost.

Success discounted: even if the group had presented proposals to management and had them approved, they were generally so demotivated that they would have paid lip-service only to the new approach – and patients would have sensed this and still been dissatisfied.

The Discounting Process

Although I have described behaviour in the examples, discounting itself is actually an internal process. It serves to maintain our frame of reference. By 'not noticing' things which would conflict with what we believe, or want to believe, we are able to avoid changing our view of the world, of others, and of ourselves. Because the discounting is outside our awareness, it is difficult to spot without feedback from other people. This is why it can be so helpful to talk things over with someone else. Coaching and counselling can be thought of as antidotes to discounting; effective coaches and counsellors help clients to see what they have been overlooking – whether that relates to their awareness of events, their understanding of the significance, or their opportunities to do things differently.

At the root of discounting is a wish that we could leave it to someone else to deal with our problems. As adults, we know that such a wish is inappropriate; however a part of us would still sometimes like to be free of responsibility. If we can act as if the problem doesn't exist for long enough, perhaps someone else will come along and deal with it for us. If we give out signals that it's too hard for us, maybe they will rescue us by taking over.

We may also adopt the other side of this avoidance tactic when someone else is trying to sidestep their responsibility. As they discount their ability, so do we. We convince ourselves that they really do need us to rescue them. Discounting in one form or another is an integral part of the dynamic of playing psychological games. We can only adopt Rescuer, Persecutor or Victim roles if we are overlooking something in the situation. Otherwise we would recognise the repetitive, predictable nature of the game and its unsatisfactory outcome.

When other people discount in different areas to us, we can often spot what they are doing. If we notice the stimulus and they don't, we know they are discounting it. Similarly, if we can see the significance, or realise there are solutions, skills and strategies that could be applied, we can identify what they are overlooking. There are also some more general ways in which discounting shows up.

If we consider first our general behaviour, then evidence of discounting might include: doing nothing, as when we do not respond to events or simply look anxious; over-adapting, when we go along with what someone else suggests without even considering whether it is right for us; agitating, as when we pace about, chain-smoke, or otherwise occupy ourselves with repetitive actions which take our energy away from problem solving; and incapacitation, when we get psychosomatically sick so we cannot be expected to do anything about the problem, or sometimes we may get so distressed or angry that we have to be restrained for our own good and for the safety of others - which still means we can't be expected to solve problems.

Occasionally, we may even become violent as a form of incapacitating ourselves; while others are restraining us we will not be expected to problem solve. I recall employing a less extreme version of this many years ago when I used to storm out and slam the door of my manager's office. This was guaranteed to earn me respite from his bad temper but at the same time I was 'allowed' not to do anything about problem solving, because who could expect someone to think when they were as angry as I was. (This approach is not recommended – unless of course you now work for that same unreasonable manager!)

At the micro level, our discounting may show up in our speech patterns. We are likely to be grandiose, claiming that things are 'always' or 'never' so. We make sweeping generalisations based on very skimpy evidence. One example may be used by us as the basis for believing that we have identified a major new trend.

We may also redefine – a process whereby we answer at a tangent or even change the subject completely. Asked if our report will be ready on time, we may respond by complaining about the lack of clerical support. Only later will our questioner realise that they still do not have our answer on whether the report will be ready. Another common example of redefining is that infuriating response "What would you like to do?" said in reply to exactly the same question.

Challenging Discounting

Dealing with redefining is relatively straightforward once we have identified that it is happening. At micro level, we can challenge (politely) the process by repeating the original question, and by querying grandiose statements. We might ask if they really mean always or never; will they tell us their evidence for generalisations; can we just make sure their previous experiences are truly relevant in the current situation.

To challenge discounting more generally, and thereby help others with their problem solving and decision making, we can operate to a sequence that relates to the typical patterns, checking that:

1. they have noticed the stimulus, they know what is happening
2. they realise that it is significant, that it represents a problem for them
3. they accept that there will be a solution, that something can be done
4. they know that they or others have the skills to act, or can acquire the skills
5. that they devise a strategy for implementation, they can produce an action plan
6. they are willing to deal with any of the ways in which implementation might be undermined, and especially with the ways in which they or colleagues might unwittingly sabotage the plan

There will be no point in asking them to consider aspects earlier in this sequence than they have reached themselves. Talking about solutions makes no sense to someone who has not even accepted that they have a problem; urging them to draw up action plans is a waste of time if they lack confidence in their ability to change.

It is as if we are standing on some steps and we are higher up than they are. I call these the Steps to Success and, as you will see in Figure 10.1, it is no use talking to someone from a higher step – they will not understand what we mean. We have to walk down to the step they are on, and preferably at least one step below that. We can then, metaphorically, take their hand and help them up to the top of the steps. We do this by prompting and questioning, and sometimes by giving information, so they become aware of the facts at each step.

Figure 10.1: Steps to Sucess

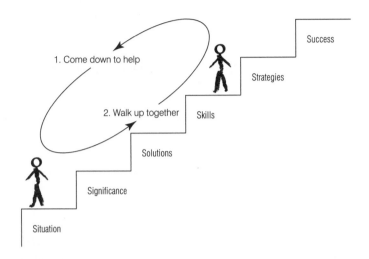

We can challenge discounting at an individual and an organisational level. As an individual, we will probably need someone else to act as 'devil's advocate' for us, to challenge us to notice the areas we are inadvertently overlooking. Within an organisation, we can probably better identify where creativity and problem solving are being lost if we are not the person who is responsible for the system. This is why quality circles come up with such good results; the members of the circle are unlikely to discount in exactly the same way as each other and as the person who initially designed the work procedures.

MORE ABOUT EGO STATES

Assuming you have avoided the dangers of discounting, there are a number of additional insights that you can gain by considering the contributions of your different ego states. In Chapter 4, I described how, from when we were small, we have been storing away memories of what happens to us and how we respond. I will now explain how the concept of ego states can help us understand why some of us seem more creative than others, and why some of us appear to have more trouble making decisions about how to solve problems.

Scientists continue to explore how much of our adult personality is due to genetics (nature) and how much to the way we are brought up (nurture). What they do generally agree on is that both have an effect. We should not be too quick to dismiss ourselves or others as being incapable of creativity. Maybe we were not so lucky in the genetic lottery and failed to get our share of innate creativity. We will still have quite a lot, as you will see if you watch any small child making toys out of whatever is available. There is still plenty of scope for removing some of the inhibiting effects that social conditioning will have had as we grew up.

Earlier, I showed that our internal ego states could be broadly described as our systems for experience (Internal Parent), evaluation (Internal Adult) and emotion (Internal Child). If we now extract from these systems the parts of most relevance to creativity, we can substitute three more qualities as in Figure 10.2.

Our **Internal Child** contains our creativity, as part of our natural responses to the world and to other people.

Our **Internal Adult** contains our ability to process information, think logically and solve problems, and therefore enables us to be competent.

Our **Internal Parent** contains the 'messages' and opinions which are significant in our lives, and seeks to ensure that we adopt solutions that conform.

Internal Child

Our Internal Child is curious and creative. As babies, we display this via our Natural Child as we begin to explore our world. We are not satisfied with looking – we want to touch things, hold them, turn them over, put them into our mouths. As we gain mobility, many more objects come within our reach. Left to our own devices, we will find and play happily with almost anything. Cardboard boxes become dens; stones become animals, cars, or food for dolls; pans become hats; stuffed toys become fierce dragons. This is our natural creativity in effect.

Figure 10.2: Creativity and Ego States

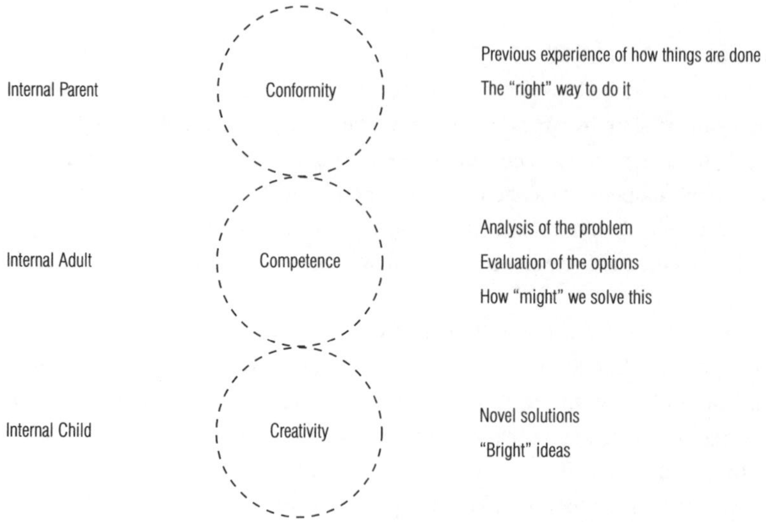

Internal Parent	Conformity	Previous experience of how things are done The "right" way to do it
Internal Adult	Competence	Analysis of the problem Evaluation of the options How "might" we solve this
Internal Child	Creativity	Novel solutions "Bright" ideas

Unfortunately, many of us experience curbs on this creativity and curiosity. Objects are moved out of reach in case we break them. We are put into a playpen for our own safety but this stops us exploring our surroundings. We may be unlucky enough to reach something dangerous and get burned by the fire or spill something hot over us from the stove. Perhaps our caregiver gets angry, so that we come to associate our actions with fear as we are shouted at, or pain as we are chastised. When we put our creative ideas into effect, we may be ridiculed. In these ways, we learn that it is not always wise to show our natural reactions to the world about us. Our Internal Child stores away a knot in the tree rings – an unhappy emotion in our memory bank – that will replay as an unpleasant sensation when we are tempted to use our Natural Child in the future.

There are also conflicts between our creativity and our need to learn from others. People teach us the 'right way to do things. We learn that pans are for cooking in and that it is unhygienic to put them on our heads. At school, more of this teaching takes place, as we discover what low marks we get if we make up our own answers to the teacher's questions instead of quoting from the textbook.

Some of us will be lucky enough to be exposed to people who encourage us to be creative. We will learn that it is okay to have bright ideas and to experiment. Those of us who were allowed to take our toys apart to see how they worked will have retained our innate sense of curiosity and will be ready to explore novel ways of solving problems. We may well go into occupations where creativity is seen as appropriate, such as inventing, advertising or entertainment.

However, by the time we are adults, many more of us will have decided long ago to push much of our original creativity underground. We will accept that our work places more demands on our knowledge and experience than it does on our ability to produce innovative ideas. We will, therefore, display to the world our Adapted Child more often than we show our Natural Child. Indeed, over the years we are likely to forget that we ever had much creative ability and come to believe that our adaptation is really us. Hence the common myth that only some of us are gifted with creativity.

Internal Parent
Reinforcing the learning and adaptation process of our Internal Child ego state is our Internal Parent. This is the repository of all the things that people tell us and demonstrate to us. We store away copies of their behaviour and replay these in the future, both internally as memories and externally as ways to act towards others. If we were encouraged to be creative, we will have filed away copies of that encouraging behaviour which we will now use to encourage others in turn. We will also be comfortable about our own creativity.

However, many of us have different recollections. For example, if we were laughed at when we wore a pan as a hat, we are likely to laugh in the same way when we see a child doing as we used to. If we were told our ideas were impractical, we will use our Controlling Parent to tell others why their ideas are impractical. Thus, the implicit messages about creativity being stupid or a waste of time are passed on through generations. Check this for yourself by recalling what happens when you offer an idea. The more truly different the idea is, the more you are likely to receive a sceptical or outrightly adverse response.

Internally, we may react negatively to ourselves at the first sign of any creativity. Inside our heads we may replicate a scene from childhood; this time we have our copy of the grown-up stored in memory and we use it in an internal dialogue with our Internal Child. We then feel uncomfortable and decide our idea is not worth pursuing. When we replay Internal Parent in this way, we may also stimulate a corresponding replay of a recording in Internal Child so that we feel discomfort that is related to the past. This feeling can be re-experienced powerfully enough in the present to stop us being creative even though other people are encouraging us to put forward ideas.

Internal Adult

Our mediator between our Internal Parent and Child is our Internal Adult. With luck, this ego state also filters the effects of other people that we have 'filed' within ourselves so that we have some protection from their conditioning. Internal Adult also deals with the demands and wants left over from childhood that may arise within our Internal Child.

Our input includes data from our Internal Parent, which has stored away our experiences of how such matters were tackled in the past. This ego state will provide us with options that we recall being used successfully on previous occasions. It will be up to our Internal Adult to analyse whether the current situation is similar enough to the past to make an option relevant.

The contribution to the process from Internal Child is two-fold; it consists of our emotional response to the situation and, hopefully, our creativity. Our Internal Adult may have to deal with feelings of discomfort if being creative led to unpleasant experiences in the past. It will also have to sift through any ideas we do have to check which ones could be implemented without too many problems. It is as if Internal Adult takes the raw material from Internal Child, imagines what would happen if the various ideas were pursued, and then develops suitable options.

In practice, Internal Adult is likely to arrive at solutions that are a mix of Internal Child creativity and Internal Parent experience. Provided we are not too cluttered with negative messages, our Internal Child can see totally new and creative ways of doing things. Provided we are not too set in our ways, our Internal Parent sees the implications of the new idea based on what happened in similar situations in the past and checks for us that the results are likely to conform enough to expectations. Internal Adult synthesises the two sets of inputs and adds any relevant external data, such as information and opinions from other people, before making the final selection of a course of action that will demonstrate our ability to be competently creative.

DECISION MAKING

The impact of our ego states in decision making is just as significant as on our creative generation of ideas and options.

When our decision making process is functioning effectively, it contains the elements shown in Figure 10.3. Our Internal Parent provides experience, Internal Child contributes an emotional aspect, and Internal Adult evaluates both of these and compares them with what is occurring externally.

In this way, we identify problems, recognise the need to find a solution, consider the advantages and disadvantages of various options, review the implications, weigh the probabilities of success, and make decisions. We may do this in fractions of a second or it may be a process that extends over days as we keep coming back to the problem.

However, we do not always manage such a balanced and considered process. If we do not listen to ourselves internally, one ego state may have too much prominence and another may be excluded from the thinking process. When this happens, we are denied an important part of the input we need for a balanced result. Because this exclusion operates as if the ego state does not exist, we will be unaware that we are not operating on the full set.

Many times a day we will make decisions without noticing we have done so. This happens when we rely on our Internal Parent to contain something relevant already; we merely scan

Figure 10.3: Decision Making and Ego States

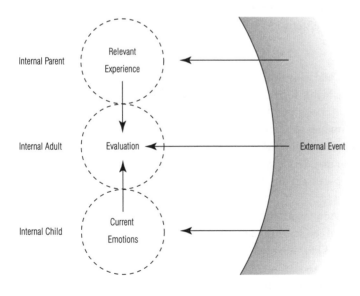

rapidly through our previous experience and use the decision we made last time. A significant advantage is that it saves time if we can recycle an earlier sequence.

When we consciously consider a decision, we have to select from the past which recordings will be most applicable to our current situation. Over the years we have decided what is important to us and what can be disregarded. We also have the facility to continually update our Internal Parent; we are likely to do this each time we make a decision that is not based in the past, recording at the same time whether the new decision was successful or not.

Exclusion of Internal Parent will mean we lack access to previous relevant experiences and the knowledge that goes with them. We will have to think the situation through as if it has never been encountered before. At the very least, this will waste a lot of time. It will probably also result in significant aspects being overlooked.

The input to decision making from Internal Child concerns our emotional responses to the potential options. There will be internal support for a decision which gets us what we want, takes account of our anxieties, results in a good feeling for us. There will be internal resistance to decisions which might have unpleasant consequences for us. Such consequences might include being left without something we want, incurring the wrath of another person, losing status in the eyes of our colleagues, having to work late instead of going out with friends for the evening – any of the things which are so important to our sense of comfort.

Because our Internal Child also contains recordings of how we felt in the past, there is the danger that we may 'rubberband' into these old recordings without being aware of it. We will repeat an old emotional response as if it were occurring in the present. This will seriously undermine the effectiveness of our decision making as it will now be based on out-of-date feelings.

Exclusion of Internal Child will result in lack of attention to how we feel about the situation. Our decisions may be highly logical but will ignore any emotional responses associated with carrying them out. Decisions that lead to overwork are often made in this mode; our normal feelings of tiredness are repressed. If we exclude our own Internal Child from decision making, we may well overlook the significance of it as far as other people are concerned. A manager may decide to introduce a new system without recognising that staff may react negatively because it interferes with their job satisfaction.

We need our Internal Adult to act as the referee, seeing the events personally by watching the players (the external ego states) and checking internally by asking the lines people (the other internal ego states) for their perspectives. And just as a referee consults the lines people, Internal Adult takes account of the situation we are in. We take in data from the environment, including noting the reactions or potential reactions to other people to any actions we might take. Rather like the referee who calls off the match when the crowd invades the pitch, except that this is an exception for them whereas a well-functioning Internal Adult ego state routinely monitors the external situation. Thus, Internal Adult balances the events around us against our responses in terms of beliefs and feelings, evaluates, and then comes to a conclusion.

Exclusion of Internal Adult occurs when our Internal Parent opinions or Internal Child feelings are especially powerful. When this happens, we make our decisions without an adequate evaluation of the current situation and the available options. We may insist on obsolete working practices because they were effective in the past, or opt to spend our money on an expensive new car when we are already in debt.

Our Internal Adult may also be weakened if exclusion occurs as the result of an interaction or in a customary style within a relationship. This is similar to the hierarchy of ego states described in Chapter 5. In such a case, one person will provide the 'thinking' from Internal Parent, and possibly Internal Adult, although this ego state may be missing altogether. The other person supplies the 'thinking' from Internal Child. The opinions and past experiences of one will be coupled with the feelings and wishes of the other. Each will feel unable to make a decision on their own.

Our decision making may also become contaminated. This occurs when the detail that belongs in one ego state 'leaks' into another. If Internal Parent contaminates Internal Adult, we think our opinions are facts and we fail to recognise the assumptions we are making. We are likely to justify our conclusions by quoting spurious connections, such as arguing that we must be right this time because we were right in the past. Prejudices are contaminations; we may quote from the specific to the general and claim that one negative proves that a whole racial group are suspect.

When Internal Child contaminates Internal Adult, our emotions cloud our judgment. We believe we are being logical because we have convinced ourselves that everyone must feel as we do. If we feel angry about the way the manager spoke to us, we are convinced that everyone would feel angry if given the same provocation. Our decision to go on strike seems to us to be the only logical option we have.

NOISICED

There will be many times when the quality of our decision making will improve if we can ensure that all ego states are actively involved. This is more likely to happen if we use a structured approach. Overleaf, therefore, I outline a simple decision making process, called NOISICED (or DECISION spelled backwards) after the first letter for each step. Applying this to a current problem you wish to resolve will generate a number of additional insights that will help you make a better balanced decision.

We cannot avoid discounting sometimes because this process occurs outside our awareness. However, we can minimise the impact by using colleagues as sounding boards, and by using a structured approach to decision making as a safety precaution before we take action.

We can also 'give ourselves permission' to be creative problem solvers, recognising that some of the messages we have stored from the past are unnecessary barriers to the exercise of our true abilities.

Need	*Why do I need to make a decision?*
	Why now?
Objective	*What do I want to achieve - in the short term?*
	What do I want to achieve - in the long term?
Information	*What information do I have about the problem?*
	What information do I have about possible decisions?
	What information do I still lack?
	How can I get it?
Strategies	*How can I achieve what I want?*
	How else?
	And how else?
	Are these the only options?
Investigate	*What is good about each option?*
	What are the snags with each option?
	How might I get round the snags?
Choose	*Which option is most likely to help me meet my objective?*
	Are there clear second and third choices?
Ego States	*Internal Parent - What does my previous experience tell me about each opinion?*
	Internal Child - How do I feel about each option?
	Internal Adult - What is the probability of success with each option?
Decide	*Which action am I most likely to be successful with?*
	What action(s) will I take to ensure I reach my objective?

CHAPTER 11: ALL THE WORLD'S A STAGE

Robin Hood

Eric lived his life as if he were Robin Hood. He took from the rich to give to the poor. Eric was a trade union convenor. He did his best to extract as much money as possible from the 'rich' management to give to the 'poor' employees.

The shop stewards were Eric's merry men (and women). Sometimes they went to negotiations (fought) together, with Eric as the leader. At other times, a shop steward might deal with a foreman (one of the knights) unaided. However, Eric was called in if the discussions involved a manager (one of the barons). Eric also took charge when the negotiations applied to the whole factory (all of Nottingham) because then the Factory Manager (the Sheriff) would be across the table.

Eric disliked the Managing Director (Prince John). He knew the MD was behind it whenever the Factory Manager introduced new production methods that meant the employees had to work harder for the same money. He wished the Chairman (King Richard) would get more involved in the running of the company. However, as far as he could see, the Chairman was too busy with public relations and keeping the city financiers happy (off at the Crusades). Eric suspected that the Sheriff of Nottingham and Prince John were conspiring to keep King Richard out of the way.

Eric wondered if the situation would ever change. Would the Chairman one day realise what was going on and sack the MD and the Factory Manager? Or would the MD and the Factory Manager find a way of getting rid of Eric? So far Eric had been careful not to give them the chance but they were always looking for ways to undermine him. At one time they had even tried offering the employees concessions in return for giving up their trade union membership. The employees had rejected the offer then but Eric knew it was getting harder all the time to persuade them to go on strike (go into the forest) when he needed to resist management's demands.

Eric, like many of us, was living out his life as if it were a well-known story.

To understand why this happens, we need to step out of the world of work for a while, and remember what it was like to be very young. The world was new to us, people were new to us, behaviour was new to us. We had to work out our own set of theories so we could know what to expect and how to act. This is very difficult for a small child, especially when the grown-ups are not always consistent.

We struggled with a mass of incoming data, doing our best to classify and sort it just like a researcher. We set up file headings so we could collect together similar ideas. We kept searching for a pattern that would help us make sense of it. Eventually, we finished up with a network of patterns, held together by the common thread that represents our way through life.

SCRIPT

This pattern formed what is called our *script*. It is our best attempt at making sense of what we observed and experienced when we were a small child. Having put together a jigsaw of so many different parts, we then allowed the pattern to slip out of our conscious awareness. However, it continues to form the basis for our subsequent behaviours and beliefs, so that we are continually reinforcing the pattern by fitting current events into it – even if we have to massage them a little to get them to fit!

Script is used here in the same way as in the theatre; to mean a story that is to be acted out before an audience. Our life script, therefore, is an unconscious plan of how we will get from birth to death. We decide on it when we are small, as a way of making sense of our world. Into its design goes a whole range of things – how we perceive the world, our observations of how the big people behave, what they and our peers do and say to us, what we overhear, the stories we are told, even the television programmes we watch. It is fascinating to see how the same themes appear in myths, fairy tales and news stories the world over: only the names of the characters change.

Take for example the story of Cinderella. Do you know anyone who works hard for an ungrateful boss (wicked stepmother) and senior colleagues (ugly sisters)? Do these wicked people take the credit for the work Cinderella does? Will a fairy godmother, or godfather, come along one day, perhaps called a mentor! And will the godparent then identify a prince, and make sure that Cinders goes to a dance (a meeting) at which she will leave behind a shoe (a project report)? Will the prince then insist on learning who really wrote the report, even though the colleagues claim it was a team effort? Will the prince then become Cinderella's new manager and treat her properly, give her jewels (a salary increase) and a castle to run (lots of responsibility)? Are you Cinderella waiting for your luck to change?

The scripts of most people are of the more mundane variety so they may not be noticeable until we know what to look out for. However, we can observe plenty of more 'exciting' scripts, when people seem set on creating problems for themselves or others. Tragic scripts involve people committing suicide or murder, becoming dictators or martyrs. They may drink themselves to death or work themselves to death. Along the way, they will affect the lives of other too, such as when the company goes bankrupt and people lose their jobs and savings.

As in the best suspense drama, we may keep much of our script secret from the other players although the audience can see what is going on. At work, it is often the uninvolved person who perceives most clearly what is happening, while those engaged in the action are too close to see the total pattern. We observe someone who seems determined to set themselves up to get the sack, and a supervisor who will become the executioner. Yet even though we may try to intervene, the employee seems unable to heed our warnings or act on our advice. This is script in action.

A major component of our script is the particular story that we invent or select. We choose the story when we are quite small, amending it as necessary so that it fits our own circumstances. For some people the selection occurs suddenly, as the result of a particularly traumatic incident such as absence of a loved one. However, most of us probably complete our jigsaw gradually, piecing things together and testing various designs until we find one that fits. We may no longer remember hearing the original version, having embroidered and embellished it to make it more suitable. If you doubt this, try comparing recollections of fairy stories with your colleagues and see what different versions emerge.

Our Role in the Story

Within our story, we allocate ourselves a role to play. We will not necessarily be the hero or heroine; our character will depend on what we have come to believe about ourselves by the time we make the selection. We may identify most with the lead, with the villain, with one of the supporting roles, or even with one of the bit parts if we have decided to be especially self-effacing. We will then somehow manage to surround ourselves with the other players that we need to move the story on. We seem to have some psychological mechanism that enables us to identify 'suitable' companions, as if we can sniff out people whose stories will dovetail with our own.

Robin Hood the Union Official will seek out companies where there is a Sheriff of Nottingham to do battle with – and if a would-be Sheriff can't find a suitable opponent he will be quite likely to act in such an unacceptable way that a suitable crusader emerges from the crowd to fight with him. Cinderella will need an organisational culture where ugly sisters can function – and may be so unassertive that quite reasonable colleagues will be tempted to take advantage of Cinders' good nature. Different Cinderellas will have different views on how long they will stay downtrodden before serendipitously bringing themselves to the attention of a godparent and prince.

Associated with our role in the story will be our beliefs about ourselves, other people and the world in general. We will have opted to be a winner, a loser, a survivor, a fighter, a saviour, a destroyer, or perhaps a mediocrity. We will therefore be operating on a basis of one-up or one-down. Others will be viewed by us as superior or inferior too. The world may seem hostile and threatening, challenging and exciting, boring and dull. Our windows on the world provide the basic frame of reference for our scripts so we will believe that we or others, or all of us, are not OK.

There are likely to be physical/emotional components too – some feelings within our body that we come to regard as normal. We may tense particular areas such as our neck or shoulders. We may even hold our head in a specific way, as British police officers must to see under their hats. Regular feelings of discomfort in our stomach, frequent migraine-type headaches, nervous indigestion, and similar ailments may form part of our pattern without us recognising the true cause. That is not to say that such problems may not also arise due to physical or genetic reasons; a clue to script is when we accept such symptoms as usual or do nothing to cure them.

Our Interpretations

Our script will contain even more specific elements that determine the way we behave on a day-to-day basis. The primary substance of these is provided for us as children by our parents and other caregivers. However, we still have considerable influence over what is actually incorporated. We listen and observe, then interpret in our own way. The same event will be dealt with quite differently by different children.

Suppose, for example, that mother is tired and feels ill. Her three year old is demanding attention and she wants to rest. She has no other adult available at present to take over the childcare while she has a short nap. In response to yet another demand from the child, she angrily tells him to go away. The child does not comprehend the circumstances; he knows only that mother is refusing his request. He therefore interprets this the best way he can, which may be to conclude any of the following:

- She means go away for ever.
- She means pester some more before she will say yes.
- Nobody loves me.
- It will be alright later on.
- If I cry she'll cuddle me.
- If I cry she'll punish me.
- If I cry she'll beat me.
- I'll wait till Daddy comes home.
- I'll never ask her again.

...almost anything, it seems, but the correct interpretation that she is tired now but still loves him and will play with him again later.

In addition to individual differences in response, our conclusions are affected by what has happened before. If this is the first time mother has been like this, we may be more shocked and therefore react as if to a major tragedy. On the other hand, we may be better able to put the event into perspective. If mother acts this way often, then we may test out alternatives whilst gradually making a decision based on the constant repetitions.

Even children who have been the target of very damaging interactions may still decide to opt for a positive conclusion. However, it is obviously much harder for a small child to remain optimistic if they are severely abused. I am not saying, therefore, that parents should not be held accountable for how they treat their children. Likewise, we should not be blamed if our childhood circumstances were such that we are psychologically damaged and continue to approach the world in the light of our early experiences.

Injunctions

A legal injunction is an order that prohibits someone from doing something. In our scripts, *injunctions* serve the same function – they are things we are forbidden to do. We may have been told them directly but we are just as likely to have inferred them as part of our creation of a framework. Typical injunctions include prescriptions against being successful, against being important, against being a child or against growing up, against thinking or against feeling, and even against existing. They sound like slogans – "Don't think!", "Don't succeed!", "Don't grow up!" and so on.

For example, when we were small we may have been told repeatedly that we did things wrong, that we were not successful like our brother or sister, that we were never going to change, that we were likely to fail our exams, and that therefore we would never hold down a good job. We might also have decided we would be unsuccessful at work because we misinterpreted it when a teacher told us it would be difficult to find employment – they were thinking of the general economic situation but we assumed they meant us!

With a *Don't Succeed* injunction, we expect to fail. We feel doomed to do so. We may, therefore, turn up at work late or inappropriately dressed. We may doubt our own ability so much that we turn down opportunities. We may be diffident, or cynical, or seem paranoid about making a mistake. There are any number of ways in which we can set ourselves up to not succeed. And each time we fail, we have reinforced the injunction. If we do this a lot, the management will seek to dismiss us, providing even more evidence for us that we cannot succeed.

Phyllis had the injunction *Don't Be Close*. She was an accountant working for a public utility. Phyllis had no injunctions directly about thinking or succeeding, so she had studied well and passed her accountancy exams with flying colours. She was now on a senior grade and in charge of several trainee accountants and bookkeeping staff. At this stage in her career, the organisation introduced a customer care initiative. Previously, as a utility they had not really thought of their consumers as customers. Now, all staff were expected to implement the new corporate mission. Part of this involved treating colleagues in other departments as internal customers. Another important aspect of the new culture was an emphasis on teamwork.

Phyllis found these two themes very difficult. She had always 'kept herself to herself' – now she needed to work much more closely with other people. In order to treat people as internal customers, Phyllis had to spend time with them finding out how her section could serve them better. It became obvious that she did not do this as well as some of the other accountants. She lacked the personal skills, so that her questioning sounded more like an interrogation: "What data do you need?" "Why do you need it?" "What will you do with it?"

In ego state terms, Phyllis came over as permanent Functional Adult, always logical but lacking any real warmth. Even Adapted Child was missing, so that Phyllis tended to skip the niceties and get straight down to business. This lack of social graces left her 'customers' feeling that she was not truly interested in them. Within her own team, there were similar problems. Her staff all had enormous respect for her accountancy expertise. However, they had become used to working very much as individuals, going to Phyllis for advice when necessary. Although there were some friendships within the group, these tended to be kept separate to their work activities. Because of her Don't Be Close injunction, Phyllis was unable to change her own style enough to establish a real team atmosphere.

Attributions

Attributions are qualities which are attributed to us. In other words, they are the characteristics that we are told to have. We may have attributed to us both negative and positive features, such as being told often when we are small that we are beautiful but clumsy. The attributions are labels, defining how an adult has determined we will be. We grow up believing that the attributes are really a part of our personality, and we are very likely to adjust our behaviour accordingly.

At work we may therefore limit our behaviour to suit. We may then be seen as stupid, slow, clumsy, nervous, highly-strung, or a host of other qualities. If people comment, we are not surprised as we feel as if we have always been like that. Even positive attributions may be a problem. This is because the qualities are being 'forced' on us. Being told we are clever or beautiful or confident when we may really feel scared and vulnerable, puts us under considerable pressure to pretend. We hide our genuine responses so as not to disappoint the grown-ups, and may eventually lose touch with our true emotions and our spontaneity.

The process of attributions demonstrates well how scripts are often passed along through generations of a family. We may be told we have the same characteristics as an older member of the family. This form of attributing also saves a lot of time; if we are told we are just like Uncle Frank we can add the detail ourselves. If Uncle Frank drank a lot, got arrested often, washed infrequently, and came to a sticky end, we now know exactly what to do to prove the attribution correct. If Uncle Frank was a pillar of society, went to church twice a week, never lost his temper and was generous to charities, we may feel obliged to demonstrate the same qualities.

Several shop assistants in a well-known department store were examples of attributions in effect. Naomi was convinced that she was sensible but not very clever – so she dealt sensibly with children who had become separated from their parents but struggled to understand the new stock control system. Phil, on the other hand, knew he was clever but clumsy. He had no problem with the stock control system but he had a habit of dropping items when he was handed them to wrap. Fortunately, he worked in the menswear department so the goods were not breakable.

Melanie had been brought up to be very assertive, like her Aunt Helen who had been a top advertising executive. When Melanie acted like Helen it caused quite a problem behind the counter in the cosmetics section. Melanie worked alongside Indira, who had grown up being told how beautiful she was. This could have been quite a helpful attribution considering her job, especially as it was also true. However, Indira tended to assume that all truly beautiful people looked like her. When she demonstrated the cosmetics, she used the colours and shadings that suited her own face.

The example of Indira shows us how even positive attributes can cause problems. Indira really was beautiful, but believed this was her only good point so became totally focussed on it. Naomi felt obliged to be sensible all the time, in the same way that Melanie persisted in acting like a confident advertising executive when her supervisor just wanted her to serve the customers.

Permissions

The key to injunctions and attributions is the lack of choice. We believe the injunctions and attributions are true and that we cannot change our character or our behaviour. Over the years, we have woven them into our scripts so they reinforce our roles. Out of awareness, we limit ourselves to repeat the same unhelpful sequences – instead of recognising that we have a range of options available to us in any situation. To counteract the injunctions and attributions, we need *permissions* – beliefs that will allow us to be autonomous, make choices about how to feel and act, and enable us to live a full life.

The most important permission is to exist; when we arrive in the world we need to experience being wanted and loved. We all receive this permission to some extent although the balance between permission and injunction varies between individuals. Other permissions we need are to be aware of sensations, to feel emotions, to think, to be close to others. Later, we need permissions to grow up and to succeed in the world.

The permissions are transmitted to us in the same ways we acquire the injunctions – through touch, hearing, sight, body language, and through intuition. We pick up some directly when our parents hug us and tell us they love us, just as we may receive some injunctions directly when they chastise us. We also interpret a lot, based on the ways we are treated. The more definitely and clearly our parents communicate positive messages to us, the less script-bound we are likely to become.

As adults, we still need some permissions. We may get these from managers and colleagues, who give us positive messages about our worth and abilities. Effective managers are well aware of the need to demonstrate their recognition of good performance. The most effective way to improve the work of a poor performer is to concentrate on what they do right.

Reminding people of their errors will usually serve only to leave them more anxious and hence more prone to problems. Telling people emphatically that they are capable of good work is much more likely to lead to successful accomplishments. This is what is meant when managers are advised to "Catch them doing something right!"

Kieran was a co-ordinator on a scheme for training unemployed young people. He was good at most aspects of his job. He got on well with the young people, he was effective at arranging work experience placements for them, he liaised competently with their off-the-job tutors. However, Kieran had a Don't Be Important injunction. He was capable of more but did not believe it. His manager, Nina, recognised this and decided to do what she could to encourage Kieran to develop himself. She used every opportunity she could to stroke Kieran for his performance. She then created new opportunities for him. Or instance, she 'found' herself double-booked in her diary so that Kieran had to represent her at a meeting with senior management. As Nina had known, he handled the meeting well and she was then able to schedule him for similar sessions in the future.

On another occasion, Kieran participated in a training workshop run by the government department responsible for the scheme. On his return, he described how he had contributed to several sessions. When the government department asked for presenters for future workshops, Nina encouraged Kieran to volunteer. The presentations, the meetings with senior managers, and Nina's constant congratulations combined to give Kieran enough permission to overcome his reluctance about being important. When Nina moved to another job, Kieran was appointed as her successor – a job he had previously thought was too 'high profile' for him.

Counterscript

One other element that forms part of the jigsaw of our script is our *counterscript*. This is a set of ways of behaving that allow us to feel we are functioning effectively. These characteristic behaviours enable us to fit in with the expectations of society. They are the drivers, or working styles, that I described in Chapter 6. They are known also as counterscript because they seem to do just that – counter the script.

However, remember the element of compulsion in these styles. We may feel that our OKness depends on them; we may get very uncomfortable if we are not acting in the prescribed way. We often start off well, getting appropriate praise for our hurrying, our perfection, our pleasing, our trying or our being strong. However, every so often we overdo it and finish up reinforcing the underlying theme of our script.

Perhaps we have a subconscious life plan that calls for us to be rejected by others. We may then generate this response in them by adopting a Please People style. In this we set out to get the approval of others but are regularly misunderstood because we persist in guessing what they want instead of asking them. Or we do things in Hurry Up, so that we get a lot done but then people find our work contains serious mistakes due to lack of attention to detail. Alternatively, if we adopt a Be Perfect theme, we may anger people by pointing out their mistakes. Be Strong will mean they can't get close to us because we keep our feelings so well hidden, whereas Try Hard will produce a pattern where we try but don't succeed at building relationships.

In Chapter 6 I have included several ideas on how you might tackle some of the drawbacks associated with these counterscript themes. I also described how we create characteristic working styles that incorporate these themes as our strengths. You might care to revisit that now with an added attention to script, and to the script payoffs I describe below.

Payoffs

We get both major and minor *payoffs* from our script process. These are the outcomes, in terms of how we feel and what we are thinking at the end of a sequence.

The severity of the major payoff will depend on the nature of our own story. If we have opted for a tragic ending, our final payoff may be an untimely death, loss of sanity or physical health, or loss of liberty. For most of us, the ending will be far less dramatic so we may collect a series of payoffs. Maybe we will settle for distress as we retire from our work, as our children leave home, as we are divorced from our partner. Or perhaps we engage in a repeating pattern of relationship problems, with significant payoffs each time as we are 'asked to leave' the organisation because of our failure to get along with our colleagues or managers.

For example, Robin Hood's payoffs may be a series of one-ups as different Sheriffs are defeated in arguments – or it may be dismissal or denied promotion if Robin angers management too much (and if the Merry Men are unwilling to support Robin by going on strike when this happens). Cinderella's payoffs may be a series of hard times followed by eventual recognition. The script may stop at this point, or Cinders may feel obliged to act like a princess for evermore – saintly, tolerant, happy ever after!

Our daily interactions may also generate many relatively minor payoffs, such as irritation or discomfort when things don't work out as we hope. These minor payoffs occur because we operate a compressed version of our script pattern. Outside our awareness, we cycle briefly through the same theme that runs through our script, constantly reinforcing it. We can identify six of these patterns, or process scripts:

never – setting yourself up to never get what you want, as when we spend a lifetime pursuing an unachievable goal. We may show this pattern at work by seeking promotion to jobs beyond our capabilities instead of enjoying what we can do.

always – spending a lifetime doing something we really don't want to do. At work, we may wear ourselves out doing the same job for years, even though we do not enjoy it (and even though we could find a different job if we really looked for one).

until – feeling obliged to complete a monumental task before we can relax. On a day-to-day basis this shows up as an inability to have fun until all the tasks are finished, even if that means working late and missing out on social occasions.

after – having fun now but knowing as you do so that you will pay for it afterwards. Rather like the reverse of until, in that you socialise first and then regret it as you go without sleep or meals in order to meet a deadline.

over-and-over – repeatedly not quite managing to achieve what you set out to do. With this pattern we slacken off just before we complete something, only to find that we then slide backwards and have to start again.

open-ended – having a script which appears to expire and leaves us not knowing what to do next. At work we may demonstrate this by appearing unsure what to do after we finish each task we have been allocated.

Identifying your own story

If you want to identify your own script, think of a fairy story or myth, or any other story that you recall was special for you when you were small. If you cannot remember having a particular story read to you when you were little, pretend that you now have to amuse a 5 year old. You can choose anything that resembles a story, such as a TV series or a film that made an impact on you in the past.

Then treat the story as a metaphor for your life, and think about:

the events in the story – are they similar in some way to what happens in your life? Is there one, long-running sequence of events or is the same short sequence being repeated?

the ending – are there alternative endings? We often remember an ending that has particular significance for us.

the character selected – which person in the story is you? Are there aspects of the other characters that are like you? Which character would other people associate with you?

Remember that your script is an unconscious life plan that you created in your mind when you were a very young child. At that time you did not have the experience of the world that you have now. You probably misinterpreted many of the things that happened around you! You also didn't know then that big people don't always tell the truth!

Having identified your overall script, consider the impact on your working life. Go over the three elements again, with a particular focus on how you earn your living.

How does the pattern of events show up in your working life? Is there a repetitive sequence, or are you functioning within one long-term story that will slowly come to a climax?

What is your probable ending? Do you dread retirement; do you have exciting plans for when you retire; do you expect to keep on working past normal retirement age?

Are you the same character all the time or do you have a separate persona that you apply at work? Would your colleagues describe you in the same way as your family might? Which characters do you need around you so you can play your part?

What impact is all this having on your behaviour at work? Are you seen as competent, effective, successful – or is an adverse impression being created?

What do you want to change? Which chapters of this book are likely to be of most use to you in the short-term? How will you plan your ongoing, long-term personal and professional development? What will you do differently in future?

You can dispense with your story or make significant changes to it now if you want to, especially if you don't like the ending. The rest of this book has been full of ideas for increasing your understanding of these unconscious processes, and suggestions for what to put in their place. The more you bring your frameworks up for inspection, the less you will be constrained unknowingly by your childhood decisions. It may take some practice to stop your mind returning to the same old grooves but it can be done.

You probably need to retain some elements so that there is a structure to your life. However, you can change it from a *deterministic* to a *developmental* script. A deterministic script is one where the play is already written and the players are merely performing it. A developmental script is more like improvisation theatre – there is a broad outline but the players have freedom to choose how to act within it – and may also be able to consider different possible endings.

The next chapter shows you what happens when people change. When you've read it, go back to your responses about your story. Then use the ideas in Chapter 13 to help you draw up a detailed plan for changing any elements of your script that you now recognise as unhelpful or particularly limiting.

CHAPTER 12: THE CHALLENGE OF CHANGE

We are constantly being told that the world has seen more change in the last century than in all the time before. And that the pace of change is accelerating all the time. Handling change has become a growth industry. There are books on change, audio tapes on change, video tapes on change, radio and TV programmes on change. The newspapers run articles and carry advertisements for coaches and counsellors who offer to help us handle change. This book itself is about change – change at the level of our attitudes – our thinking, feeling and behaviour. Before we look finally at how you might plan to change, let's consider the context we operate in nowadays.

We now have changes operating on a global scale. We also know more about what is happening, thanks to international television and the internet. We have become used to companies working across national boundaries. Recession has hit many parts of the world, just as it had when I wrote the first edition of this book, so once again we have to get used to redundancies as organisations change their structures and staffing levels. Most of us expect to have more than one occupation in our lifetimes, and some of us struggle to find even a first job.

It can take up to four years before we adjust fully to a significant transition, even one as apparently routine as a job change. An average time for someone to feel in command of a new job is around two years. The pace of change can easily overtake us, so that we move on again without ever reaching full competence.

I doubt if any of us can remain totally unaffected by change. We may enjoy the challenge or dread the results; we may welcome change or have it forced upon us; but we are not likely to feel neutral about it. Most of us, therefore, would find it helpful to understand the processes of change and transition. As individuals, this knowledge can be reassuring as we experience normal but worrying reactions to change. If we are managers, it will enable us to plan change in ways that cause least stress to those affected.

THE COMPETENCE CURVE

Given time, we will eventually emerge from the change process whether or not we have been lucky with the responses of other people. We will go through some identifiable phases. Knowledge of these phases can in itself be helpful, as it reassures us that we are behaving as most other human beings would. The phases that seem to apply most commonly are shown in figure 12.1 The Competence Curve.

Immobilisation

During Phase 1 we may well seem to be *immobilised* for a while. In imposed changes, such as redundancy, this could even be labelled shock. We need time to absorb the change and to compare our old expectations to the new reality.

Our competence drops as we appear to be marking time, doing nothing – maybe even not coping. There are several explanations for this. We probably lack information about the new situation so don't know what to do. We may be afraid of doing it wrong and appearing stupid, so that our fear of the unknown shows up as paralysis. Or perhaps we simply lack the motivation to make the change work.

Even with a change that we chose and planned, a psychologically healthy person needs a short period for simply experiencing being in a new situation before they are expected to take action.

Denial

Phase 2 involves *denial*. We act as if our behaviour patterns from the past will still be appropriate. Again, even if we have chosen the transition, we hope our existing skills and knowledge will still be useful. Some of them will, but severe problems due to denial may

Figure 12.1: The Competence Curve

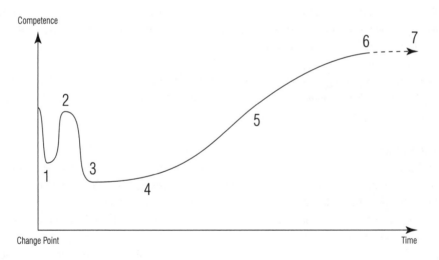

1. Immobilisation
2. Denial
3. Frustration
4. Acceptance
5. Development
6. Application
7. Completion

arise because we fear failure, and rationalise that what worked for us in the past should still work now. Perhaps we feel a threat to our level of competence and skill, making us reluctant to experiment with new behaviours. Or we may be simply custom-bound or in a rut.

Strangely, we may actually appear to be performing better during this phase than in Phase 1. This is because we now start applying our existing skills and knowledge, and are therefore seen to be achieving things. Unfortunately, we will not be using behaviour that relates to the current job; this will gradually become evident. People will start to question our grasp of reality, or think we are being deliberately obtuse. We, on the other hand, are unaware of our denial and continue to behave in the way that was successful previously. Slowly, we allow our defence systems to weaken and start to notice the need for change.

Frustration

In Phase 3 we go through a period of *frustration*. We now recognise we need to behave differently but we don't know how. Our frustration arises because we feel incompetent during our efforts to apply new approaches. Indeed, others too may perceive us as incompetent as we struggle with new skills, new knowledge, new situations – and this means we become even more conscious of our shortcomings. In some cases, we turn our frustration against others, and seek to blame them for our position. Even when we chose the change, we can blame others for not helping us enough, not training us properly beforehand, even for not warning us against the problems we now face.

Feeding into our frustration will be the potential overload due to our genuine need to learn new approaches. We may also fear a loss of status through decreased competence, and the loss of our power base or our network of contacts.

So in Phase 3 we struggle to work out how we should be different, what new skills do we need, what qualities are required in the new situation. We are likely to need to do a great deal of thinking about this.

Acceptance

At Phase 4 we move into *acceptance*. We let go of the attitudes and behaviours that were comfortable and useful in the past. We now have the answers from Phase 3 and can start the process of becoming us in the new situation. We now focus on consolidating our identity in our changed role. We develop our own views on how the job should be done, how we should relate to others, and how they should relate to us. We resolve in our own minds the questions about our status, our beliefs about the situation, and our view of the organisation. In particular, we work out how we fit in the new scheme of things.

During Phase 4 we may still appear incompetent to a degree. We are working out our identity in the changed situation, so although we have now accepted the change there will still be temporary problems where we do not as yet have the necessary skills, as well as because we are still thinking about our new role rather than doing it.

Development

All being well, we will move on to Phase 5: that of *development*. In this phase, we concentrate on developing the skills and knowledge required in the new situation. This phase represents our move, psychologically, into our personal learning cycle. We recognise the reality of our experience – that we are in a new situation and need a new set of behaviours. We review the situation and compare it with the past to identify differences. We analyse the differences and determine what new skills we will need – and then set out to acquire them. Now we will benefit from attending training programmes, having a coach, or other ways of learning.

Out competence will be seen to rise gradually as we learn what we need to do within our new identity.

Application

In Phase 6 we move on to *application*, when we put into practice the new skills we've been learning. There will still be occasional moments of frustration, such as when our new skills are not quite practised enough, or we identify yet another area where we lack knowledge.

Generally, though, we now become increasingly competent at operating in the changed environment. We make decisions about the most effective techniques and then become skilled at using them. Our knowledge increases so that others come to regard us as the appropriate expert in our field. Our competence rises steadily.

Completion

Entering Phase 7 means we have *completion*. We now feel comfortable and competent once again – so much so that we are no longer conscious of having experienced a transition. We are really into the new situation and have ceased to compare it, favourably or unfavourably, to our position before the change. We start thinking about what new challenge we would like; we are ready for the next change.

In summary, we have progressed through the following phases:
1. **Immobilisation** - our competence drops; we seem to do nothing, to withdraw or mark time
2. **Denial** - our competence appears to rise; we act as if nothing has changed and go on as we used to
3. **Frustration** - our competence drops again; we know we need to change but don't know how
4. **Acceptance** - our competence begins to rise; we start exploring options that might be appropriate to the new situation
4. **Development** - our competence continues to rise; we develop our new skills and knowledge so as to become a competent performer
5. **Application** - competence is consolidated; we apply our new skills within our new situation

7. **Completion** - maximum competence is evident; we are through the transition and are no longer consciously aware of the change

Lauren worked as a supervisor in an electronics company that was taken over by a much larger organisation. The new management believed in acting quickly, so they very soon announced a number of changes. These included having fewer supervisors so Lauren was given a new job as an Assistant Buyer in the Purchasing Department.

When first told of the job change, Lauren felt stunned. When required to move the next day into the Purchasing Office, Lauren began trying to supervise the clerical staff there. They left Lauren in little doubt that they reported to someone else, so within a few days Lauren was feeling pretty frustrated and resentful. It took several weeks before Lauren finally accepted that there was no real possibility of returning to a supervisory role in the foreseeable future, and started to think like a buyer.

Once that stage was reached, Lauren was able to consider the new job more objectively, and to identify some training needs. Working with a Senior Buyer as a mentor, Lauren then set about learning a range of new skills. Because Lauren already had a good knowledge of the company and its products, the transition into the new job was relatively quick. Within a few months, Lauren was performing competently as an Assistant Buyer. It was, however, several months later that Lauren stopped secretly dreaming of a return to supervision and began to plan a career as a buyer (but that's another story...).

CYCLES OF DEVELOPMENT

We can understand the phases of change better if we compare them to the normal developmental stages of a human being. There are seven of these stages, and they occur in cycles throughout our lives. In addition to cycles timed accordingly to our age, we also experience shorter periods triggered by specific events.

The first full cycle occurs when we are young and we therefore have certain 'developmental tasks' to complete in each stage. Few of us succeed totally and as we recycle through the equivalent period in later life, we have another opportunity for growth. However, we are also at risk of experiencing the same problems as occurred for us before. Unfortunately, we may then simply repeat the same strategies that were unsuccessful for us in the past.

We can envisage this process as a spiral, as shown in Figure 12.2. We complete our first full revolution by the time we are 19 years old. As important events occur in our lives, smaller spirals are started. There may even be smaller spirals within smaller spirals, rather like those sets of Russian dolls where you continue to find a smaller doll inside each one you open.

If we are very unlucky, we have changes occur in our lives whilst we are at a point on our major spiral that is not comfortable for us. We may even have a series of changes, each sparking off its own limited spiral on the back of another. Loss of job may lead to loss of friends, the next job may require relocation, this may take us away from family, and so on. The accumulation of spirals then adds to our stress. Even those of us who are at a good stage in life, feeling confident and capable, can be jolted severely by an unexpected change.

Pleasant changes will also stimulate new spirals. Marriage around the same time as promotion, a new baby in the family, an exciting new project to work on, passing an exam – even a break for a holiday can generate a small spiral. Add several together and it may feel as if everything in our life is going well, but it may also be one of those occasions when we experience first-hand how people get stressed through good news.

Figure 12.2: Cycles of Development

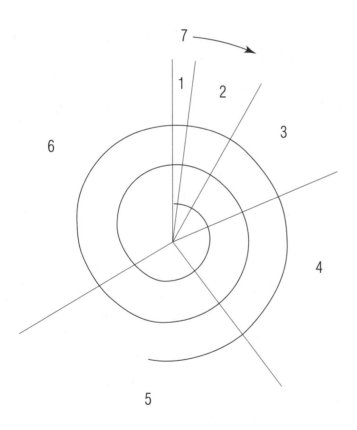

1. Being
2. Exploring
3. Thinking
4. Identity
5. Skills
6. Integration
7. Recycling

Stage 1: Being - From when we are born until we are about six months old, we need to experience just being in the world. To do this, we need a situation where we feel secure and wanted and loved. This affirmation must be there for us without requiring us to behave in any particular ways; we lack the ability to act on parental wishes at this age. If the people around us cannot provide such an atmosphere, we will grow up needing to rework this stage. Until we do, we may have problems centred around our belief in our right to exist. These may show up as an inability to relax.

Stage 2: Exploring - During the period from six to eighteen months, we want to be doing things. We start by exploring objects with our eyes, hands and mouths. We become increasingly mobile and want to move around. It is still important to us that our caregiver is around to go back to but we need the freedom to do things on our own. If we are thwarted in this stage, as adults we may be reluctant to enter new situations.

Stage 3: Thinking - Eighteen months to three years is our approximate time for developing our thinking ability. We start to reason things out for ourselves and to make our own decisions. We want to choose whether to wear a warm coat or to play in the rain. We object strongly if adults attempt to impose such choices on us. If we are not allowed to develop our thinking skills we will find it hard to form our own opinions in later life.

Stage 4: Identity - From three years to six years we are working out our identity. Who do we intend to be? Cultural and gender norms are significant here but we also consider what style to adopt. Will we be sensitive or tough, frivolous or serious? Do we plan to be the cop or the robber, a worker or a layabout, a leader or a follower? Without a clear sense of our identity, we may grow up unsure of our role in life, or with rigid views that limit our potential development.

Stage 5: Skills - Once past six years old, we are ready to spend the next six years acquiring the skills we need to get by in the world. We observe how adults behave and copy whatever fits with the identity we have adopted for ourselves. During this time, we also incorporate a whole range of opinions and values that will enable us to view the world in a structured way. Obviously, we will be limited as adults insofar as we fail to acquire significant skills or values. The competencies of our role models during this stage will be critical.

Stage 6: Integration - Having reached about twelve years old, we seem to start again as if we were babies. However, this tie we move at twice the pace. By the time we are eighteen, we will be finishing a repeat of our first twelve years. At the end of this time, we will have integrated the different aspects into a whole, rather like putting a skin around the facets of our personality. Failure to achieve this will leave us somehow fragmented, as if we have not yet finished growing up.

Stage 7: Recycling - We now start the process of recycling through the stages. As we pass through each stage, we will seek to take care of any needs that we were unable to deal with before. Sometimes we notice evidence of these issues for ourselves or others. Perhaps we observe that someone generally lacks life skills, or does not appear to trust their own thinking. Maybe they seem immature, or are unwilling to start new tasks without direct supervision. Alternatively, we may come into contact with people who are over-compensating. They insist on solving problems alone, or have very rigid views about what helping strategies they are prepared to accept.

Spirals within spirals

I have described the stages as they occur over months and years. I also said that we have smaller spirals initiated by events in our lives. Figure 12.3 illustrates this. These may span months and years but they might equally last for minutes and hours only. As you read the following example, keep in mind that we will be experiencing also the impact of the major lifetime spiral, and of any other spirals that may be in effect at the same time.

Figure 12.3: Spirals within Spirals

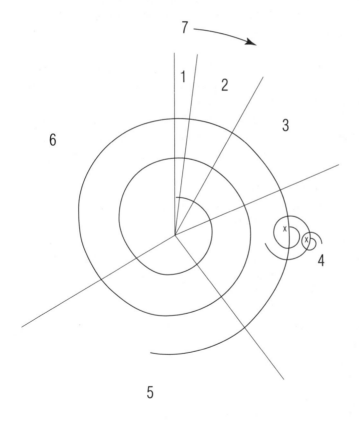

x = Change Point

Any problems will be multiplied when stages overlap in which we have 'unfinished business'. Fortunately, the same multiplier effect will occur for any stages in which we are particularly strong.

Let us take the sort of change that happened to Lauren, and that will happen to most of us at some time – starting a new job. This will generate its own spiral that will last for several weeks at least. Depending on the complexity of our work, it may be measured in months or years. Think about the last time you were in this situation. Assume for our purposes that this job is in a section that is new to you, that you do not already know your future colleagues, and that you will be undertaking different duties from your previous work.

What typically happens? You are probably shown briefly where your new desk or work station is. You may then be taken round and introduced to your new colleagues. Or you are told to start work immediately. In some cases, you attend an induction or skills training programme before you get anywhere near your new place of work. Generally, what happens bears only limited relationship to an effective way of handling such a change. If we use the cycles of development as our model, then we can predict that a job change will initiate its own spiral. What then would be the ideal process to follow?

First, we need time for **being**. A short interval for us to simply get used to being at our new place of work. The reassurance that we are welcomed by our new manager, who is pleased that we are here. Perhaps a chance to absorb our surroundings, look at the view (or lack of), put personal possessions away safely. What we do not want is to be pressured into starting work the instant we arrive. Just a few minutes may be all that is necessary to enable us to feel we have arrived and are wanted.

Second, we want time for **exploring**. We want to do this at our own pace. We need to walk around the building and register where various amenities are situated. We may take time to visualise our own location on the site. We may appreciate directions but will probably prefer to go alone so we can pay attention to what we see. An important part of this exploration will be the opportunity to meet people and find out what they do. It will help if they have been warned to expect a new face. Introductions will not be as useful if we are escorted to meet a large number of new people in a short time.

Third, we now want to do our own **thinking** about the job. We need a manager who encourages us to do this, and is then willing to discuss our views. We need information sources such as job descriptions, procedures manuals, task instructions. We want to be able to ask others about their views of the job. Then we want to work out how we see our new job. We do not want a manager who tells us we must do the job exactly as they specify. We do want a manager who will answer our questions and listen to our ideas with interest.

Fourth, we move into creating our own **identity** in the job. In some organisations, this is provided for by having performance standards set jointly by manager and subordinate. We need to believe that we have an element of choice over what sort of worker we will be. This need for self-determination is more often recognised as appropriate for managers, who are expected to have their own management style. It is just as important for those with other types of job. If this choice is denied us, we are likely to accept the decision of the organisation grudgingly and may even become rebellious.

Fifth, we are now ready to learn the **skills** required to do the job. Organisations that thrust people into training too early will not gain the full benefit. We need to have a good idea of the job itself, and our personal identity within it, if we are to make maximum use of training. Only then can we select what we need to know. Otherwise we must rely on the trainer to predict our training needs instead of working in partnership with them. Motivation to learn is much higher when we know why we are learning.

Sixth, we want to **integrate** the previous stages. As we undertake the tasks of the job, we are pulling together our prior efforts of exploration, decision making and learning. Gradually, we begin to feel that we are performing as we should. We may rework some of the earlier stages to cover parts we missed. Perhaps we have more people to get to know. Maybe we will change our style now we know the organisation better. If we are prevented from making these adjustments, we will not achieve our full potential.

Seventh, we begin the **recycling** stage. We have completed our transition into the new job. We will now move through each stage again but with far less impact. The effect of this particular spiral will fade. Soon, we will forget that we changed our job. We will function at our peak level until some other change comes along.

MANAGING CHANGE

If we are a manager, we have a responsibility for the way in which we impose change on others. We can combine what we know about the stages of development with the phases of change to generate ideas for making transitions easier. We can then ensure that the changes we are involved in cause as little pain as possible. Even if we are not a manager, we are likely to be called upon sometimes by friends or colleagues who are finding change stressful. There are several ways in which we can help other people to find the easiest route around the spiral.

Phase 1: Immobilisation/Being - those affected by change need time to experience the change. They also need information, although they are probably not in a condition to absorb it. Non-directive coaching and counselling approaches are helpful here – letting someone talk, listening to them attentively, reflecting key words back so they can structure their thoughts better. Advising them of sources of information is also useful, as is giving them written information that they can retain and study later.

Phase 2: Denial/Exploring - this is probably the most difficult stage for the would-be-helper. If the individual denies the change, we can't even discuss it with them. Patience is needed, perhaps accompanied by occasional carefully phrased questions about their objectives and their use of techniques which we recognise as inappropriate in the new situation. If in doubt, keep quiet – too much pushing will only drive them further into denial. Keep in mind that the denial is subconscious so they are unaware of it.

Phase 3: Frustration/Thinking – here we need lots of tolerance and good humour – especially if they start blaming us for the problems. Empathetic listening is now best, letting them know that we too might be angry and frustrated were we in their position. Remember empathy is not sympathy – we can relate to how they feel and still expect action from them. Avoid any temptation to wallow in mutual misery.

Phase 4: Acceptance/Identity – at last we can start to discuss the new situation with them and expect them to want to start resolving problems. Our comments must, however, be focussed on their own recognition of what is needed. Too much advice too soon will interfere with their need to work out their own identity in the new situation.

Phase 5: Development/Skills - this is a much easier phase to deal with. Advice, coaching, teaching are all appropriate now as they start actively to build up their new skills and knowledge. At last, they will be open to comments based on the previous experience of others – now you can say things like "When I did it, I …". Off-the-job training may also be useful during this phase, and contacts with others who have ideas to offer.

Phase 6: Application/Integration – we may find that our involvement now is greater than during the previous phase, when we perhaps sent them elsewhere for training. Our role is to provide plenty of encouragement and reinforcement as they apply their new skills. It may also be appropriate to remind them of 'old' skills that could usefully be applied in the new situation.

Finally, at **Phase 7: Completion/Recycling** – no more help is needed. The person is now established in the new situation and is ready to begin the process of assisting others to handle change.

DEALING WITH CHANGE

You may be unlucky enough to work in an organisation where change is not managed well. There is still a lot you can do to help yourself deal with this. Keep in mind your needs as you go through the phases, as summarised below:

- **Stage 1: Being** - we need reassurance that people are pleased we are around.
- **Stage 2: Exploring** -we need their patience while we find our own way.
- **Stage 3: Thinking** - we need their tolerance as we test out our thinking.
- **Stage 4: Identity** - we need acceptance as we define our identity.
- **Stage 5: Skills** - we are ready for coaching and training.
- **Stage 6: Integration** - we need encouragement as we settle into the new situation.
- **Stage 7: Recycling** - we are on our way.

Whether or not your organisation sets up change processes that are helpful, you can do a lot to help yourself. You can also plan positive change experiences in your personal life or if you are self-employed. The next time you are due to go through a change, use the following checklist to identify ways of making your own transition less stressful.

Immobilisation/Being: *take time to get used to the idea of change. Arrange for some periods when you can be alone; plan ways to look after yourself so that you relax – a hot bath, your favourite TV programme, a walk in the woods.*

Review your previous accomplishments and remind yourself how competent you are. Plan also to be with the sort of friends who will still want your company even if you are anxious about the change.

Denial/Exploring: *be aware that this phase exists. It may be difficult to help yourself through something which is generally outside awareness. Watch out for signs that you may be acting as if your situation is unchanged. Ask someone you trust and respect to give you feedback if they notice you behaving inappropriately.*

Actively explore your current circumstances. Make approaches to people and ask them questions. Use this period as a stimulus to making contact with people you do not know. Focus on the opportunities to do things and visit places.

Frustration/Thinking: *recognise that any anger or frustration you feel is normal. Punch a pillow or stick pins in a model instead of saying things to others that you will later regret. Engage in energetic exercise to let off steam.*

Talk to someone you respect about how you see your circumstances. Ask others who have been through a similar change about their experiences. Prepare a written plan of what you think needs to happen.

Acceptance/Identity: *you will now be starting to come to terms with 'life after change.' Accept that it will require a change in you as a person. See this as a major development opportunity. Take advantage of this chance to decide how you want to be.*

Look back over the times you were less effective than you wished. Plan now how to change your behaviour so as to avoid these pitfalls in the future. This is the beginning of the rest of your life; an ideal time to review what is important to you and whether values and beliefs have changed in any way.

Development/skills: *now you are ready to acquire the skills and knowledge you require for continued success. Look around to see what you can learn from people who are already successful in your new field. Who can you model yourself on, who can you go to for advice, how did they get their expertise?*

Check out what training is available, both on-and-off-the-job. Prepare a schedule of programmes you need. Remember to cover skills, knowledge and application. Consider other ways of learning, such as through projects, by voluntary work, through self-study.

Application/Integration: *use your new skills wisely. Remember the resolutions you made in the Identity stage about how you now want to appear to others. Apply your learning within your own clear framework of values and beliefs. Monitor your progress and make adjustments as necessary.*

Completion/Recycling: *congratulate yourself. Relax and start to help others deal with change. Get ready for the next change – and the next opportunity to grow and develop.*

CHAPTER 13: WHAT NOW

Chapter 12 concentrated on what happens when 'big' changes occur. However, life is also full of 'little' changes – and even the big changes are made up of lots of smaller parts. Also, if we want to become more effective in our relationships with other people, we need to be able to initiate changes in our own behaviour – and many of these will need to consist of a series of small changes.

In this final chapter, therefore, I'm going to describe how you can use some of the TA concepts to ensure that your small changes are made effectively, and that they add up to a coherent action plan for development and growth.

ACTION PLANS

You can probably guess at this point that there will be ways in which we sabotage ourselves even when we plan to change. One common technique for making sure we don't really change is to have action plans that are vague. Then we never know whether we have achieved our aims or not. We may also choose actions that are outside our power to achieve, or that are not really worth doing. To overcome these potential sabotage mechanisms, we need to meet the criteria for 'proper' objectives:

- **measurable** - so you will know when they have been achieved - the Parent ego state
- **manageable** - so you are capable and have the resources and authority to achieve them - the Adult ego state
- motivational- so you really want to achieve them - the Child ego state

Measurable

To ensure your action plans contain objectives that are measurable, you need to answer questions such as:

- *What exactly am I planning to do?*
- *How will I behave?*
- *In what situation(s)?*
- *With which people?*
- *When will I do this?*
- *How will I know I have achieved my objective?*

'Get on better with Harry.' is not specific enough. We need something like 'Spend five minutes at least three times a week chatting casually with Harry about his hobbies.' This tells us what, how, when, with whom. It is measurable – we can check during the week that we are on target so we don't have to chat to Harry three times on Friday afternoon.

Measuring progress is very important. It provides reinforcement when we can congratulate ourselves on doing what we planned. Without adequate measures, we miss the satisfaction of knowing we have achieved our objectives. We also need the measure so we can decide when we have incorporated the change into our usual behaviour; then we can move on to the next challenge.

Manageable

The manageable element has a different set of considerations. For example, do you currently find Harry very difficult to talk to? If so, is it realistic to plan to spend most of your week with him? Three five-minute chats is probably manageable. Set the target higher and you might well find it too hard to achieve.

Objectives need to be selected so that we have a good likelihood of attaining them. Picking the biggest problem to tackle first is not the best route to success. Instead, start with something that can realistically be accomplished – you can always be more ambitious later if you find it was too easy.

Manageability also relates to power to act. We can only change our own behaviour, not anyone else's. Chatting with Harry is only acceptable as an objective if we are sure that Harry will agree to talk to us. If he is likely to walk away and ignore us, the objective is not achievable.

Motivational

We need to balance manageable with motivational. How challenging and worthwhile are our selected objectives? There is no point having an action plan about things which are not important or are simple to put into effect. If we could easily go and chat to Harry a few times a week why not just do it now we realise it would improve our relationship. It hardly justifies being part of an action plan, which should be reserved for significant developments.

We get little feeling of satisfaction from making easy changes. We need to tackle something that we recognise as a real challenge, so that we will have an incentive to persevere. Otherwise, our reaction is likely to be "So what?" after we have implemented our plan.

Objectives also need to be motivating in the sense that they contribute to our overall effectiveness. It may be nice to get to know Harry but hardly worthwhile if he is leaving the organisation shortly (unless we want to continue the relationship, or see Harry as a useful test case on which to improve our ability to relate to others).

Elephants and Rabbits

The way we frame our objectives is also significant. Compare the action planning process with eating an elephant – you can do it if you go for small pieces at a time. Changing our behaviour or attitudes can be equally indigestible if we tackle too much at once. Picking a few priority areas allows us to spread the elephant eating over a sensible timeframe.

"Whatever you do, don't think about rabbits!" When someone says that to you, what do you think about? It is virtually impossible not to think about rabbits, even if it is only fleetingly. To avoid someone thinking about rabbits, we need to tell them to think about something else, such as elephants perhaps!

The think-rabbit syndrome applies directly to action planning. If we concentrate on our weaknesses, we are likely to reinforce them. We should instead identify alternative objectives that would have the effect of cancelling out our weaknesses. For example, to stop interrupting other people, focus instead on listening to the end of their sentences. To improve a relationship, look for things you have in common; don't approach them thinking 'I must not lose my temper' or you will very likely do just that.

OVERCOMING SELF-SABOTAGE
The idea of action planning is not new; neither are the criteria I have mentioned. However, there are some useful elements within TA enables that we can add into the planning process. In particular, the concepts of internal ego states, strokes and working styles/drivers are valuable frameworks for checking the way our objectives have been selected and structured.

Internal Ego States
The concept of internal ego states allows us to consider in more detail the decision making process involved in our action planning. Thus, our Internal Parent holds opinions and is a store of previous experience, including recollections of how we and others have behaved in similar situations to those covered by our action plan. Our Internal Child contains our anticipated feelings about being in the circumstances specified in the action plan, often mixed up with emotional memories from previous incidents. Our Internal Adult thinks logically about our plans, considering options and implications and weighing up the probabilities of success. If we are to succeed in our stated objectives, all three internal ego states need to be in broad agreement.

Our Internal Parent will want to check that the plan is based on reliable precedents, even if we cannot identify an exactly similar set of circumstances. This ego state will also be in action when we consider our value systems and beliefs about the right ways to act. A logical course of action selected by Internal Adult will not be implemented successfully if it is out of line with our principles. Our Internal Parent is also the ego state that wants our objectives stated in measurable terms, so we can check that we've done what we were supposed to do!

Our Internal Child will put energy and enthusiasm into plans that we feel comfortable and excited about. This ego state will unconsciously undermine decisions which ignore our feelings of scare or anxiety. This does not mean we cannot do anything we feel nervous about; it means that we need to use the resources of our other ego states to reassure the Internal Child that the concerns will be taken care of. Perhaps we will plan some relaxation before we enact a stressful change in behaviour, or set up a reward for ourselves as an incentive to make the extra effort. It's our Internal Child that makes sure we only put effort into things that we are motivated about.

Our Internal Adult looks for evidence that the objective is well-founded. In this ego state there is a danger that we see the logical solution and take insufficient account of our opinions and feelings. If we are used to doing this, we may have lost touch with our own underlying motivations. We then act rather like a computer, without the necessary attention to all aspects of the decision. We may also underestimate the responses of other people, expecting them to appreciate the logic of our actions in the same way that we do. Internal Adult ensures that our objectives are manageable and realistic.

Stroking Patterns

When we change our behaviour in line with our action plans, our stroking patterns will also shift. If we make significant modifications to our behaviour, we may want more recognition, or strokes, to reinforce our sense of well-being as we put extra effort into the change.

We can add the concept of strokes to our action planning by considering:

- How do I get stroked now? For what?
- What strokes might no longer be available if I change?
- How can I make up the deficit?
- How can I get extra strokes/recognition for the changes?
- How will I reinforce my success?

It is important to remember that human beings settle for negative strokes if insufficient positive ones are available. We would rather be shouted at than ignored. The behaviours you now want to change may well have been providing a steady supply of negative strokes, as people expressed their dissatisfaction to you in a multitude of ways. Introducing a more skilful way of interacting may prevent the negative strokes being given, before the positive stroking pattern comes into effect. In that case, make sure you organise extra strokes temporarily from other sources, such as by spending more time with friends while you develop new ways of relating.

Working Styles versus Drivers

Planning to change behaviour is somewhat stressful for all of us, so our drivers tend to creep in to our action plans and stop us getting the benefits of our working styles.

Hurry Up shows up when we want to tackle everything in a rush. We draw up an action plan with many items, all to be completed in a very short time. We then accomplish the changes only superficially, so we fail to reap the full benefits. Or we select our priorities so quickly that we overlook significant areas that we should be working on.

Be Perfect is in effect when we aim to produce the perfect action plan, with just the right priorities and a great deal of detail on how we will implement the changes. This takes us so long that we never quite finish drawing up the plan anyway. Or we make each objective so complex that it would take hours to put any one of them into effect – so we never have a long enough period to get started.

Please People affects us by requiring that whatever we do has the approval of other people. We may ask a colleague to tell us what should be in our action plan. If the colleague wisely refuses, we may ask friends or family members, or go back to check with our manager. We want someone else to determine our priorities in case we get it wrong. Or we worry about upsetting other people if we make changes to our own behaviour.

Try Hard is about trying but not succeeding. We tackle lots of things enthusiastically but never quite finish them. Our action plan is therefore likely to be crammed with good ideas, which we will initiate and then get bored with. We will have several objectives, so we can move between them anytime there is a danger that we might actually achieve one of them. We may even get bored with doing an action plan, and sidetrack ourselves by starting to experiment with alternative layouts for the plan – and maybe even alternative designs for the action planning section.

Be Strong driver means we keep a stiff upper lip. We stay calm and emotionless. We fail to see why we need an action plan anyway, as we are loathe to admit to having any weaknesses. Our speciality is coping in crises, without help from anyone else. We may grudgingly put down one or two loosely worded items to satisfy our manager but will do our best to avoid facing up to any shortcomings. We cannot imagine why we would want to change when we are in control of everything already.

Check your own action plans for signs of any of the drivers – then work out how to reword your objectives to avoid the pitfalls and get the benefits of working styles instead.

PLANS INTO ACTION

Checking ego states will ensure your choices are balanced, considering strokes will remind you to include encouragement and reinforcement in your plans, and looking out for drivers will identify the characteristic ways you might sabotage your own efforts.

Another important element to take into account is the choice of situations in which to implement the action plans. Learning new ways of behaving towards other people is like learning to ride a bicycle – we are acquiring skills we did not have before. We did not simply get on a bicycle for the first time and pedal off; we went through a process of practising separate actions and eventually being able to perform several functions at once.

First we learned to pedal strongly enough to keep our balance. We probably fell off a few times until we got this right. Hopefully, we had picked a quiet spot to learn this and not a busy road. Then, if we got it wrong we did not fall in front of a car. Learning new people skills also needs a quiet spot – in other words we need to select carefully the environment in which to make the change. We should defer using the new behaviour in front of other people who could cause us harm, until we have practised enough to be confident and will not lose our balance.

We may also find that our new approach lacks the impact we hoped for. Perhaps it seems false, even to us. It may certainly feel disjointed. On the bicycle, it took time before we could pedal, watch the traffic, give hand signals, stop efficiently and without leaving the saddle precipitously. Similarly, with people skills we have to practise before we can readily pull together the sequence of judging the situation, determining our desired outcome, interacting in an appropriate style, matching body language, tone and content, responding to the other party.

This need to co-ordinate may make our behaviour seem stilted and artificial. This is a normal problem and it signifies that you are well on the way to making a definite change in behaviour. Practice will take care of the rough edges. You might usefully plan to rehearse as I suggested earlier. Keep in mind also that your first attempts in the 'real world' may still seem stilted. If so, people may not react as you hoped. Resist the temptation to give up at that point – persevere and the skills will suddenly come together.

One final warning. Human beings have an unfortunate habit of seeing what they expect to see (and hearing what they expect to hear). When you change your behaviour, don't be surprised if other people respond just as if you are still doing what you've always done. Be ready for this and persist!

I recall a time, a few years ago, when I had been working with a colleague who regularly criticised my ideas. We would then have an argument. After a few months of this, I moved on to a new project and met the colleague only occasionally – but each time I did we had another argument.

Then, one day I became aware that something had changed. Our infrequent conversations seemed stilted. Suddenly, I realised what had been happening. He had stopped criticising me. Instead, he had started to ask me questions, listen to my replies, and make favourable comments about my work. Unfortunately, I was still trying to argue with him!

My expectations were so entrenched that it took at least three occasions before I recognised what was happening. As soon as I did, I changed my reactions to him and we started to have some very friendly and constructive discussions.

The moral is, of course, that we need to be alert and open-minded in our responses to other people. I'd carried on replying in the old pattern, as if he were still criticising, long after he'd changed. Fortunately he persisted – but he could so easily have become disillusioned and stopped putting the extra effort into our interactions. So, double check your own behaviour around anyone you don't get on with, and remember to persevere with the changes that you make.

I wish you well on your personal path to greater self awareness, increased options, and deeper closeness with other human beings.

APPENDIX 1: WINDOWS ON THE WORLD QUESTIONNAIRE

Please note that this questionnaire is included here for your personal use only. It is a copyrighted item and may not be reproduced. Copies are available for purchase in packs of 25 from Sherwood Publishing www.sherwoodpublishing.com

Circle the number next to the statement in each group that best describes you.

Be honest with yourself – don't just pick whatever you think is the 'best' answer.

A	1	I tend to interrupt others when they are speaking
	2	I prefer to take a back seat in groups and let others take the lead
	3	I do my best to avoid situations where you're expected to give an opinion
	4	I let other people finish what they are saying before I speak
B	1	I usually think that other people know best
	2	I stand up for myself when I feel that I'm right and expect others to do the same
	3	I insist that I'm right and expect others to go along with me
	4	I don't see any point in pushing my ideas as people rarely appreciate them
C	1	I resist making decisions or taking advice from others
	2	I let other people make decisions for me
	3	I make my own decisions based on what I feel is right and appropriate
	4	I often make decisions for other people
D	1	I tend to keep my voice low and avoid eye contact to prevent attention being drawn to me
	2	I sometimes speak loudly and expect to make quite an impact
	3	I can't be bothered to communicate much
	4	I generally match my level of communication to suit the circumstances
E	1	I tend to blame and find fault with others
	2	I sometimes hide my feelings and just go along with others
	3	I do my best to understand the feelings of others before letting them know how I feel
	4	I don't often feel that strongly about anything

F	1	I let others get what they want but I often feel resentful about it
	2	I talk through problems before they occur and find ways of coping with them when they do
	3	I make sure that things turn out the way I want them to
	4	I really don't mind if other people get their own way
G	1	I hold back on decisions so that others will make them for me
	2	I tend to avoid facing problems and keep putting decisions off until tomorrow
	3	I deal with my own problems and make my own decisions
	4	I provide solutions for people who seem unable to decide for themselves
H	1	I consider myself capable and equal to others
	2	I consider myself weaker and less capable than others
	3	I consider myself stronger and more capable than others
	4	I consider that most people are weak, including me
I	1	I avoid taking responsibility as it only gets you blamed when things don't work out
	2	I accept my responsibilities and am clear about what others are responsible for
	3	I take on responsibility for as much as possible, including the work of others
	4	I prefer it when someone else takes responsibility and I can follow their lead

To analyse your scores turn to the next page

Windows on the World - Scoring

Step 1. Using the chart below, circle the A, B, C or D that is alongside the number that you chose for each question. Then add each column to get a total score.

Q.A	4	A	2	B	1	C	3	D
Q.B	2	A	1	B	3	C	4	D
Q.C	3	A	2	B	4	C	1	D
Q.D	4	A	1	B	2	C	3	D
Q.E	3	A	2	B	1	C	4	D
Q.F	2	A	4	B	3	C	1	D
Q.G	3	A	1	B	4	C	2	D
Q.H	1	A	2	B	3	C	4	D
Q.I	2	A	4	B	3	C	1	D

Total A	Total B	Total C	Total D

Step 2. Now draw a bar chart of your scores by making horizontal lines at the score points.

Total score

8

7

6

5

4

3

2

1

0	A - win-win	B – lose-win	C – win-lose	D – lose-lose
	assertive	accommodating	aggressive	apathetic

APPENDIX 2: PERSONAL STYLES QUESTIONNAIRE

Please note that this questionnaire is included here for your personal use only. It is a copyrighted item and may not be reproduced. Copies are available for purchase in packs of 25 from Sherwood Publishing www.sherwoodpublishing.com

This questionnaire is also available in French and German.

INSTRUCTIONS

For each statement, allocate a score to show how much the behaviour is like the way you behave:

not true for me   0   partly true for me   1   moderately true for me   2   extremely true for me   3

ITEM	SCORE	
1.		I tell people firmly how they should behave.
2.		I tend to reason things out before acting.
3.		I do as I'm told.
4.		I behave sympathetically towards people with problems.
5.		I really enjoy being with other people.
6.		I enjoy taking care of people.
7.		I enjoy solving problems in a systematic and logical way.
8.		I tell people what to do.
9.		I let people know how I really feel without embarrassment.
10.		I am polite and courteous.
11.		I do the opposite to what people expect.
12.		When someone is new, I make an effort to show them where everything is.
13.		I can stay calm in a crisis.
14.		When I know I'm right, I insist that others listen to me.
15.		I ask a lot of questions when I'm curious.
16.		I am very enthusiastic about my work.
17.		People seem to expect me to know the answer.
18.		I'm asked to take care of new members of staff.
19.		I get on well with people who are polite to me.
20.		I keep on thinking logically even under pressure.

SCORE

21.   My working style is systematic and logical.

22.   I dress to match the sort of outfits that other people wear to work.

23.   I do things for people when I think they can't manage for themselves.

24.   I can quote my previous experience when problems occur.

25.   People tell me I'm creative and inventive.

26.   I prefer to take control rather than following someone else's lead.

27.   I fuss over people too much.

28.   I'm over-emotional compared to others.

29.   I expect my manager to set my terms of reference.

30.   I take all points of view into account when making decisions.

31.   I encourage people to test out their own capabilities.

32.   People complain that I'm bossy.

33.   I spend time enjoying myself.

34.   People tell me I'm especially courteous.

35.   I'm noted for my even temper and balanced comments.

36.   I show my feelings whether I am happy or sad, so that people can congratulate or sympathise with me.

37.   I've looked after someone even though they could have managed on their own.

38.   I'm tempted to analyse jokes, which spoils them for others.

39.   People do as I tell them.

40.   I go along too readily with what other people want.

Personal Styles Questionnaire - Scoring

Step 1. Transfer your scores to the summary below, against the question numbers, and add up each column.

	SCORE		SCORE		SCORE		SCORE		SCORE
1		4		2		3		5	
8		6		7		10		9	
14		12		13		11		15	
17		18		20		19		16	
24		23		21		22		25	
26		27		30		29		28	
32		31		35		34		33	
39		37		38		40		36	

Total

Controlling	Nurturing	Functional	Adapted	Natural
Parent	Parent	Adult	Child	Child

Step 2. Now draw a bar chart of your responses by marking horizontal lines at the score points.

Total score

24

21

18

15

12

9

6

3

0

Controlling	Nurturing	Functional	Adapted	Natural
Parent	Parent	Adult	Child	Child

APPENDIX 3: INTERNAL EGO STATE QUESTIONNAIRE

Please note that this questionnaire is included here for your personal use only. It is a copyrighted item and may not be reproduced. Copies are available for purchase in packs of 25 from Sherwood Publishing www.sherwoodpublishing.com

This questionnaire is also available in French.

INSTRUCTIONS

For each statement, allocate a score to indicate how much it matches your own thinking.

| not true for me | 0 | partly true for me | 1 | moderately true for me | 2 | extremely true for me | 3 |

ITEM	SCORE	
1.		I have strong opinions on some subjects.
2.		I like to balance the pros and cons before I make a decision.
3.		Children should be taught to respect their elders more.
4.		Most of my parent's views are totally out-of-date.
5.		I feel upset when people are angry.
6.		I take a moment to assess a difficult situation before I respond.
7.		I often go with a hunch when making a decision.
8.		I think about the implications before I do something.
9.		I rely on my experience a lot to make decisions.
10.		I can observe other peoples' reactions without necessarily feeling the same way.
11.		I often feel more mature than other people.
12.		I often feel as if I'm a lot younger than I really am.
13.		I am comfortable sharing decision making when relevant.
14.		I sometimes hide my true feelings from others.
15.		Sometimes I think other people behave childishly.
16.		I prefer it when someone else has to make the decisions.
17.		I have updated some of the views I learned from my parents.
18.		I expect to make my own decisions all the time.
19.		I resent it when people tell me what to do.
20.		I share many of the views of my parents.
21.		I can learn from younger people.

Internal Ego State Questionnaire - Scoring

Step 1. Transfer your scores to the summary below, against the question numbers, and add up each column.

	SCORE	SCORE	SCORE
1	2	4	
3	6	5	
9	8	7	
11	10	12	
15	13	14	
18	17	16	
20	21	19	

Total

Internal	Internal	Internal
Parent	Adult	Child

Step 2. Draw a chart of your responses by marking horizontal lines at the score points for each ego state.

Total score

24

21

18

15

12

9

6

3

0

Internal	Internal	Internal
Parent	Adult	Child

APPENDIX 4:   WORKING STYLES QUESTIONNAIRE

Please note that this questionnaire is included here for your personal use only. It is a copyrighted item and may not be reproduced. Copies are available for purchase in packs of 25 from Sherwood Publishing www.sherwoodpublishing.com

This questionnaire is also available in German and Romanian.

INSTRUCTIONS

For each item, give a score between 0 and 8, where 8 is totally like you, 4 is average and 0 is totally unlike you.

ITEM	SCORE	WHAT I TYPICALLY DO:
1.		I tend to wait until the deadline is near before I work on a task.
2.		I like to organise my work area efficiently.
3.		It is important to maintain harmony in working relationships.
4.		I enjoy starting new projects.
5.		I am very good at staying calm during a crisis.
6.		I work steadily and conscientiously at whatever is required.
7.		I am good at seeing the whole scope of a task and showing initiative.
8.		I enjoy encouraging people and doing things to help them.
9.		I plan ahead thoroughly so that I am ready for any problems that arise.
10.		I enjoy having lots to do (even if I complain about it sometimes).
11.		It is important to check so that there are no mistakes.
12.		I am usually more enthusiastic than other people.
13.		I am usually more balanced and even-tempered than other people.
14.		I am usually intuitive and sensitive to other people's feelings.
15.		I can usually finish tasks more quickly than other people.

Table continues on next page

16.	Sometimes people seem to think that I'm overly critical about standards of work.
17.	Sometimes I make mistakes because I am working so fast.
18.	Sometimes people act as if they resent it when I am only trying to help them.
19.	I sometimes miss deadlines because I find it hard to ask for help even when I have too much to do.
20.	I tend to start several projects but have trouble finishing any of them.
21.	People sometimes complain that I make tasks too big because I consider so many possible aspects.
22.	People sometimes seem to think I am aloof and unfriendly.
23.	I have problems saying no to people even when I already have too much to do.
24.	I feel impatient when people spend too much time discussing what to do.
25.	I sometimes miss deadlines because I need longer to check my work.

To analyse your scores, please turn to the next page.

Working Styles Questionnaire - Scoring

Step 1. Transfer your scores to the summary below, against the question numbers, and add up each column.

ITEM	SCORE		SCORE		SCORE		SCORE		SCORE
1		2		3		4		5	
10		9		8		7		6	
15		11		14		12		13	
17		16		18		20		19	
24		25		23		21		22	

Total

	Hurry Up	Be Perfect	Please People	Try Hard	Be Strong

Step 2. Now draw a bar chart of your responses by marking horizontal lines at the score points.

Total score

40

35

30

25

20

15

10

5

0

	Hurry Up	Be Perfect	Please People	Try Hard	Be Strong

APPENDIX 5: MANAGER WORKING STYLES QUESTIONNAIRE

Please note that this questionnaire is included here for your personal use only. It is a copyrighted item and may not be reproduced. Copies are available for purchase in packs of 25 from Sherwood Publishing www.sherwoodpublishing.com

For each item, give a score between 0 and 8, where 8 is totally like your manager, 4 is average and 0 is totally unlike your manager.

ITEM	SCORE	MY MANAGER:
1.		Sets very short deadlines for work to be done.
2.		Gives very thorough instructions on how things should be done.
3.		Can be very encouraging.
4.		Is enthusiastic and exciting to have around.
5.		Is calm and thoughtful whatever the circumstance.
6.		Has a strong sense of duty to the organisation.
7.		Has so many new ideas that it's hard to keep up.
8.		Shows an interest in me as a person.
9.		Can spot mistakes in most things.
10.		Talks fast and tends to interrupt.
11.		Takes a lot of care over quality of work.
12.		Goes off on tangents instead of finishing one thing at a time.
13.		Tells people what to do in a controlling manner.
14.		Avoids making decisions in case someone is upset.
15.		Gets a lot of work done very quickly.
16.		Complains about unimportant details.
17.		Comes late to meetings and is always in a hurry.
18.		Insists on helping me when I don't really need help.
19.		Is unemotional and even unfeeling at times.
20.		Turns small tasks into major projects - and then delegates the boring parts.
21.		Seems to judge my performance by how enthusiastic I am.
22.		Seems to judge my performance by how uncomplaining I am.
23.		Seems to judge my performance by how well I get on with other people.
24.		Seems to judge my performance by how fast I work.
25.		Seems to judge my performance by how accurate I am.

Manager Working Styles Questionnaire - Scoring

Step 1. Transfer your scores to the summary below, against the question numbers, and add up each column.

ITEM	SCORE		SCORE		SCORE		SCORE		SCORE
1		2		3		4		5	
10		9		8		7		6	
15		11		14		12		13	
17		16		18		20		19	
24		25		23		21		22	

Total

Hurry Up   Be Perfect   Please People   Try Hard   Be Strong

Step 2. Now draw a bar chart of your responses by marking horizontal lines at the score points.

Total score

24

21

18

15

12

9

6

4

0

Hurry Up   Be Perfect   Please People   Try Hard   Be Strong

APPENDIX 6: STROKE MYTHS QUESTIONNAIRE

For each question, indicate a score between 0 and 4, where 0 means *Not at all like me* and 4 means *Very much like me.*

Afterwards, transfer your scores to the chart that follows.

ITEM	SCORE	QUESTION:
1.		If you praise people, they stop trying so hard.
2.		I get paid to do my job so I do not need a lot of compliments.
3.		It is very bad mannered to refuse a compliment.
4.		I am nervous about asking for direct feedback.
5.		It is boastful to tell people what you are good at.
6.		I rely on other people to know what I am good at and make sure I get that kind of work.
7.		I just assume that my work is okay when my manager doesn't criticize me.
8.		I am willing to accept the blame even though it is sometimes not really my fault.
9.		I feel embarrassed when people praise me.
10.		People get paid to do their job and should not need lots of compliments.
11.		My performance appraisal has not been done when it should have been but I understand that my manager is too busy.
12.		I feel I don't deserve praise, especially when other people have helped me.
13.		I notice that sometimes people get given projects that I would be able to do better.
14.		I rarely see anyone do a job as well as it should be done.
15.		When someone makes personal comments about me, I don't make a fuss even though I may not like what they say.

To analyse your scores, please turn to the next page.

Stroke Myths Questionnaire - Scoring

Step 1. Transfer your scores to the summary below, against the question numbers, and add up each column.

ITEM	SCORE		SCORE		SCORE		SCORE		SCORE
1		2		3		4		5	
10		9		8		7		6	
14		12		15		11		13	

Total

	Don't Give	Don't Accept	Don't Reject	Don't Ask	Don't Stroke Yourself

Step 2. Now draw a bar chart of your responses by marking horizontal lines at the score points.

Total score

40

35

30

25

20

15

10

5

0

	Don't Give	Don't Accept	Don't Reject	Don't Ask	Don't Stroke Yourself

SUGGESTED FURTHER READING

Berne, Eric , *What do you say after you say Hello?* Corgi 1975 – if you want to read what was written by the originator of TA

Dyer, Wayne, *Gifts from Eykis, Pulling Your Own Strings* and *The Sky's the Limit,* published years ago, still available and well worth reading for ideas on how to liberate ourselves from self-imposed limitations (Wayne Dyers' later writing is not the same style).

Harris, Thomas , *I'm OK, You're OK,* Pan 1973 – an excellent introduction to the range of TA ideas that were developed during the 1960's

Hay, Julie, *Transactional Analysis Introductory Course* – workbook and audiotape recording of a course, Sherwood Publishing 2001 – see www.sherwoodpublishing.com – a complete programme, 7 hours of recording, run to an internationally-agreed syllabus and often referred to as the TA 101

Hay, Julie, *Dealing with Difficult People* - workbook and audiotape recording of a workshop, Sherwood Publishing 1998 – see www.sherwoodpublishing.com – combines TA and NLP (neuro linguistic programming)

James, Muriel and Jongeward, Dorothy, *Born to Win,* Signet 1978 – another early book on TA that is still going strong, this one is very easy to read

Levin, Pamela , *The Cycle of Life,* The Nourishing Company 2007 – Pam explains the cycle of development and includes suggestions for dealing with developmental issues – see www.yourcycleoflife.com

Peck, M Scott , *The Road Less Travelled,* Rider 1988 – an excellent book about our need to be close to other human beings

Claude Steiner, *Scripts People Live,* Bantam Books 1975 – this concentrates on scripts in their various forms

Abe Wagner, *The Transactional Manager,* Prentice-Hall 1981 – TA with a specific focus on being a manager

GLOSSARY

Page numbers refer to the start of the main explanation(s) of the item in the text

A

acceleration - 113 - 'type' of person within AP³ framework

acceptance – 160 – fourth stage on the competence curve; when we take on a new identity

active/alone - 111 - 'type' of person within AP³ framework

active/people - 109 - 'type' of person within AP³ framework

Adapted Child – 43 – one of the ego states, or personal styles, we have available for interacting with others; used appropriately this style is courteous; used inappropriately it becomes either submissive, rebellious or withdrawn

adapted imago – 101 – third stage of mental image we form about a group, when we are resolving in our mind the relative leader/ follower positions of the group members

adjusted imago – 100 – second stage of mental image we form about a group, as we get to know people

Adult – ego state: see Functional Adult, Internal Adult

after – 156 – one of the process scripts; based on belief that you'll pay for pleasure later

alienated imago - 102 - what happens when we fail to attain an attached imago; failure to connect with the group

always – 155 – one of the process scripts; based on having to keep doing the same thing

anticipatory imago – 98 – first stage of mental image we form about a group, before we know all of the group members

AP³ – 105 - framework that draws together several TA concepts into a model of 5 types of people

application – 161 – sixth stage on the competence curve; when we begin to apply new learning

assessing cube - 105 - alternative name for AP³: framework that draws together several TA concepts into a model of 5 types of people

attached imago – 102 – final stage of mental image we form about a group, after we know them and have resolved leadership issues; imago for getting on with the work of the group

attitude - 5 - shorthand label for blend of beliefs, behaviours and emotions

attribution – 152 – element of script; characteristic that is 'attributed' to us by others so that we grow up believing we have to be like they say (e.g. clumsy, clever)

autonomy – 19 – script-free; being truly aware of the present, knowing you have alternative courses of action available to you, and that you can connect to other human beings

B

BAR – 26 – to assertiveness: stands for Beliefs, Actions, Reinforcements, which form a closed, self-reinforcing cycle

being – 164 - first stage in our cycle of development; when we need to know that we are welcome without having to perform

Be Perfect – 77 – one of five characteristic working styles, or drivers; means that we pay great attention to detail but may miss deadlines through needing to check so carefully

Be Strong – 80 – one of five characteristic working styles, or drivers; means that we are calm in a crisis but may appear unfeeling

blamer – 34 – position on the miniscript where we blame others for failure (ours or theirs) to maintain behaviour in line with our unrealistic expectations

C

channels of communication – 57 – ways we communicate through different combinations of ego states, or personal styles

Child – ego state: see Adapted Child, Internal Child, Natural Child

Closeness – 130 - used here to mean a way of spending time in open, trusting, genuine connection with others

competence curve – 158 – diagram showing the variations in level of competence after a change, and the stages we go through: immobilisation, denial, frustration, acceptance, development, application, completion

complementary transaction – 59 – an interaction between people in which the ego states used are complementary i.e. they 'match' in some way so that the conversation continues as it started (note: it may not always be useful to continue a conversation e.g. if someone is being unreasonable)

completion – 162 – final stage on the competence curve; when we are no longer conscious of the change

conditional stroke – 90 – unit of recognition that is only there 'on condition' that someone has done something; tends to be recognition for performance, appearance, etc

contamination – 145 – when our Internal Parent or Child takes over but we think we are operating from Internal Adult; when we are affected by prejudices and fantasies but believe we are being rational

Controlling Parent – 45 – one of the ego states, or personal styles, we have available for interacting with others; used appropriately this style is firm; inappropriately and it becomes bossy and autocratic

counterscript – 154 – apparently script-free behaviour which is in fact based on the theme of the script; shows as our driver, or unhelpful aspect of our working style

crossed transaction – 60 – an interaction between people in which the ego states used are not complementary i.e. they do not 'match' so that the conversation is disrupted in some way (note: it may be useful to do this when an interaction is being conducted in an unhelpful way)

cycles of development – 162 – cycle of stages in our development to adulthood, that then repeat throughout life; also repeated over shorter time spans related to significant changes in our lives: being, exploring, thinking, identity, skills, integration, recycling

D

denial – 159 – second stage on the competence curve; when we may act as if nothing has changed

despairer - 34 - alternative name for payoff at end of miniscript sequence

deterministic script - 157 - usual form of script, where we are constrained by a 'life story' that we chose when still a small child (see also script)

development – 161 – fifth stage on the competence curve; when we are ready to acquire the new skills we need

developmental script - 157 - outline script within which we can improvise (see also script)

discounting – 133 – process by which we unknowingly 'overlook' some aspect of the situation or people's abilities; we may discount at six levels:
the stimulus (what is actually happening), significance (that it is a problem), solutions (that things could be resolved), skills (that someone is able to do something about it);
strategies (that plan can be devised); success (that we or others can succeed)

disposition diamond – 15 – diagram representing three levels at which our windows on the world operate: beliefs, behaviour and emotion

drama triangle – 118 – diagram which shows three roles taken on when people play psychological games: Persecutor, Rescuer, Victim

driver – 33, 76 – position at start of miniscript sequence; unhelpful aspect of our characteristic working styles; compulsive ways of behaving that become more evident when we are stressed; consist of Hurry Up, Be Perfect, Please People, Try Hard and Be Strong

E

egogram – 48 – way of drawing a bar chart of our ego states to reflect the amount of time we spend in each of them *ego states* – 38 – also called personal styles; five ways of interacting, or transacting, with others, each style having positive and negative applications: Controlling Parent, Nurturing Parent, Functional Adult, Adapted Child, Natural Child (see also Internal Ego States)

exclusion – 143 – when we consistently do not use one of our ego states

exploring – 164 – second stage in our cycle of development; when we need to investigate and do things for ourselves

F

Functional Adult – 46 – one of the ego states, or personal styles, we have available for interacting with others; used appropriately this style is logical; used inappropriately it becomes overly-analytical. See also Internal Adult

frustration – 160 – third stage on the competence curve; when we feel frustrated because we must change

G

games – 117 – more accurate label is 'psychological games': unconsciously programmed ways of behaving that result in repetitive interactions with others leading to negative payoffs

Gotcha – 121 – name of psychological game; repetitive unhelpful sequence of interactions with others

group imago, imagoes – 98 – mental image(s) we have in our heads about the group; four stages: anticipatory, adjusted, adapted, attachment (or alienation)

H

Harried – 117 – name of psychological game; repetitive unhelpful sequence of interactions with others

hierarchy of ego states - 67 - way within hierarchies that managers tend to opt for Parent ego state behaviour while subordinates typically go into Child ego state behaviour

Hurry Up – 76 – one of five characteristic working styles, or drivers; means that we do everything quickly but may make mistakes in our haste

I

iceberg - 3 - metaphor for understanding how our behaviour is affected by what goes on beneath the surface and how others decide our personality based on a restricted range of information

identity – 164 – fourth stage in our cycle of development; when we need to decide who we are, how we intend to be as a person, as a worker, as a parent etc.

imago, imagoes – 98 - see group imago

immobilisation – 159 – first stage on the competence curve; when we feel surprised or shocked

I'm not OK, You're not OK – 11 – belief that you and others are lacking in some way, lose/lose; one of the life positions or windows on the world

I'm not OK, You're OK – 11 – belief that others are better than you, lose/win; one of the life positions or windows on the world

I'm OK, You're OK – 10 – belief about self and others that incorporates mutual respect, win/win approach; one of the life positions or windows on the world

injunction – 151 – element of script; something we believe we are forbidden to do (e.g. don't grow up, don't be successful)

INOK-YNOK – 11 – abbreviation for I'm not OK, You're not OK

INOK-YOK – 11 – abbreviation for I'm not OK, You're OK

integration – 164 – sixth stage in our cycle of development; when we pull together the earlier aspects of our development

Internal Adult – 53, 142 – internal ego state in which we process what is happening, check with Internal Parent and Child, evaluate options and decide how to respond to events

Internal Child – 49, 140 – internal ego state which 'contains' our current emotional responses and 'stores' our memories of previous occasions

internal ego states – 49 – set of three internal 'filing' and 'processing' systems by which we experience and make sense of the world: Internal Parent, Internal Child, Internal Adult

Internal Parent – 52, 141 – internal ego state that 'contains' our opinions and values and 'stores' our experiences and copies of other people

IOK-YNOK – 11 – abbreviation for I'm OK, You're not OK

IOK-YOK – 10 – abbreviation for I'm OK, You're OK

K

Kick Me – 124 – name of psychological game; repetitive unhelpful sequence of interactions with others

L

life positions – 9 – see windows on the world

Lunch Bag – 117 – name of psychological game; repetitive unhelpful sequence of interactions with others

M

measurable, manageable, motivational - 171 - criteria for objective setting; relate to Parent, Adult, Child ego states

miniscript – 33 – short sequence (may take only seconds) in which we start with mythical belief about the need to act in a certain way, and then fail to do so and feel one-down; may also include element where we blame others for our failure; finishes with feelings of despair

N

Natural Child – 41 – one of the ego states, or personal styles, we have available for interacting with others; used appropriately this style is friendly, creative and curious; used inappropriately it presents as immature and overly-emotional

negative stroke – 89 – unit of recognition that reinforces a view of the world in which someone is not OK

never – 155 – one of the process scripts; based on never getting what you want

NOISICED – 145 – decision spelt backwards; initials of structured decision making process: need, objective, information, strategies, investigate, choose, ego states, decide

Nurturing Parent – 44 – one of the ego states, or personal styles, we have available for interacting with others; used appropriately this style is caring; used inappropriately it becomes smothering and stops other people developing their own skills

O

open-ended – 156 – one of the process scripts; based on not knowing what to do once the plan has been achieved

over and over – 156 – one of the process scripts; based on nearly but not quite getting there

P

Parent – ego state: see Controlling Parent, Internal Parent, Nurturing Parent

passive/alone - 111 - 'type' of person within AP³ framework

passive/people - 112 - 'type' of person within AP³ framework

pastime – 128 – way of spending time making small-talk; literally 'passing time' with others

payoff – 34, 155 – final, negative result of mental or behavioural sequence, feeling bad in some way; may refer to the end of a racket or game, of a miniscript sequence, or of script itself

permission – 153 – belief that we need to have in order to fulfil our potential in life; 'antidote' to injunctions or attributions (e.g. it's OK to succeed, you can take your time)

personal styles – 38 – also called ego states; five ways of interacting, or transacting, with others, each style having positive and negative applications: Controlling Parent, Nurturing Parent, Functional Adult, Adapted Child, Natural Child

Persecutor – 118 – role on drama triangle; way we behave during psychological games: psychological role, not to be confused with real persecutors

playing – 129 – used here to mean a way of spending time in enjoyable activities, without work-based goals, with other people

Please People – 78 – one of five characteristic working styles, or drivers; means that we want people to like us but may then be reluctant to challenge appropriately

Poor Me – 124 – name of psychological game; repetitive unhelpful sequence of interactions with others

positive stroke – 89 – unit of recognition that reinforces an I'm OK, You're OK view of the world

Potency Pyramid –126 - diagram which shows how we need to be to avoid psychological games: powerful, responsible, vulnerable

powerful - 126 - position on Potency Pyramid

PRO Success - 31 - stands for Positive Beliefs, Resourceful Actions, Okay Outcomes, which form positive self-reinforcing cycle to combat BARs

process scripts – 155 – themes of our unconscious life plans, and of short repetitive sequences of our behaviour; six themes are: never (get what you want); always (have to keep doing the same thing); until (can't have fun until all the work is done); after (you'll pay for pleasure later); over and over (keep on not quite getting there); open-ended (don't know what to do once the plan has been achieved)

psychological games – 117 – unconsciously programmed ways of behaving that consist of repetitive interactions with others leading to negative payoffs

psychological stamps – 35 – the way we save up 'bad' feelings to justify our behaviour later; like collecting trading stamps or vouchers in order to claim a 'prize' (e.g. enough irritations from poor customer care 'justify' losing our temper with the next shop assistant we meet)

R

racket – 21 – behaviour that somehow manipulates people, as in gangster protection rackets, but done outside our conscious awareness; substitute for genuine emotions; familiar, habitual response that does not solve the problem

racket system – 26 – way in which we maintain our unhelpful but customary behaviour; consists of closed loop of beliefs, which influence our behaviour, which

affects the reactions of other and therefore generates reinforcements of our beliefs

Rebuff – 122 – name of psychological game; repetitive unhelpful sequence of interactions with others

recycling – 164 – final stage in our cycle of development; we have now completed a cycle and are ready to start again

refracted transaction - 69 - transaction in which recipient 'mistakes' which ego state is being used by the sender

Rescuer – 118 – role on drama triangle; way we behave during psychological games: psychological role not to be confused with real rescuers

responsible - 126 - position on Potency Pyramid

ritual – 128 – way of spending time in ritualised interaction, such as exchanging greetings; where each person 'knows' what they are supposed to say

rubberband – 50 – process whereby we 'flip back' into the past without realising we have done so; a re-experiencing of a past event as if it were happening now, or a replay of someone else's behaviour from the past as if it were our own in the present

S

script – 148 – unconscious life plan, or story, that we 'choose' when young as a result of our interpretations of our interactions with the people around us, particularly our parents or other caregivers

SHNOK – 10 – abbreviation for Somebody Here is Not OK; any of the three unhelpful life positions or windows on the world

skills – 164 – fifth stage in our cycle of development; when we are ready to acquire the skills we need

stamps – 35 – see psychological stamps

Steps to success – 138 - metaphor for understanding the various levels of discounting and how to help someone overcome their own discounting

stopper – 33 – position on the miniscript where we feel one-down due to failure to maintain behaviour in line with our unrealistic expectations

stroke – 88 – unit of human recognition, any way in which we let another person know we recognise their existence; may be positive or negative, conditional or unconditional, and vary in intensity

stroke exchange – 93 – way in which we seem to 'swap' strokes, such as complimenting someone who has just complimented us, or returning the insult when someone is rude to us

stroke filters - 116 - way in which windows on the world distort the receipt of strokes

stroke myths – 95 – set of mythical rules that constrain us from giving or receiving strokes freely

stroking pattern (1) – 91 – individual pattern of strokes we give and receive

generally and in specific groups of people such as family, friends, work colleagues

stroking pattern (2) - 96 - organisational pattern of what gets recognition, how strokes are given and to whom

switch – 121 – moment in psychological game when 'players' change roles (e.g. Rescuer switches to Persecutor); also moment when ulterior transaction comes to the surface, or social, level

T
TA – 4 – abbreviation for transactional analysis

thinking – 164 – third stage in our cycle of development when we need to think for ourselves

time structuring – 127 – set of ways in which we spend our time: alone, rituals, pastiming, working, playing, psychological games, closeness

transaction – an interaction between people: see complementary, crossed, refracted and ulterior transactions

transactional analysis (1) – 4 – body of theories and techniques, with unifying philosophy, for understanding human behaviour and developing autonomy and community

transactional analysis (2) – term originally used literally to mean analysing transactions in terms of ego states but this is now commonly referred to as transactional analysis proper: see channels of communication *transactional analysis (3)* – 125 – name of psychological game; repetitive unhelpful sequence of interactions with others

Try Hard – 79 – one of five characteristic working styles, or drivers; means that we put lots of enthusiasm into trying anything but may move on to new things before we finish our current project

U

ulterior transaction – 62 – an interaction between people in which there is another message being transmitted 'below the surface'

unconditional stroke – 90 – unit of recognition that is given because the person 'exists', i.e. they do not have to do anything to 'earn' it; tends to be about aspects of a person that are not linked to performance e.g. family, sense of fun

until – 156 – one of the process scripts; based on not being allowed to have fun until all of the work is done

Uproar – 123 – name of psychological game; repetitive unhelpful sequence of interactions with others

V

Victim – 118 – role on drama triangle; way we behave during psychological games: psychological role not to be confused with real victims

vulnerable - 126 - position on Potency Pyramid

W

wavelengths - 38 - metaphor for how our ego states show up in behaviour and are picked up by others

windows on the world – 9 – set of ways in which we perceive the world, as if through windows with particular beliefs built into them so they distort what comes through to us; also called life positions

working – 129 – used here to mean a way of spending time engaged in goal-directed activity, with others

working styles – 73 – set of five characteristic ways of working, each with benefits and drawbacks; also known as drivers when we are stressed and therefore getting mostly the drawbacks; consist of Hurry Up, Be Perfect, Please People, Try Hard and Be Strong

Y

Yes but... - 119 – name of psychological game; repetitive unhelpful sequence of interactions with others